Descriptive and Objective Floriculture

NIPA GENX ELECTRONIC RESOURCES & SOLUTIONS P. LTD.
New Delhi-110 034

About the Authors

Professor Harminder Singh Baweja presently Director, Directorate of Horticulture and Food Processing, Govt. of Uttarakhand. With over 30 years of experience in teaching, research and administration, Dr Baweja has worked on key positions like Managing Director, HP State Agriculture Marketing Board (HPSAMB), besides holding the post of Director, Horticulture, in Himachal Pradesh. Has joined as Assistant Scientist in the Department of Floriculture & Landscaping, UHF Nauni and served the University as Scientist, Principal Scientist and Professor and Head (Officiating) Deptt. of Floriculture and Landscape Architecture, UHF, Solan. Dr Baweja has published excellent research publications, extension bulletins, popular articles, 13 Book Chapters and also authored 03 Books. He also performed his duty with different technical and policy making committees of colossal importance. Has visited Rome and attended "World Union of Wholesale Markets (WUWSM) Conference in 2017, visited various Wholesale Markets in Madrid, Kent (UK), Spain viz., Villa Del Prado (Wine Pack House), New Spital Fields Fruits and Vegetable Markets, London Retail Market as well as Borough Market (Wholesale and Retail Food Market) in South Wark in the vicinity of London Bridge (London) with an objective of updating and strengthening of agri-markets in Himachal Pradesh. Visited Dubai, U.A.E to study various markets viz., Al Aweer Central Fruit and Vegetable Market, Dubai as well as main vegetable market in central Abu Dhabi, United Arab Emirates for exploring the potential of export of various vegetables, fruits and flowers to U.A.E from India in general and Himachal Pradesh in particular as a member of the Governing Council, Crop Diversification Promotion of Japan International Cooperation Agency (JICA)-ODA project headed by Hon'ble Agriculture Minister of Himachal Pradesh during the period from 12th February, 2013 to -2nd January, 2018. Has attended a number of International Conferences.

Handled a number of externally funded projects worth Rs Crores and associated as a Member of the Governing Council, headed by the Chief Secretary, HP, for Horticulture Development Project of worth Rs. 1134 crores, a World Bank Funded Project. Worked with Himachal Pradesh State Agricultural Marketing Board (HPSAMB), Shimla and developed seven Market Yards with total budget out lay of 2979.64 lakhs, developed three Fruit and Vegetable Collection Centres in Himachal Pradesh. Associated with different technical and policy making committees, having experience as member of committees, Board of Management, Finance Committee, Research and Extension Councils of different Government as well as Private organizations.

Dr Anil Kumar Verma, Doctorate in Horticulture (Post Harvest Technology) from Dr. Y S Parmar, University of Horticulture and Forestry, Nauni, Solan (HP) has published more than 150 research papers, review articles and popular articles in National and International journals. Has also authored 13 books viz. Nutritional Guide to all ages, Food Safety, Pushp Beej Utpadan–Ek Vayavsai., Swarojgar: Sushak Pushp Utpadan., Question bank on Post Harvest Technology, Post Harvest Technologies for Commercial Floriculture, Objective Horticulture, A Practical Manual–Analytical Chemistry and Mathematical Application in Post harvest Technology, A Practical Manual–Practical Chemistry Application in Post harvest Technology, Plum and apricot prasanskran etc. Also has been conferred Dr Rajendra Prasad Puruskar 2014 for Technical book in Hindi by ICAR, Dr JS Pruthi memorial award 2014, and Kejriwal award 2016 for best research papers by All India Food Processors' Association (AIFPA).

Dr Anil Gupta has obtained his graduation as well as post-graduation in Horticulture (Post Harvest Technology) from Dr. Y S Parmar, University of Horticulture and Forestry, Nauni, Solan (HP). Has published more than 100 research papers, review articles and technical articles in National and International journals. Has authored 9 books and written 15 book chapters. Has received ICAR Dr Rajendra Prasad Puruskar 2014 for Technical book in Hindi, Dr JS Pruthi memorial award 2014, and Kejriwal award 2016 for best research papers by All India Food Processors' Association (AIFPA). He has published one design patent as well as four technology patents and is associated as a research advisor for GI Tag on apricot kernel oil. Life member of reputed journals and also appointed as reviewer for journals in field of Food Science and Technology.

Dr Dharminder Kumar presently working as Associate Professor in the Regional Horticulture Research and Training Centre, Jachh, District Kangra, Dr YS Parmar, University of Horticulture and Forestry, Himachal Pradesh. Has written eight competitive examination books in different field of horticulture (both in Hindi as well as in English), more than 20 Research papers in National and International Reputed Journals. Released two two varieties i.e. One in lettuce and one in Red Cabbage. Having a long experience of teaching, research and extension and guided M.Sc and Ph.D. students in field of Horticulture (Vegetable Science). Also handled a number of externally funded projects, as Principle Investigator and

Co- Principle Investigator. Has been a Life member of different International and National Journals and Societies. Has published 28 Research papers in different reputed international and national journals and also authored 10 books.

Dr. Parminder Kaur Baweja presently working as Senior Scientist (Agrometeorology) is Ph. D. in Environmental Management. Has area of Specialization as Microclimatic studies on horticulture crops, crop-weather forecasting, climate change impacts. Has attended a number National and International Seminar/symposiums and also received awards for research presentations. She received Pride of Solan-2017 award her for contribution towards society.

She has 22 years experience in the field of Crop-Weather-Relationship studies, environment management, teaching and research. Has authored and published more than 20 Research Papers, a number of extension bulletins including Gramin Krishi Mausam Sewa Bulletin, Has worked on different projects like Crop-weather relationship studies in tomato, capsicum, peach and apricot, formulation of Crop-weather calendars for important crops, formulation of Ergographs for major crops of the area and weather forecasts based crop management practices. Delivered various farmers' scientists' talks, radio and TV Talks besides transmitting Agromet Advisory Bulletins to Press, Media for wider publicity of Weather based crop management practices. Organized Farmers' Awareness Camps at different locations in District Solan. Has handled a number of externally funded projects, as Principle Investigator and Co- Principle Investigator/Nodal Scientist.

Descriptive and Objective Floriculture

Harminder Singh Baweja
Director
Directorate of Horticulture and Food Processing
Govt. of Uttarakhand. (India)

Anil Kumar Verma
Department of Food Science and Technology
Dr. Y S Parmar, University of Horticulture and Forestry
Nauni, Solan, Himachal Pradesh

Anil Gupta
Department of Food Science and Technology
Dr. Y S Parmar, University of Horticulture and Forestry
Nauni, Solan, Himachal Pradesh

Dharminder Kumar
Associate Professor
Regional Horticulture Research and Training Centre
Jachh, District Kangra
Himachal Pradesh

Parminder Kaur Baweja
Sr. Scientist (Agrometeorology)
Director Extension Education
Dr. Y S Parmar, University of Horticulture and Forestry
Nauni, Solan, Himachal Pradesh

NIPA GENX ELECTRONIC RESOURCES & SOLUTIONS P. LTD.
New Delhi-110 034

NIPA GENX ELECTRONIC RESOURCES & SOLUTIONS P. LTD.

101,103, Vikas Surya Plaza, CU Block
L.S.C.Market, Pitam Pura, New Delhi-110 034
Ph : +91 11 27341616, 27341717, 27341718
E-mail:newindiapublishingagency@gmail.com
www: www.nipabooks.com

For customer assistance, please contact
Phone: + 91-11-27 34 17 17 Fax: + 91-11- 27 34 16 16
E-Mail: feedbacks@nipabooks.com

ISBN: 978-93-91383-27-5

Composed and Designed by NIPA.

Preface

Floriculture is developing as an area of high technology- based frontier interdisciplinary subject on scientific excellence and is recognized as most remunerative profession with a much higher potential for returns per unit area than most fields and even some other horticultural crops. It has progressed both scientifically and commercially due to concentrated efforts made by floriculture scientists.

India has a wide variety of climate and soil on which a large number of ornamentals are grown. After liberalization, the floriculture industries witnessed a sudden rise in the export arena. As per National Horticulture Database, the area under floriculture production in India is 305 thousand hectares with a production of 2301 thousand tonnes loose flowers and 762 thousand tonnes cut flowers during the year 2019-20. Floriculture is now commercially cultivated in several States like Andhra Pradesh (19.1%), Tamil Nadu (16.6%), Madhya Pradesh (11.9%), Karnataka, West Bengal, Mizoram, Gujarat, Orissa, Jharkhand, Haryana, Assam, Chhattisgarh, Himachal Pradesh and Uttrakhand. India's total export of floriculture was Rs. 575.98 Crores/77.84 USD Millions in 2020-21. The major importing countries were USA, Netherland, UK and Germany. There are more than 300 export-oriented units in India, out of which 50% are based in Karnataka, Andhra Pradesh and Tamil Nadu.

The Government of India has identified floriculture as a sunrise industry and accorded it 100% export oriented status. Owing to steady increase in demand of flower floriculture has become one of the important commercial trades in Agriculture. Hence, commercial floriculture has emerged as hi-tech activity-taking place under controlled climatic conditions inside greenhouse. The new seed policy had already made it feasible to import planting material of International varieties. It has been found that commercial floriculture has higher potential per unit area than most of the field crops and is therefore a lucrative business. Indian floriculture industry has been shifting from traditional flowers to cut flowers for export purposes. The liberalized economy has given an impetus to the Indian entrepreneurs for establishing export oriented floriculture units under controlled climatic conditions Agricultural and Processed Food Products Export Development Authority (APEDA) is responsible for export promotion and development of floriculture in India.

Floriculture products mainly consist of cut flowers, pot plants, cut foilage, seeds bulbs, tubers, rooted cuttings and dried flowers or leaves. The important crops in the International cut flower trade are rose, carnation, chrysanthemum, gerbera, gladiolus, gypsophila, orchids, archilea, anthurium, tulip, and lilies. Floriculture crops like gerbera, carnation, etc. are grown in green houses. The open field crops are chrysanthemum, roses, gaillardia, lily marigold, aster, tuberose.

India has a rich heritage of ornamental floriculture. It is evident from ancient literature that Indian flowers have been associated in social life since times immemorial and used for diverse purposes such as offerings to God, floral ornamentals for ladies, decoration on auspicious ceremonies and for preparation of perfumes. Recently floriculture has become increasingly popular as commercial commodity with considerable potential for export. Monumental literature have been developed by concentrated efforts of multidisciplinary competent floriculture scientists which provides an illustrated account of important ornamental species and cultivars, germplasm status and their usages, propagation, nursery management, techno-economics, conventional breeding, induced mutagenesis, new varieties, cytogenetics, tissue culture, characterization of varieties, management of disease, dehydration of flowers, etc. It is not possible to analyze all research topics and related publications. The early literature survey indicates that the Floriculture research in India was started before the Second Five-Year Plan at Indian Botanic Garden, Howrah; Lalbagh, Bangalore and National Botanical Research Institute, Lucknow. Research Institute, Regional Station, Katrain; Botanical Survey of India (BSI), Howrah (Calcutta) and BSI, Shillong.

Keeping in view the growing importance of floriculture a need was felt for a book designed for students in floriculture. We hope that this book has covered all the questions in a systematic manner according to the syllabus as well as keeping in view the competitive examinations. No book can claim to be perfect.

We are thankful to New India Publishing Agency (NIPA) for their efforts in producing this publication.

The authors are hearty grateful to all colleagues and friends for their moral support during completion of present manuscript.

This book will help all and serve as a comprehensive guide to those who want to prepare for competitive examinations like M.Sc. and Ph.D admissions in Agricultural/Horticultural Universities, ICAR Institutes and other competitive examinations viz; ARS, SRF, JRF, Civil Services held at National level. It is earnestly hoped that the students of floriculture and post- harvest technology will find this book quite useful and prove beneficial to its readers.

Suggestions for further improvement are invited and will be immensely acknowledged.

Authors

Contents

1

Classification

Floriculture is the aesthetic branch of horticulture that deals with the cultivation of ornamentals, annuals, biennials and perennial plants as well as with their marketing. Flowers symbolize beauty, purity, peace and love. In India, it is a dynamic and expanding industry showing an impressive annual growth rate.

Classification of Flower Crops

The flowering plants can be classified broadly on the basis of their species, genus, family, plant part used or type of flower plants. They are further classified as cutflowers, cut foliage, turfgrasses, groundcovers, hedges, accents, specimen plants, avenue trees, screens, topiaries, fillers and others.

A. Classification on basis of life span

1. **Seasonal flowers:** These complete their life cycle within one calander year and need to replant every year. Thesc flowers have short life span ranging from 4-6 months. For example; marigold, chrysanthemum, gladiolus, aster etc.
2. **Perennial flowers:** The flowers have life span extending beyond one calendar year and do not need replacement year after year. The life span ranges from 2 years in case of tuberose; 5 years in case of crossandra, to over 8 years in case of rose or over 10 years in some jasmine varieties.

B. Classification on basis of end use

1. **Traditional flowers:** These are offered in religious and social ceremonies, used as an adornment by womens, offered for worship at home or temples. Flowers are used singly or in form of garlands or strung together loosely. Examples are jasmine, rose, chrysanthemum, marigold, crossandra and tuberose, etc.
2. **Non-traditional flowers:** These are used strictly for decorative purposes, referred as cut flowers and are generally harvested with a long stem. The flowers in non-traditional use are arranged in vases, pots, bouquets

and are mostly consumed during social functions. These flowers are also known as modern flowers. Examples are gladiolus, rose, carnation, gerbera, orchids, etc.

3. **Industrial use flowers**: Some flowers are used as raw material in the industries for extraction of essential oil, perfumes and cosmetic products and also for preparation of some edible products like gulkand. Rose oil, rose water, jasmine oil, concretes, gulkand and attar are some of the commercial products manufactured in processing units/perfumeries.

C. Classification on basis of their use

1. **Lawn or Turf grasses:** The grasses grown for aesthetic purpose in the landscape or for any outdoor recreational use. They are usually maintained at a low height. Examples: Bermuda grass, carabao grass, zoysia grass, creeping bent grass, perennial rye grass.
2. **Cut flowers**: The plants grown for their attractive flowers with long shelf life. Examples: anthurium, chrysanthemum, gladiolus, orchids, rose.
3. **Cut foliage**: The plants grown for their attractive foliage which are cut for floral decoration. Examples: ferns, fishtail palm, Song of India, Song of Jamaica.
4. **Edge Crops**: The short statured plants grown to serve as barrier between the lawn and garden, to highlight gardens, or to create stand-alone gardens; also called *border plants*.
5. **Ground covers**: The aesthetically appealing plants grown in the landscape primarily to suppress weed growth and to control, retard or prevent soil erosion by covering and binding loose, bare soil. It is oftenly used en masse to produce a carpeting effect. Examples: *Alternanthera versicolor*, *Cuphea*, travelling jew, creeping peanut, Vietnam rose.
6. **Hedges**- The plants grown at the edges of pathways or boundaries and continuously pruned to knee-high height or upper but below eye level. Examples: *Duranta*, hedge bamboo, Chinese holly, dwarf santan.
7. **Specimens**: The plants having showy features, or with unique characteristics which make them pieces of conversation or botanical curiosity, or otherwise desired as collector's item. They are ideally planted in isolation rather than massed with other plants, and easily become focal point in the landscape. Examples of potential specimens: queen of flowering trees (*Amherstia nobilis*), palms.

8. **Shade crops**: These are generally trees, shrubs, trellised vines and lianas which are grown mainly to provide shade singly or with supporting trellis.

9. **Avenue trees**: The trees and shrubs grown, more or less equidistant, beside roads and streets. Palms are also used. Examples: acacia (raintree), katuray, narra, date palm.

D. Classification on the basis of plant type

a) Woody plants

1) Trees
2) Shrubs
3) Vines and ground covers

b) Herbaceous plants

1) Flowers
2) Vines and ground covers
3) Grass/turf

c) Potted plants, houseplants, gift plants

2

Short Notes

1. **Scooping:** It involves `Removing' of basal plate and destroying the `Central Shoot' of the bulb, thus encouraging the formation of bulblets round the cut edges of the scale leaves. Scooping is achieved by using a special knife or a spoon with a `Sharpened edge' to leave a `Concave depression' at the base of bulb. The depth of the cut is important, because the bulblets are formed on `cell tissues' at the lowest point of the `scale leaves'. If the cut is too deep, the `basal cells' responsible for meristem development will be removed, resulting in poor bulblet formation. If the basal plate is not adequately removed, it will inhibit `bulblet formation'. The time required to reach flowering is 3 to 4 years, bulb size is 8-12 cm in diameter.

2. **Scoring**: Scoring is almost identical to scooping, except for the preparation of the "Base" of the bulb. Scoring is generally used on large-diameter bulbs (16-20 cm) where scooping is difficult. The Base of the bulb is prepared by making 2 or 3 incisions through the "base plate", sufficiently deep to destroy the Central growing shoot and to "induce" the dormant axillary buds to sprout. Proliferation of the bulblets from the base of the scale is far "less" generous than with scooping but their growth rate is greater, reducing the time needed to reach flowering to "2 to 3 years".

3. **Tunicate bulbs (Laminated bulb)**

    - Laminate or tunicate bulbs (Daffodil, Tulip).
    - True bulbs have fresh modified leaves called scales.
    - A disk of hardened stem tissue is called basal plate.
    - Laminate bulbs have outer bulb scales which are dried and membranous provide protection from drying and mechanical injury to the bulb.
    - The fleshy scales are in the continuous concentric layers, so that structure becomes more or less solid.

4. **Non-tunicated or scaly bulbs**
   - Typically represented by lillium species.
   - These bulbs do not possess the enveloping dry covering.
   - The scales are separate and are attached to the basal plate.
   - In general, the non-tunicated bulbs are easily damaged and must be handled more carefully than the tunicated bulbs.
   - They must be kept continuously moist/wet because they are injured by drying
   - Scales are thicker and loosely wrapped i.e., in Lillies
5. **Senescence:** Senescence is the final phase in the ontogeny of the organ, in which a series of normally irreversible events are, initiated that leads to the cellular breakdown and death of organ. In higher plants it is of three types i.e., Population senescence; individual plant senescence; and determinate organ senescence. Senescence is also defined as the deteriorative processes that are natural cause of death.
6. **Aging:** Aging refers to the Processes Acquiring Maturity with the passage of time. Normally an increment of time, which may or may not be accompanied by physiological changes including senescence. Aging thus includes a much `wider span' of physiological processes, which may either "weaken the organism or to be neutral" (with respect to the capability of biological organism to survive. Senescence in contrast refers to changes providing for the `endogenous regulation' of death.
7. **Growth pattern of corm:** Gladiolus and crocus growth pattern are typical examples of corm, with gladiolus semi-hard to tender. In areas with severe winter, the corm must be stored over winter and planted in spring. At time of planting the corm is a 'vegetative structure', new roots develop from its base, one or more buds to develop leaves. Flower initiation takes place within `few weeks' after the shoots begins to grow, and at the same time the base of `shoot apex' thickened. Succeeding year, new corm begins to form above the old corm. Stolons like structure bearing miniature corm or cormels on the tips develop from base of new corm. The new corm continues to make food material. At the end of summer when the foliage dries, there are one or more new corms and a great number of cormels. The corms are dug out and stored over winter until they are planted in the next spring.
8. **Growth pattern of rhizome:** Rhizomes grown by elongation of the growing points, at terminal ends and on lateral branches. Length also increases by growth in the intercallary mesostem, in the lower part

of internodes. As the plant continues to grow and the older parts die, several branches arising from a plant may eventually become separated to become ‘individual plant’ of ‘a single clone’. Rhizomes exhibit consecutive vegetative and reproductive stages, but growth cycle differs in two ways:

i) In patchymorph rhizomes of `Irish’, a growth cycle begins with the initiation of growth of `lateral branches’ on a flowering section. This flowering stock dies but these new lateral branches produce leaves and grow vegetatively during the remainder of that season. Continuous growth of underground stem, storage of food and production of floral bud at conclusion of vegetative period depends on photosynthesis. Consequently, foliage should not be removed during these periods. A flowering stock is produced in a `following spring’ and no further terminal growth can take place. In general, plant with this structure, flowers in spring and grows vegetatively during summer and fall.

ii) Plants with heptomorph habit as a general rule with exception grow vegetatively during beginning of growth period and flowers later in the same period. The length of time during which individual rhizome remain vegetative varies with kind of plants. Some bamboo species remain vegetative for many years but then they change abruptly and the entire plant produces plant. In some rhizomes plants like blueberry, rhizome development is increased by higher temperature and long photoperiod and is correlated with vigorous above ground growth.

9. Important annual flowers

S.N.	Popular name	Scientific name	Family	Native
1.	Acroclinum (Paper flower)	*Acroclinum roseum*	Asteraceae	Australia
2.	Ageratum (Floss flower)	*Ageratum houstonianum*	Asteraceae	Central America
3.	Anchusa	*Anchusa capensis*	Boraginaceae	South Africa
4.	Chrysanthemum	*Chrysanthemum sp*	Asteraceae	North Africa, Europe
5.	Snap dragon, dog flower	*Antirrhinum majus*	Scrophulariaceae	South America
6.	African daisy	*Arctotis stoechadifolia*	Asteraceae	South Africa
7.	Aster	*Callistephus chinensis*	Asteraceae	China, Japan
8.	Bells of Ireland	*Molucella laevis*	Labiateae	Mediterranean region
9.	Brachycome	*Brachycome iberidifolia*	Asteraceae	Australia
10.	Calendula	*Calendula officinalis*	Asteraceae	South Europe
11.	California poppy (Pot marigold)	*Eschscholzia californica*	Papaveraceae	California (USA)
12.	Candytuft	*Iberis sp*	Crucifereae	Europe
13.	Carnation	*Dianthus caryophyllus*	Caryophyllaceae	Europe
14.	Cineraria	*Senecio cruentus*	Asteraceae	Canary Islands
15.	Clarkia	*Clarkia elegans*	Onagraceae	California, USA
16.	Parrot Bill	*Clianthus dampieri*	Leguminoseae	California, USA
17.	Teak seed	*Coreopsis tinctorea*	Asteraceae	California, USA
18.	Corn flower	*Centaurea cyanus*	Asteraceae	Europe, Britain
19.	Cosmos	*Cosmos bipinnatus*	Asteraceae	Mexico
20.	Dahlia	*Dahlia variabilis*	Asteraceae	Mexico
21.	Daisy	*Bellis perennis*	Asteraceae	Europe
22.	Dimorphotheca (African daisy)	*Dimorphotheca aurantiaca*	Asteraceae	South Africa
23.	Gamolepsis	*Gamolepsis tagetes*	Asteraceae	South Africa
24.	Gazania	*Gazania splendens*	Asteraceae	South Africa
25.	Baby breath	*Gypsophila elegans*	Caryophyllaceae	Caucasus region
26.	Everlasting or Straw flower	*Helichrysum bracteatum*	Asteraceae	Australia
27.	Hollyhock	*Althea rosea*	Malvaceae	China
28.	Ice Plant	*M. criniflorum*	Aizoaceae	South Africa

S.N.	Popular name	Scientific name	Family	Native
29.	Lady's lace	*Pimpnella monoica*	Umbelliferae	India
30.	Larkspur	*Delphinium hybridum*	Ranunculaceae	Europe
31.	Linaria	*Linaria bipartita*	Scrophulareaceae	Spain, Morocco
32.	Linum (flax)	*Linum grandiflorum* Var. *rubrum*	Linaceae	North Africa & Europe
33	Lupin	*Lupinus hartwegis*	Luguminoseae	North America
34.	Mignonette	*Reseda odorata*	Residoceae	North Africa
35.	Mimulus (Monkey flower)	*Mimulus tigrinus*	Scrophulariaceae	Western part of North & South America
36.	Nasturtium	*Tropaeolum majus*	Tropaeolaceae	Mexico & South America
37.	Nemasia	*Nemasea strumosa*	Scrophuliaraceae	South Africa
38.	Nigella	*Nigella damascene*	Ranunculaceae	North Africa
39.	Pansy	*Viola tricolor* Var. *hortensis*	Violaceae	Europe
40.	Petunia	*Petunia hybrids*	Solanaceae	South America
41.	Phlox (Strawflower)	*Phlox drummondii*	Polemoniaceae	USA
42.	Rudbeckia (Cone flower)	*Rudbeckia bicolour*	Asteraceae	North America
43.	Salvia (Sage flower)	*Saliva splendens*	Labiateae	South America
44.	Saponaria (Soapwart)	*Saponaria vaccaria*	Caryophyllaceae	Europe
45.	Butter fly flower, Poor Man's orchid	*Schizanthus wisetonensis*	Solanaceae	Chile& Peru
46.	Shirley Poppy (corn poppy)	*Papaver rhoeas*	Papaveraceae	Europe
47.	Statice (Sea lavender)	*Limonium sinuatum*	Plumbaginaceae	Mediterranean Region
48.	Stock	*Matthiola incana*	Crucifereae	Mediterranean Region
49.	Sweet Alyssum	*Alyssum mauritimum*	Crucifereae	Western Asia and Europe
50.	Sweet pea	*Lathyrus odoratus*	Leguminosae	Europe
51.	Sweet Sultan	*Centaurea moschata*	Asteraceae	Caucasus region
52.	Sweet William	*Dianthus barbatus*	Caryophyllaceae	Northern France
53.	Venidium	*Venidium fastvosum*	Asteraceae	South Africa
54.	Verbena	*Verbena hybrida*	Verbenaceae	South America
55.	Wall flower	*Cheiranthes cheiri*	Cruciferae	Europe

10. History of gardening

- The art and science of growing ornamental dates back to 3000 BC.
- Arboriculture developed in Vedic time during 3000-2000 BC.
- Girls use flowers of champaka and jasmine for decorating their hairs and wear flowers of Siris in ears.
- Botanically, champaka is *Michelia champaca* and Siris is *Albizzia lebbek.*
- Poet Kalidas has made reference of Sandal paste in his writings.
- According to Vatsyayana, house/ Palaces of Kings had a pleasure garden generally known as Vriksavatika and Purpavatika.
- Ashoka tree, known as (*Saraca indica*) relates to Sita whereas Kadamba tree (*Anthocephalus cadamba*) was associated with life of Krishna.
- Description of flowers and gardens in Sanskrit classics like Rigveda (3000-2000 BC); Ramayana (1200-1000 BC) and Mahabharata (500 BC).
- Ashoka tree (*Saraca indica*), Padma tree/Lotus (*Nelumbo nucifera*), Tulsi (*Ocimum sanctum*) and Peepal (*Ficus religiosa*) found high place in worship.
- Lord Gautam Buddha attains Enlightenment under tree Peepal in Bodh Gaya. Sal, Ashoka and Plaksha are associated with Ram.
- Plaskha is scientifically *Butea monosperma.*
- Planting of Avenue tree was taken by Ashoka in 233 BC.
- Concept of developing a Garden in the enclosed space was introduced by Mughals (Babur) in India during 16th and 17th century.
- Babur in Baburnama mentioned some indigenous ornamental trees like *Hibiscus rosa-senensis*, oleander and white jasmine.
- Babur introduced scented Persian rose in India.
- Mother of NurJahan is credited with Otto of rose.

11. Colour schemes

- Natural colour: green, which dominates throughout the year.
- Red colour dominates during winter.
- Yellow colour dominates in spring.

Types of colour schemes: The colour schemes are basically of three types:

i) Monochromatic schemes: Only one colour is used.

ii) Analogous/hormonous colour scheme: According to wavelength of colour.

iii) Contrast colour scheme: Opposite colour of wheel.

VIBGYOR means:

V	I	B	G	Y	O	R
↓	↓	↓	↓	↓	↓	↓
Violet	Indigo	Blue	Green	Yellow	Orange	Red

Primary colours: Blue, yellow, red

Secondary colours: Violet, Indigo, Green, Orange

Black + White colour = grey colour

Complimentary/contrast colours: Blue & orange, Red & green, Violet & yellow

12. Cultivation of Jasminum

- Plants are grown as both shrubs and climbers
- Flowers and buds are used for making garlands, bouquets and veni.
- Flowers are also used for production of perfumed hair oils and attars.
- Oil is extracted from *Spanish jasmine* (*J. grandiflorum*).
- *J. sambac* (Arabian jasmine) is reported to be used in China for flavouring tea.
- Out of total world production of Jasmine concrete, 50% is supplied by France alone.
- Origin place of Jasmine is tropical and sub tropical region.
- Three important species used for commercial cultivation are:
- *J. sambac* (Arabian jasmine): Native to West Indies
- *J. officinale* (Common white jasmine): Native to Persian origin
- *J. grandiflorum* : Native to Afghanistan
- Distribution: *J. auriculatum* (India), *J. flexile* (India), *J. humile* (tropical Asia) and *J. wallichianum* (Nepal).

Cultivation: Warm climate combined with copious rainfall and sunny weather contributes long duration of flowering season.

Soil and climate: Preferred well drained sandy loam to clay loam soil. Cool house species should be kept at 7-13°C and store species at (13-18°C) during September to March. Soil pH: 6.5-7.5.

Fertilizers/ manures

- N 60g + P_2O_5 120 g singly or together enhanced flower and essential oil yield.
- Highest flower yield when treated with N and P_2O_5 350 and 300 kg/ hectare respectively.
- Application of 60:120:120g/plant along with 10 kg of FYM applied in two splits is optimum.

Pruning: Done in January to ensure higher flower yield, cut branches at 90 cm height, leaving 9-11 shoots.

Yield: 1 ton flowers give 2.5 kg concrete.

13. Post harvest management of orchids

Harvesting: Harvesting should be done in the evening. All equipments should be sterilized. When individual *cattelya & cymbidium* flowers are cut, the peduncle should immediately be inserted in a tube of water. In Hawaii and Singapore some *Dendrobium* and *Aranda* growers immerse the entire sprays of flowers in water for 15 minutes before packing and shipping. Orchids are harvested when fully opened.

Grading: No standard grades for orchids. In case of *Cattelya* flower both "Colour and size" are considered while pricing. While grading; spike length, number of open flowers, unopened buds, arrangement of flowers on a spike and number of side shoots/spike are taken into consideration. In solitary flowers like cattelaya, both flower colour and flower size are considered.

Storage: Stored at 5-7°C for 10-14 days. Use of modified atmosphere can often usefully substitute for the low temperature. Most of the orchids are stored at 7-10°C. *Cymbidium* and *Paphio redilum* are stored at -0.5 to 4°C.

Packaging: An ideal package should be airtight, water proof, strong enough to withstand handling. *Cymbidium* spikes are packed "100 flowers' in a box. Standards boxes are used for packaging of *cattelya* flowers. *Dendrobium* is packed in (4 dozon sprays) per box. Orchids have `Non-thermic' properties, hence packed in corrugated boxes of different sizes.

1. Scorpion orchids are packed in bunches of 5-10 while small packages used for dendrobiums.
2. Arenda flowers are individually wrapped in tissue papers and packed.
3. Fan shaped varieties like 'Golden Shower' are packed in such a way that they lie with the flat side on top of each other.
4. Care should be taken when blooms packed individually, few pieces of shredded wax paper is to be put between sepals and petals and around the tip.

Vase-life: Lower 0.75 cm of the peduncle is cut and flower is inserted into tube of water. In spray type orchids, the basal 2.5 cm of the stem is cut upon arrival. Placed in warm water at 38°C with a preservative and hardened off at 5°C. Orchid flowers are sensitive to ethylene. Modified atmosphere storage under 10% CO_2 for 4 days could extend the bench life by 4 days. Foliar application of 500 ppm aluminium chloride lengthens the vase-life of Oncidium.

Transportation: Orchids are sensitive to wilting, hence the cut ends of spike are wrapped with water saturated cotton during long distance transport.

14. Specific use of chemical retardants

Growth retardants: They reduce plant height and are mostly synthetic compounds that either slow down cell division or inhibit cell elongation. They are very specific to plant species in their action. Very old, but little used retardant is Phosphon-D. Foliar sprays of SADH are used commonly in chrysanthemum, azaleas whereas Chlormequat (CCC spray) drenches are used in begonia, geranium and poinsettia. Ancymidol is active in lilies, hyacinths, tulips.

- **Chrysanthemum:** Plant treated with MH (1000 to 2000 ppm) at three time intervals after planting reduces the plant height.
- **Rose:** CCC application at 5000-10,000 ppm to cultivar Celebration decreases plant height.
- **Marigold:** Growth regulation was observed with 500 ppm cycocel and 700 ppm TIBA in seedling of marigold Cv Fantasy.
- **Tuberose**: Etheral sprayed after 40 days of planting noticed reduction in plant height. Rhizome treated with GA_3 (100 ppm) for 24 hours have smaller plant height.
- **Carnation:** Reduction in height of main shoot and length of laterals with 2000 ppm MH is recorded.

- **Daffodils:** A dip of daffodils in BA (100 ppm) + 2, 4-D (22 ppm) retards senescence.

15. Important species as cut flowers

- In *Lilium, Pollyana,* Elite, Grand Paradise are Asiatic type whereas; Star Gazer is oriental type.
- Tulip: Apeldoorn, Golden Apeldoorn are promising.
- Daffodil: Gigantic Star, Carlton & Dutch Master
- Hyacinth: Anna Marie, Jan Bose and Amsterdom, Gypsy Queen.
- Carnation: Red Corso, Espana, Candy.
- Gladiolus: Priscilla, Trader Horn, Wind Song, Marvellous, Yellow Dreams.
- Chrysanthemum: Snowdon, Mountaineer in standard and Ajay, Birbal Sahni in spray.

16. Important species used as pot plant

1) *Crocus species*
2) *Hyacinthus orientalis* (Gypsy Queen, Jan Bose Amsterdom)
3) *Iris hollandica*
4) *Iris reticulata*
5) *Muscari armeniacum*
6) *Narcissus species*
7) *Tulips species* (Apeldoorn, Golden Apeldoorn)
8) Lilies: Pollyana, Elite, Paradise, Star Gazer

17. Foliage plants: These plants are valued for their beautiful foliage and grow well in shade or partial shade. In the garden such conditions are available under the "trees or artificially constructed greenhouse or the buildings". These are also used for interior decoration in pots, wooden crates etc. Important foliage plants are Aspidistra, Chlorophytum, Caladium, Dieffenbachia, Moranta and Monstera.

1) Asparagus: Native to South Africa is tuberose rooted belongs to family liliaceae.
2) *Aspidistra elator* belongs to liliaceae family.

3) *Caladium hortulanum* (Araceae) also called syngonium.

4) *Coleus blumae* (Labiateae) is propagated by seed and terminal cuttings.

5) *Dieffenbachia spp.* (Araceae).

6) Crotons (*Coliaeum variegatum*) belong to Euphorbiaceae family and propagated by air layering.

7) Dracaena (Liliaceae).

8) *Chlorophytum sp* (Ribbon plant) belongs to family liliaceae.

18. Important Parks and Gardens

Name of park/garden	Special features
Sayaji Park, Baroda (Gujarat)-1879	Siyaji park in Baroda named after Maharaja Sayaji Rao to cover 40 hectare area. About 8000 various ornamental trees are there in garden. The garden has a toy train, a grant wheel, children park and traffic training centre for children. The Baroda museum is situated in the park (opened in 1894). The park has a Zoo. The most important attractive part of the garden is the bandstand i.e., on one hectare area. The formal portion of garden has arbour-like band stand, paved walks, and green lawns, music besides changing multi-colour light.
Mandor garden, Jodhpur, (Rajashtan)- 1724-1749 AD.	The garden is 5 km away from Jodhpur. This garden was laid out by Raja Abhai Singh in the desert region of Rajasthan. Lawn, the flower beds, trees, shrubs add beauty to this garden.
Rose Garden, Chandigarh, 1966	The garden is among the biggest rose gardens of the world. Top position goes to Jackson and Perkins of New York. The garden covers 10 hectare area and has more than 36,000 rose types. **Other famous Rose gardens** - The Rose garden, Parque Bagatelle (Paris) - Parque del oeste Madrid (Spain) have 30,000 roses. - Pare Qe La group (Geneva) - Queen Marryrose garden and Regent park (London) - Golden walk, Cartwell (England)
The Mughal Garden, Pinjore (Haryana)- 17th Century	The garden is situated near Kalka. Lay out by Fidai Khan. The original name of place is Panchapnea or Panjpur has association with five Pandavas. Area under garden is 25 hectare and garden is divided into six terraces. The Main gate is at the highest terrace, while the remaining five appear in a decending order.
Shalimar Garden, Srinagar-1619-1630 AD	Jahangir initiated the garden work and extended by Zafar Khan. The garden is connected with Dal Lake (16 m Canal). On both sides of canal, trees are planted. The garden has three terraces. In two terraces only their stone bases are left while third terrace is meant for ladies, have a magnificent black stone pavilleon and surrounded by a reservoir.

Name of park/garden	Special features
Achabal, 1620	Built by Nur Jahan. The spring air in achabal is the largest in Kashmir. Six vertical waterfalls situated in the garden.
Lal bagh Bangalore (Karnataka), 1760	Lal bagh was built by Hyder Ali in a total area of 50 lakh heactare area.
Governmental botanical garden, Ootacamund- 1848	Situated in Nilgiris hills. The garden has six major sections.
Sim's park, Coonor, Tamil Nadu-1874	The park was established by JD Sim. The total area of garden is 15 hectare.
Botanic garden, Coimbatore,Tamil Nadu-1908	The garden was established by Department of Agriculture.
The Byrant Park KodaiKanal,Tamil Nadu-1909	Total area of garden in 10 lakh hectares
The Indian Botanic Garden, Sibpur Kolkatta, (West Bengal)- 1787	The garden is situated in twin city on the opposite side of the river hoogly. 200 year old banyan tree is important feature of this garden. The garden has 26 lakes, the total area of garden is 150 hectare.
Llyod botanic garden Darjeeling, West Bengal-1878	Situated in Middest of the Himalayas. The garden has 24 hectare area. Garden is laid out by Sir George King, the then Superintendent of Royal Botanic Garden.
National Botanical Research Institute (NBRI), Lucknow-1789-1814	The NBRI was laid out by Nawab Sardar Ali Khan and improved by Nawab Wajid Ali Khan and named after his wife Sikander Mahal Begum. The main objective of the garden is to disseminate knowledge for establishing scientifically planned garden.
Horticultural Research Institute, Saharanpur-1750/ 1817	Laid by East India Company in 1817. Falconii, Jameson and Duthies, have worked in this garden
Rashtrapati Bhawan Garden, New Delhi-1929	The architecture of the Palace is a mixture of Indian and Western style. The area under garden is 134 sq meters.
Other gardens	Mediterranean garden- Yalta
	Osaka garden, Japan
	Lal bagh, Bangalore-1760
	Brindavan garden, Mysore
	Llyod botanic garden, Darjeeling, 1878
	Baradari garden- Patiala
	Shalimar garden- Lahore
	Chasma-e-shahi garden- Srinagar
	Rock garden, Chandigarh
	Agri-Horticultural Society garden-Kolkatta-1872
	Government Botanic garden, Ootacamond-1848

19. Pot (flowering) plants

1) *Calceolaria herberohybrids* (Pocket book plant) belong to Scrophulariaceae family. Requires cool temperature below 15°C for flower initiation.
2) *Campanula isophylla* (Pocket book plant) belongs to family Campanulaceae. It is a long day plant need 16, 15 & 14 hours at night temperature of 12-15 °C, 18°C, 21°C respectively.
3) *Capsicum sp* and *Solanum pseudocapsicum* (Chrismas cherry) belongs to family solanaceae.
4) *Clerodendron thomsoniae* (bleeding heart) belongs to family Verbenaceae. The development of flowers is delayed under long days.
5) *Exacum affine* (German Violet) belongs to family Gentinaceae, propagated by seed.
   - Shade loving plants are mainly grown in pots and highly prized for their ornamental foliage and called foliage plants or pot plants.
   - Pot mixture: 2 parts garden soil + 1 parts sand + 2 parts leaf mould + 1 part farm yard manure.
   - Re-potting should be done in rainy season or February-March. At the time of repotting, extra shoot cut off. Feed pots with liquid manure containing bone meal and spray systemic fungicide.

20. Famous Gardens in India

1 Lalbagh: Bangalore (KN)

2 Brindavan Garden: Mysore (KN) – Biggest formal Garden

3 Sim's Park: Conoor (Tamil Nadu)

4 Byrant Park: Kodaikanal (Tamil Nadu)

5 The Indian Botanical Garden: Sibpur, Calcutta (WB)

6 Lyod Botanical Garden: Darjeeling (WB)

7 National Botanical Garden: Lucknow (UP)

8 Rastrapathi Bhawan Garden: New Delhi

9 Buddha Jyanti Park: New Delhi

10 Pinjore Garden: Haryana

11 Rose Garden : Chandigarh (Punjab)

12 Mandoor Garden : Jodhpur (Rajasthan)

13 Syaji Park : Baroda (Gujarat) Branching palm

14 Roshana park : New Delhi

21. National Flower of the Different Countries

1 Lotus : India Egypt

2 Rose : England, Iran, New Sealand

3 Narcisuss : China

4 Chrysanthamum : Japan

5 Tulip : Netherlands

6 Lily : Italy, Canada

7 Corn flower : Germany

8 Daffodil : Wales

9 Carnation : Spain

10. Golden rose : USA

11 Cresent : Pakistan

12 Water tily : Bangladesh

22. Flower for Different Purposes

Name	Purpose	Name	Purpose
Rose	Love	Daffodil	Regard
Carnation (white)	Women's love	Amary lillies	Pride
French Marigold	Jealously/ Sorrow	Iris	Message
African Marigold	Vulgar mind	Lily	Purity
Pansy	Thoughts	Stock	Luxary
Narcisuss	Self esteem	Sweet Pea	Departure

23. Annuals

- Summer Annuals: Seeds are sown during February-March.

  Zinnia, Kochia, Portulaca, Tithonia, Gaillardia, Sunflower, Cosmos, Gomphrena, Coreopsis etc.

- Rainy annuals: Seeds are sown during June-July.

  Balsam, Cock's Comb, Amaranthus, Gaillardia, Gomphrena etc.

- Winter annuals: Seeds are sown during September-October. They are able to tolerate low temperature during winter

  1. For fragrant flower: Mignonette, Carnation, Sweet pea, Sweet Sultan, Sweet William, Sweet Alyssum and Stock.
  2. For hanging Basket: Daisy, Nasturtium, Verbena, Phlox, Portulaca.
  3. For shady situation: Salvia, Cineraria.
  4. For rock garden: Ice plant, Nasturtium, Verbana, Phlox.
  5. For screening purpose: Hollyhock, Sweet pea
  6. For pots: Carnation, Antirrhinum, Aster, Petunia
  7. For dry flower: Statice, Helichrysum, Acroclinum, Lady's lace.

- Blue colour (flower) annuals: Corn flower, blue larkspur, ageratum and Linaria.
- White flower annuals: Allysum, China Aster, Mathiola, Nigelia, Phlox, Papaver, Zinnia and Stock.
- Yellow and orange flower annuals: Pot marigold, *Dimorphetheca*, *Eschacholtiza*, *Tegetes*, Zinnia, Wall flower, Coreopsis and Helichrysum.
- Self pollinated annuals: Lupin, Sweet pea, Salvia.
- Often cross pollinated: Antirrhinum, Larkspur, Linaria, Phlox, Pansy.
- Short long day: Campanula, White Clover
- Tender annual: Oxalis
- Hardy annuals: Digtalis, Rudbeckia, Viola.
- Long day flowers: China aster, Calendula, Delphinium, Gardenia, Stock, Antirrhinum, Petunia, Rudbeckia, Sweet Willium
- Short day flowers: Chrysanthemum, Cosmos, Kalanchoe, Poinsettia Amaranthus, Salvia, Aster.
- Day neutral flowers: Carnation, Balsam, African Violet, Tuberose, Dianthus, Gompherena.

24. Colour Scheme in gardens

1. Green colour dominant throughout year in garden.
2. Warm colour: Red in winter.
3. Yellow colour: in spring.
4. Red, yellow, blue: Primary colour
5. Orange, green, violet: Secondary colour
6. White, black, grey: Neutral colours
7. Cream, pink and shades:Tertiary colours
8. Red, orange and yellow: Warm colours
9. Green and blue: Cool colours

25. Hedge and Classification: When shrub is planned on boundary for fencing, it is called as hedge.

- Planting time: July – August.
- Spacing: Tall 60-90 cm, dwarf; 20-30 cm
- When hedge attain height of 15 cm, they whould be topped back to 10 cm height

Classes of hedge

1. **Tall protective** (1-3 mt ht): *Inga dulcus*, Karoda, Bouganvillea, *Accasia ferrestina.*
2. **Dwarf protective** (1 m ht): *Euphorbia bojori*, *Opuntia spp, Agave spp*, *Pedilanthus spp*.
3. **Tall ornamental**: Mehandi, *Duranta*, *Casurina*, *Hibiscus*, *Hamelia patems*, *Thevatia peruviana*, *Murryaa peniculata*.
4. **Dwarf ornamental**: *Acalypha, Clerodendron, Thumbergia*, *Lantana spp.*

26. Edge: When low growing plants are grown on the border of plot they are called as edge plant. They hardly grow upto 20-30 cm. Examples are Alterranthera, Justicia, Eupatorium, *Iresine lindenii.*

27. Topiary: It is an art of training the plants into different shapes. Examples are *Duranta plumeri*, *Sesberia egyptica*, *Inga dulcus, Acasia modesta, Murraya panniculata.*

28. Lawn (Heart of Garden)

Important grasses:

1 Bermuda grass: Cyadon dectylon (Doob or Haryali)

2 Korean grass: Zoysia japonica

3 Manilla grass: Zosia matrella

4 Korean velvet grass: Zoysia tenuifolia

5 Carpet grass: Axonopus affinis

Planting of grasses

1 Dibbling of roots: Most common and cheapest method of planting

2 Seedling

3 Turfing: Quickest method

4 Bricking: to replace the few unhealthy patches in well maintained lawns

Disease of lawn

1. Fairy Ring: Caused by fungus *Marasmius ordeades*
2. Pale or yellow lawn: Due to N_2 deficiency
3. 60-75% area of garden should be devoted to lawn
4. Seed rate: 12 kg/ Acre or 25-30 kg/ hac or 25 g/m^2
5. Weeds occur in lawn: *Cypruss rotandus*, *Baphorbia spp*
6. Glyphosate: Most widely used pre-emergance herbicide for lawn
7. In shady region: Kentucy grass is grown

29. Style of Gardening

1. Formal style: Plan is symmetrical. Persian and Mughal Garden are formal.
2. Informal style: Plan is asymmetrical. It reflects naturalistic effect of total view and represents natural beauty. Rose garden of Ludhiana, English Garden and Lal Bagh are informal.
3. Free style: Combination of both formal and informal style. English Garden and Lal Bagh are free style.

30. Gardens

Features of Mughal Garden are:

1. Terraces
2. Running water
3. High protecting wall
4. Entrance gate
5. Baradari
6. Terminal building

Symbol of some plants and flower trees

1. Cypress - immortality
2. Flowering trees - Renewal of life.
3. Kachnar - Youth and life.
4. Running water - Life

Main features of Japanese Gardens

1 Trees

2 Ornamentla water

3 Garden lanterns

4 Garden Pagoda

5 Garden Bridges

6 Dry landscape

7 Gate + fences

8 Wells

Main features of English Garden

1. Herbaceous border -discovered by William Robinson
2. Cottage Garden: - discovered by G Jekyell
3. Lawn
4. Rockery

31. Flower Arrangement

1. Japanese style of gardening: **Ikebana**
2. Natural Ikebana where piled flowers are used: **Moribana**
3. Free flower arrangement: **Jiyubana**
4. English flower arrangements: **Morimona**
5. In western style, flowers are 1½ times taller than flower vase.
6. Straight material with uneven height are used: **Zeneika**
7. Beautiful sculpture is created by using wood, stone, rocks: **Zeneibana**
8. Emphasis is given on spritial and religious background, only few flowers are used: **Japanese flower arrangement.**
9. Emphasis given on mass flower arrangement: **English flower arrangement**.

32. Bonsai: Japanese art of growing miniature trees and shrubs by extreme dwarfing. Origin of bonsai is China. In Maime bonsal: Plant height is 15-20 cm.

33. Oil Extraction

Rose:

i) *Rosa damascena*: 0-05%

ii) *Rosa bourboniana*: 0-04%

iii) *Rosa centifolia*: 001%

iv) *Rosa moschata*: 0-04%

Jasmine

i) *Jasminum auriculatum*: 0.29% (Maximum oil recovery)

ii) *J. grandiflorum*: 0.25-0.30%

34. Status of Aromatic and Medicinal Plants

- Highest number of medicinal spp are under family – Asteraceae
- Maximum demand in the world market is of Senna leaves, Isabgol seed, and Cassia tora seeds.
- India is 1st largest producer of Kewada oil, Senna, Isabgol.

- India is the largest exporter of – *Psyllium* and Senna leaves
- China is the major producer of Geranium oil and Citronella oil.
- World production of essential oil is dominated by Brazil (40%) followed by USA (20%) and India (15%).
- Essential oil is the odoriferous steam volatile constituents of aromatic plants.
- National Aromatic and Medicinal Plant Board is situated at New Delhi
- Central Institute for Medicinal and Aromatic Plants is located at Lucknow
- National research centre for Medicinal and Aromatic Plants is located at Anand –Gujrat.

3

Explanatory Notes

Lotus

(*Nelumbo nucifera*)

Family: Nymphaeaceae/Nelumbonaceae

Origin: Southern Asia

Flower colour: White to deep pink

Plant part used: Flower (almost all parts)

Basic chromosome number: X=8

Somatic chromosome number: 2n =16

- Flower of *antiquity*.
- National flower of *India*.
- Considered to be a Sacred flower and symbol of Goddess *Lakshmi*.
- In Sanskrit the words *Padma* ,*kamala* and *pankaja* refer to lotus
- The family Nymphaeaceae has two genera *Nymphaea* and *Nelumbo*.
- Water Lilly belongs to Nymphaea whereas Lotus to Nelumbo.
- It is a tropical deep water aquatic plant need warm climate (20-30°C).
- Lotus may go into dormancy during cooler climate.
- Nelumbo has two species viz; *N. nucifera* and *N. lutea*
- *N. lutea* (American lotus) with yellow flowers is native to North America.
- *Nelumbo nucifera* is commonly known as Sacred Lotus, the Hindu Lotus, Indian Lotus, the East Indian Lotus or the Chinese Lotus.
- All parts of lotus are usd as food; rhizomes are used as vegetable; eaten as pickle, chips; carpels are also edible and are very nutritious; petals used as soup garnishing etc.
- It is propagated by rhizome, divisions and seeds

Rose

(*Rosa* spp.)

Family: Rosaceae

Origin: North Hemisphere (Himalayas)

Flower colour: Red (commonly)

Plant part used: Flower

Basic chromosome number: X=7

Somatic chromosome number: 2n =14

- Queen of flowers.
- National flower of England, Iran, UK.
- Symbol of beauty, convey message of love.
- Commercial method of propagation: T budding
- Best time for budding: November to February
- Rootstock: *R. multiflora* (Edward rose) most commonly used rootstock of western India.
    - *Rosa indica* var *odorata* – most commonly used rootstock in North India.
    - Dog rose: *Rosa canina.*
    - Cabbage rose: *R. centifolia*
    - Thornless rose: *R. pendulina, R. bourboniana*
    - French Rose: *R. gallica*
    - Musk Rose: *R. moschata*
- Good quality blooms are produced in winter.
- Rose requires ligh throughout the year.
- BK Roy Choudhary: 1st Indian Rose breeder who raised var Dr S D Mukarjee in 1935.
- BS Bhattacharajee (Father of Rose breeding) was 2nd rose breeder, evaluated var Ramkrishnadev.
- Dr BP Pal evolved 1st rose var *Rose Sherbet.*

- Bud union is most susceptible to low temperature than any other part of Rose.
- Winter chilling is necessary in flower bud formation in *Rosa damascena.*
- Preservative solution: 1-3% sugar + 100-300 ppm HQC.
- var `La France' produced by Guillot (1867).
- About 80% of rose flowers are utilized for rose water, 10% attars and 1-2% pankhuri and 8% for gulrogan and gulkand preparation.
- **Hybrid Tea Roses** (Hybrid Perpetual × Tea Roses)

La France is considered as First hybrid tea rose (1867)

- Bedding varieties.
  - Yellow: Vasant, King Ransom, Golden Giant
  - Orange : Scarlet Superstar
  - Pink : Confidence, First Prize, Sonia
  - Red: Crimson Glory, Happiness
  - Bronze: Sunset Song
  - Lavender: Blue Moon, Anurag
  - White: June Bride, Tushar
  - Colour blend: CarelessLove, Kiss of Fire
- Hybrid Perpetual: First hybrid perpetual was developed by Princess Helene.
- Floribundas: Hybrid Tea × Polyanthas (1924). Also called Hybrid polyanthas.
  - 1st var-Rodhatte, produced by poulesen (1912)
  - Red: Week Jock, Jantar-Mantar
  - Orange: Independence, Shola
  - Yellow: Ali Gold, Gold Bunny
  - Pink: Queen Elizabath, Junior Miss
  - White: Iceberg, Himangini
  - Bicolour: Red Gold

    - Colourblend: Banjaran
    - Bicentennial: Charisma Madhura
- **Grandiflora**: Hybrid Tea × Floribundas
    - 1st var: Buccaneer (1952)
    - Swati Rashmi, Montezuma (1955), Queen Elizabeth (1954).
- **Polyantha**: *R. multiflora* × *R. wichuriana* × *R. chinensis*
    - 1st var La Paquerette (1875)
- **Climbers**: Sympathe, Delhi White Pearl, Breath of life, Golden shower America, Swan Lake, Delhi Pink Pearl.
- **Ramblers**: American Pillar (1902), Excelsa (1909), Albertine
- **Miniature roses** (Baby or fairy roses): Ideal for growing in pots. Desert charm, Red Flush, Delhi Scarlet, Summer Butter, Party Girl, Puppy Love, Snow Carpet, Yellow Doll, Cindrella.
    - Siriped and hand painted: Sidhartha, Madhosh
    - Exhibition varieties: Christian Dior, Eiffel Tower, Garden Party, Mischief, Pusa Sonia, Show Girl, First Prize, Raktagandha.
    - Scented varieties: Lafrance, Seventh Heaven, Pusa Sugandha, Blue Moon.
    - Cut flower: Gladiator, Happiness, Super Star, Sonia Mercedes, Arjun, Ratkagandha, Sindhoor.
- Most of varieties take about 60-75 days for blooming after pruning.
- Wintering of roses is very common in western part of India.
- Pulsing treatment is done to increase shelf-life.
- Most costly oil: Rose oil.
- Miniature roses are resistant to pest and diseases.
- Limp neck – Rose disorder.
- Most common rootstock in European countries: *R. cannina*
- Flowering in hybrid tea roses: 42 days after pruning.
- Flowering in Floribundus: 45 days after pruning.
- The waxy residue left after extraction of essential oil through distillation is known as concrete.

- Die back is the main fungal disease in roses.
- Bent neck is the physiological disorder characterized by bending of cut rose stems after harvesting.

Gladiolus

(*Gladiolus tritis*)

Family: Iridaceae

Origin: South Africa

Plant part used: Flower spike

Basic chromosome number : X= 15

Somatic chromosome number: 2n = 30, 60, 120

- Most popular bulbous flowering plant.
- Gladious a Latin word means sword. It is also known as Sword Lily.
- Gladiolus was coined by Pliny the Elder (AD 23-79).
- Optimum temperature for growth: 16-30°C
- Optimum temperature for corm storage is 4-5°C.
- It require open sunny situation.
- Longer day length improves spike quality.
- The point where scale is attached to the corm is called Node.
- Planting time: July-December, spacing 20 x 30 cm^2.
- Corm should be treated with 0-2% Bavistin before plantation.
- Ethylene chlorohydrine is used to break dormancy of corms.
- Gladiolus is a 7 months crop.
- Hilling is important operation of Gladiolus.
- Preservative solution: 20% sucrose + 200 ppm HQC.
- Dormancy of corm broken by storage at 4-5°C for 3-4 month.
- Corm and cormels are the important planting material.
- Seeds require: 15-20 days to germinate.
- For cut spikes storage temperature: 1-2°C for 2 weeks.

- Fluoride toxicity seen on tip of leaves, absorbed from air.
- Toxicity is due to heavy application of super phosphate, rock phosphate which contains hydrogen fluoride.

Carnation

(*Dianthus caryophyllus*)

Family: Caryophyllaceae

Origin: Mediterrarean region

Plant part used: Flower spike

Basic chromosome number: X= 15

Somatic chromosome number: 2n = 30

- Quantitatively long day plant. Cyclic lighting is effective.
- It is a cool season crop.
- Ideal temperature range: 10-20°C.
- Night temperature should not be less than 10°C and more than 18°C.
- Carnatin occupies a prime position in International cut flower market.
- Pinching is regular practice in carnation.
- Disbudding is regular practice in carnation and is most important in standard varieties.
- Staking is also done in carnation.
- Pre-conditioning of cut flower in solution of $AgNO_3$ is important to avoid ethylene injury and prolong shelf life.
- Sim carnation has great commercial importance.
- Sim group need regular pinching.
- Perpetual flwering carnations are commercially used as cut flowers.
- Calyx splitting is a serious problem affecting quality of flowers.
- Types of carnation:

A) Perpetual: *D. caryophyllus* × *D. chinensis*. These may be standard or spray type, having longer stock length.

B) Marguerite: *D. chinensis* × *D. caryophyllus*. Flowers are single or double.

C) Malmaison: Flowers are large, double with well filled centre. It has pink flowers. Princess of Wales, Mr Martin Smith

D) Royal: Malmaison × Perpetual (Royal Fancy, White Perfection)

E) Modern : Pico

- Pinching:

  1st : 4th week after planting (July) – (6th pair of leaf)

  2nd: 7th week after planting

1) Single pinching: Below 6th node: to get early crop.
2) Pinch and a half regular princing + half pinching: Steady production.

   Double pinch: To delay flowering period

Chrysanthamum

(*Dendranthema grandiflora*)

Family: Asteraceae

Origin: China

Plant part used: Flower and spike

Flower colour: Almost all except blue

Basic chromosome number: X= 9

Somatic chromosome number: 2n = 36, 45, 54.

- It is a short day plant.
- Common name: Guldaudi, Autumn Queen, Glory of East, Queen of East
- Symbol of Royality in Japan.
- National Flower of Japan.
- Disc florets: Centre.
- Ray Florets: Outer.
- Blooming period: September-October.
- Propagation: By root suckers or terminal cuttings.
- Suckers: For small flowered, cuttings for disease free, long time, fails.

- Pinching: To encourage side branches for cut flower.
- Disbudding: To encourage single crown branch for standard flower.
- Yellow, white colours are preferred for cut flowers.
- Urea is not applied as it causes phytotoxicity.
- Use of Alar/Phosphon is very effective in producing better size blooms, on dwarf plants.
- Disc florets are perfect while ray florets are pistillate.
- Axillary shoots produce buds called crown buds
- Harvesting: July-August-September
- Pinching: Most important for cascade (Japanese) formation
- Pinching is also known as stopping.
- Regular incurve, irregular, regular reflex, irregular reflex, intermediate, quilled, spoon, anemone, single and semi double are ray florets arrangement of large chrysanthemum flowers.
- Anemone, button, single Korean, decorative, pompon, semi quilled, quilled, stellate and cineraria are ray florets arrangement of small chrysanthemum flowers.
- It has shallow fibrous root system which is sensitive to water logging.
- Lighting in greenhouse is done for normal growth during inadequate natural light.
- International variety
    i) Kokovarouri – Standard type – Yellow
    ii) Nanako – Spray type – yellow

Marigold

African (*Tagetes erecta*)

French (*Tagetes petula)*

Family: Asteraceae/Compositae

Origin: Mexico (Central America)

Plant part used: Loose Flowers

Basic chromosome number: X= 12

Somatic chromosome number: 2n = 24, 48

- Marigold is a quantitative short day plants.
- Flowers are sold in market as loose or as a garland.
- Requires mild climate for luxuriant growth.
- Optimum temperature: 18-30°C
- Nugget is a triploid variety of marigold.
- Seed rate: 1-15 kg/hectare. Seeds count about 300-350 seeds per gram.
- Best flowering noticed during winter months (October to April).
- Weeds are major problem and 3-4 weedings are required.
- Plucking of flowers should be done in cool hours of the day (preferably evening).
- It is a cross pollinated crop.
- Damping off is the major disease of marigold.
- Ketones are the base material for synthesizing aroma chemicals.
- French marigold thrives best in light soil.
- Application of CCC growth retardant @3000ppm prolongs flowering period in African marigold.

Jasmine

(*Jasminum* spp)

Family: Oleaceae

Origin: Mexico

Basic chromosome number: X= 13

Somatic chromosome number: 2n = 26, 39, 52

- It is grown in tropical climate and is known as native of tropical and sub-tropical region.
- It is a perennial crop.
- Jasmine is a climbing, erect shrubby plant may be deciduous or evergreen.
- Poet's jasmine: *J. officinale;* Chameli: *J. grandiflorum*

- Different spp of *Jasminum*
    1. *J. sambac*: Arabian Jasmine, Tuscan jasmine, Bela, Mogra.
    2. *J. grandiflorum*: Royal or Spanish jasmine, chameli, Mallai, Pitchi (Flowering time: March-September)
    3. *J. auriculatum*: Thum, Jai, Mullai (Maximum recovery of oil)
    4 *J. multiflorum*: Kakada, Fussy jasmine. (Non-scented jasmine)
    5 *J. arborescence*: Tree jasmine, Bela (Flowering: November – May).
    5 *J. carophyllum*
    6 *J. flexile*: Climbing jasmine.
    7 *J. humile*: Yellow jasmine.
- Propagation: By semi hard wood cutting.

  Pruning
    1) *J sambac* (Arabian or Tuscan jasmine): October end.
    2) *J grandiflorum* (Spanish/common jasmine): Mid December
    3) *J auriculatum*: White flowers produced in December-January.
- For extraction of Jasmine concentrate – fully open flowers are plucked.
- Flowering in Jasmine starts from second year.

Orchids

(*Cymbidum* sp and *Dendrobium* sp)

Family: Orchidaceae

Origin: Tropical countries

- Bulbophyllum is largest genera of orchids.
- Orchids are the most beautiful flowers in God's creation.

Group of orchids:

- Epiphytes : Dendrobium, Vanda, Bulbophyllum
- Lithophytes (Terrestial): Cymbidium

Plant morphotology

- Monopodial : Venda, Vanilla, Renanthera

- Sympodial: Cattleya, Cymbidium, Dendrobium, Bulbophyllum
- Propagation: A) Division: Cattleya, Cymbidium, Dendrobium

  B) Cutting: Venda
- Netherland: Largest producer of temperature orchids (*Cymbidium*).
- Thailand: Largest producer of tropical orchids (*Dendrobium*).
- Orchids include about 800 genera and 35000 species.
- Orchidaceae is the largest family among flowering plants.
- Flower have 3-sepals and 3 petals, hence called as – Tepals.
- Seed – Endosperm absent (Exalbuminous).
- Commercial propagatioin method: Tissue culture.
- In orchids light requirement is 2000-6000 Foot candles.
- Day temperature vary from 15.5-21°C and night temperature 10-15.5°C.
- Epiphytic orchids are commonly grown in media containing tree fern fibre, osmuda figre, coconut husk, bricks, charcoal etc.
- Most common method for multiplication of sympodial orchids is division.
- Harvesting influence keeping quality
  - Cattleya harvested: 3-5 days after bud split or dehisce.
  - Dendrobium harvested when 2-3 buds are still unopened.
  - During warm weather, blooms are harvested at early development stage.

Tuberose

(*Polyanthes tuberosa*)

Order - Asparagales

Family - Agavaceae

Origin: - Mexico

- Latin word tuberose meaning Swollen or tuberous; Polianthes means grey flower.
- In Hindi tuberose is called Rajnigandha means *night fragrance* (Rajni = Night, gandha = Fragrance)

- In Bengali – tuberose is called Rajoni-gondha meaning *scent of the night.*
- In Singapore, it is called ye Lai Xiang means *fragrance that comes in night.*

Lavendula

(*Lavendula angustifolia*)

Order - Lamiales

Family - Lamiaceae

Binomial name - *Lavendula officinalis* Mill

Origin: Western Mediterranean region

Plant part used: Flowers

- *Lavendula angustifolia* is known as common lavender, true lavender or English lavender.

Lavender

(*Lavendula species*)

Family: Lamiaceae

Origin: Europe

Plant part used: Floweand flowering tops

Basic chromosome number: X=6

Somatic chromosome number: 2n = 48, 54

- *Lavendula angustifolia* (True lavender), *L. latifolia* (Spike lavender), *L. intermedia* (Lavendin) are three important species of lavender.
- USSR is a major producer followed by France and Bulgaria.
- *L. angustifolia* is polyploid. Lavender is mostly cross pollinated.
- It is a temperate plant, flowers in long day conditions.
- Light loam to calcareous soils, pH 7.0-8.4.
- Propagation: True lavender by seeds and Lavandin always by cutting (10 cm).
- Oil is obtained from `Flowering tops' and recovery is 1-2 percent.

- Harvesting: Flower cut with 12 cm stem.
- Main chemical constituent: Linalool (27.6-48.0%).
- Fertilizers: N and P (40:40 kg/ha each) at time of planting. N = 60 kg/ ha in 2-3 splits.

Alstroemeria

(*Alstroemeria caryophyllae*)

Family: Alstroemeriaceae

Origin: Tropical America.

Plant parts used: Flowers

Basic chromosome number: X=8

Somatic chromosome number: 2n = 16

Anthurium

(*Anthurium acutifolium*)

Family: Araceae

Origin: Columbia and Peru

Plant parts used: Flowers

Basic chromosome number: X=15, 16

Somatic chromosome number: 2n = 30, 32

Bird of Paradise

(*Sterlizia alba*)

Family: Musaceae

Origin: South Africa

Plant parts used: Flowers

China Aster

(*Callistephus chinensis L.*)

Family: Asteraceae

Origin: China

Plant parts used: Flowers

Basic chromosome number: X=9

Somatic chromosome number: 2n = 18

Crossandra

(*Crossandra undulaefolia*)

Family: Acanthaceae

Origin: East Indies

Plant parts used: Flowers

Basic chromosome number: X=15, 20

Somatic chromosome number: 2n = 30, 40

Dahlia

(*Dahlia coccinea*)

Family: Asteraceae

Origin: Mexico, Central America

Plant parts used: Flowers

Basic chromosome number: X=16

Somatic chromosome number: 2n = 32, 48

Narcissus

(*Narcissus astureinsis*)

Family: Amaryllidaceae

Origin: Northern France

Plant parts used: Flowers

Basic chromosome number: X=7, 10

Somatic chromosome number: 2n = 14, 20

Tulip

(*Tulipa biflora*)

Family: Liliaceae

Origin: Asia minor

Plant parts used: Flowers

Basic chromosome number: X=12

Somatic chromosome number: 2n = 24

Zinnia

(*Zinnia elegans*)

Family: Compositae

Origin: Mexico

Plant parts used: Flowers

Basic chromosome number: X=11, 12

Somatic chromosome number: 2n = 22,24

Palmarosa

Family: Gramineae

Origin: India

Plant part used: Flower and leaves

Basic chromosome number: X=10, 20

Somatic chromosome number: 2n = 20 (var. Motia);

2n = 40 (var. Sofia)

- Palmarosa is indigenous to India.
- India is the major producer followed by Brazil, Indonesia.
- Highly cross pollinated.
- *Cymbopogon martini* var motia, *C. martini* var Sofia are two important species belongs to family Gramineae.
- Recovery of oil: 0.4-0.6%
- Geraniol percentage in Motia = (65 to 80%); Sofia = (36 to 60%).
- Propagation: By seeds during May-June.
- Loam to light sandy loam; pH= 9.

- Harvesting: Full bloom stage, 7-10 days after flowering.
- Trishna developed at CIMAP, Lucknow Jamrosa developed at RRL, Jammu.

Citronella

Family: Gramineae.

Origin: Sri Lanka

Plant part used: Leaves

Basic chromosome number: X=10

Somatic chromosome number: 2n = 20

- Citronella is a tropical plant, thrive in Humid tropical.
- It is a perennial crop and remains for 5 to 6 years.
- *Cymbopogon winterianus* Jowett is java citronella.
- *Java citronella* and *Ceylon citronella* are native to Sri Lanka.
- Source of oil: Leaves oil recovery of citronella is 1%.
- Varieties (*Java citronella*): Manjusha, Mandakii are clonal selection and have 30-40% higher yield.
- New variety: Bio-13.
- Soil: Light loam; pH 5.8 to 8.0.
- Propagation: Propagated by splitting the clumps and each clump must have 1-3 tillers.
- Spacing: 50 cm row to row and 50-60 cm plant to plant.
- Harvest after 3 to 4 months of planting to induce tillering, leaves are harvested 15 cm above ground.
- Only leaf blade is harvested leaving the leaf sheeth.
- Crop yield: 100 kg/hectare (1st year); 150 kg/ hactare (2nd year).
- 20:40:40 kg NPK/hectare is basal dose during planting.
- Main chemical constituent: Citronellol (13.4-15.7%).
- Indonesia, China, Thailand and India are main producers.
- Java citronella has 75-85% total alcohol, whereas Ceylon citronella has 55-65% total alcohol.

Patchouli

(*Pogostemon cablin*)

Family: Labiatae

Origin: Phillipines

Plant part used: Branches and leaves

Basic chromosome number: X=17

Somatic chromosome number: 2n = 34

- Harvesting starts after 5-6 years of planting at stage when foliage starts turning pale green to light brown and gives typical patchouli odour.
- Only leaves and branches are harvested.
- Well drained, medium loam, fertile soil, rich in organic matter is preferred.
- Moderate temperature (30-35°C) with very high humidity favours the growth.
- Fertilizers: Phosphorus is beneficial in South India.
- Oil yield: 1.8 to 3% oil.
- Major chemical constituent: Patchouli alcohol (33.7%).
- Indonesia is the largest producers of oil account for 95% of world production.
- Leaves have glands which secrets Red oil.
- Real patchouli (*Pogostemon cablin*) never flowers.
- Roots, stems, branches, stalk and leaves all parts contain oil.
- Most of oil is present in top three leaves.

Basil

(*Ocimum basilicum* Var *glabrata*)

Family: Lamiaceae

Origin: India

Plant part used: Leaves and tender shoot part

Basic chromosome number: X=12

Somatic chromosome number: 2n = 24

- Basil is derived from Greek word Basilica means Royal plant.
- It is variously called Sweet basil, French basil and Common basil belongs to family Lamiaceae; Sub-family Ocimoideae.
- Parts used for extraction of oil: Leaves and tender part of shoot.
- Long days and high temperature is good for growth and oil products.
- Propagated by seed/tender shoot tip.
- Harvesting stage: Full bloom stage.
- Soil temperature and moisture directly correlated to essential oil content.
- *Ocimum species* are cross pollinated.
- Oil is present in leaves.

Fox glove

(*Digitalis purpurea*)

Family: Scrophulariaceae

Origin: Europe

Plant part used: Leaves

- It is a biennial herb, cross pollinated.
- Honey bees are main pollinators.
- Part used: Leaves.
- Source: Glycoside (0.93-0.99%).
- Harvesting stage is Rosette stage.
- Leaves of Fox glove contains glycosides namely digitoxin and gitoxin.
- Silt loam to clay loam soil is best.
- Temperature required: 20-30°C is good.
- Seed rate is 8kg/hectare.

Opium

(*Papaver somniferum* L.)

Family: Papaveraceae

Origin: Western Mediterranean Region of Europe

Plant part used: Green but fully ripe capsule

Basic chromosome number: X= 11

Somatic chromosome number: 2n = 22

- Opium is known as Joy plant in South France belongs to Family Papaveraceae; Sub family Papaveroideae.
- Type of fruit is Capsule.
- Opium is extracted from green but fully ripe capsule.
- Morphene obtained: 7-17%; Codeine obtained: 21-44%.
- Opium is self pollinated.
- Kirtiman, Chetak, Trishna are important varieties.
- India is the major producer of *Opium* alkaloid in world.
- Capsule contains 70% of total morphine.
- Opium is used in manufacturing of heroines.
- Trishna is resistant to mildew.
- Seed rate: 5-6kg/hectare
- Planting time: Nov. to April
- Spacing: 30 × 10cm

Solanum

(*Solanum viarum*)

Family: Solanaceae

Origin: India

Plant part used: Yellow berries

Basic chromosome number: X= 12

Somatic chromosome number: 2n = 24

- *Solanum viarum* syn *khashianum* belongs to family Solanaceae; sub-family: Leptostemonum.
- Solasodine contents vary from 1.00-1.75% on DWB in berries.

- Fertilizers: N: P: K= 80:40:40 kg/hectare.
- Planting time: February-March.
- Harvesting: Berries are harvested when they turn yellow.
- *S. viarum* is susceptible to *Fusarium oxysporum*.
- Wilt is the major disease.
- Spacing: 50 × 50cm

Belladona

(*A. belladonna*)

Family: Solanaceae

Origin: Central and Eastern Europe

Plant part used: Leaves and roots.

- Belladona *(A. belladonna)* is a cross pollinated crop.
- Seed rate: 4 kg/hectare.
- Spacing: 30 × 45cm

Senna

(*Cassia angustifolia*)

Family: Leguminoseae

Origin: South Africa

Plant part used: Leaves and pods.

Basic chromosome number: X= 13

Somatic chromosome number: 2n = 26

- It is a self pollinated crop.
- Source: Sennosides-A, B, C

Isabgol

(*Plantago ovata*)

Family: Plantaginaceae

Origin: India

Plant part used: Seed/ husk

- Harvesting: When crop turn yellow and spike turn brownish.

Scented Geranium

Family: Geraniaceae

Origin: South Africa

Plant parts used: Flowers

Basic chromosome number: X=9

Somatic chromosome number: 2n = 90

Lemongrass

Family: Gramineae

Origin: Malabar Coast of India.

Plant parts used: Leaves and seeds

Basic chromosome number: X=10

Somatic chromosome number: 2n = 20

Rosemary

Family: Labiateae

Origin: Spain, South Africa.

Plant parts used: Leaves and seeds

Basic chromosome number: X=12

Somatic chromosome number: 2n = 24

4

Multiple Choice Questions

1. Carnation is a
   a) Short day plant   b) Day neutral plant
   c) Long day plant   d) None of these
2. Lotus in Sanskrit is known as
   a) Water lily   b) Padma
   c) Kamala   d) Pankaja
3. The National flower of India is
   a) Rose   b) Jasmine
   c) Lotus   d) Kachnar
4. Rose is the national flower of
   a) UK   b) USA
   c) Iran   d) All of these
5. National flower of China is
   a) Chrysanthemum   b) Narcissus
   c) Tulip   d) Lily
6. National flower of Japan is
   a) Rose   b) Chrysanthemum
   c) Tulip   d) Lily
7. National flower of Netherlands is
   a) Tiger lily   b) Tulip
   c) Daffodil   d) All of these
8. Lily is the national flower of
   a) Italy   b) Iraq
   c) Turkey   d) All of these

9. Who is the present (year 2011) DDG (Horticulture) in ICAR, New Delhi?
   a) Dr KL Chadha b) Dr BP Pal
   c) Dr HP Singh d) Dr MS Swaminathan

10. Who is the present (year 2011) Director General of ICAR, New Delhi?
   a) Dr BP Pal b) Dr S Ayyappan
   c) Dr MS Swaminathan d) Dr KL Chadha

11. The largest cut flower producing country in the world is
   a) Netherland b) Colombia
   c) Armenia d) USA

12. India contributes nearly_____ percent to the global flower market
   a) 15 b) 2
   c) 10 d) 0.49

13. The biggest international flower market is located at
   a) Alsmeer b) Colombia
   d) New Delhi d) London

14. The highest per capita consumption of cut flowers is found in
   a) India b) USA
   c) Germany d) Switzerland

15. World trade in foliage plants is about (billion US$)
   a) 5 b) 2.5
   c) 10 d) 15

16. Name the country which has maximum share of foliage plants in the world market
   a) India b) China
   c) Denmark d) Netherland

17. Which of the following is considered as number one flower in International cut flower market?
   a) Rose b) Chrysanthemum
   c) Carnation d) Orchid

18. Maximum consumption of cut roses is during
    a) Valentine's day b) Mother's day
    c) New Year eve d) Christmas day
19. How many private units are engaged in export of flowers in India?
    a) 500 b) 200
    c) 100 d) 300
20. In India, the maximum area is in which flower crop?
    a) Marigold b) Tuberose
    c) Jasmine d) Rose
21. Which one is growing in largest area as long stem cut flower in our country?
    a) Chrysanthemum b) Rose
    c) Gladiolus d) Orchid
22. Free style garden are nothing but
    a) Symmetrical gardens b) Formal gardens
    c) Informal gardens d) Mughal gardens
23. Ground layering is most common in
    a) Carnation b) Rose
    c) Begonia d) Chrysanthemum
24. Herbaceous stem cutting is a propagation method used for
    a) Carnation b) Begonia
    c) Hollyhock d) All of these
25. Golden shower takes _____ years to flower.
    a) 15 b) 10
    c) 20 d) 2
26. *Lagerstroemia indica* is a
    a) Flowering climber b) Flowering shrub
    c) Foliage tree d) Flowering annual

27. Removal of undesirable leaves from the tree is known as
    a) Disbudding b) Deblossoming
    c) Defoliation d) Defruiting
28. Removal of undesirable flowers from plant is
    a) Defruiting b) Deblossoming
    c) Defoliation d) Disbudding
29. Removal of undesired branches by picking auxiliary buds is known as.
    a) Clipping b) Nipping
    c) Topping d) Budding
30. Vista vision is a theme for
    a) Landscape b) Japanese garden
    c) Persian garden d) Mixed garden
31. Which of the following is/ are cheapest or easiest method for lawn making
    a) Turfing b) Turf plastering
    c) Dibbling d) None of these
32. First DG of Indian Council of Agricultural Research was.
    a) Dr M S Swaminathan b) Dr B P Pal
    c) Dr G S Randhawa d) Dr M S Randhawa
33. Which of following is winter season foliage annual?
    a) Coleus b) Poinsettia
    c) Croton d) Kochia
34. Male sterility is common in
    a) Petunia b) Marigold
    c) Antirrhinum d) All of these
35. Thimma is an important cultivar of
    a) Rose b) Bougainvillea
    c) Tulip d) Carnation

36. Corm dormancy in gladiolus is due to
    a) Linoleic acid b) Linolenic acid
    c) Stearic acid d) All of these
37. Pyrethrum is extracted from.
    a) Leaves of *Nicotiana tobaccum* b) Flower of tobacco
    c) Flower petals of chrysanthemum d) Stems of carnation
38. Banjaran a cultivar of rose belongs to which category?
    a) Floribunda b) Polyantha
    c) Hybrid tea d) None of these
39. Dahlia is propagated by
    a) Tubers b) Rhizomes
    c) Tuberous roots d) Seeds
40. Bending of plants towards light is called
    a) Hydrotropism b) Phototropism
    c) Chemotropism d) Geotropism
41. Maximum rose oil is produced in
    a) Bulgaria b) Alsmeer
    c) Italy d) China
42. Gladiolus is asexually propagated by
    a) Corms b) Rhizome
    c) Bulb d) Tuber
43. Bulbil is a common feature in
    a) Tulip b) Gladiolus
    c) Dahlia d) Tiger lily
44. Cormel is a swollen end of
    a) Fibrous root b) Primary root
    c) Stolon d) Auxiliary bud

45. Which of the following is an "English flower arrangement"?

a) Jiyubana b) Ikebana

c) Morimona d) Zeneika

46. Dahlia was introduced by Agri-horticultural Society of India for the first time at Kolkata in the year

a) 1935 b) 1857

c) 1882 d) 1905

47. Chrysanthemum in India is known as

a) Daud b) Harsingar

c) Guldaudi d) Mum

48. In China and Japan, chrysanthemum is known as

a) Hill queen b) Autumn queen

c) Japanese queen d) Guldaudi

49. Dr MA Kher was associated with

a) Chrysanthemum b) Carnation

c) Rose d) Chinaaster

50. Bharat Sundari is a famous cultivar of

a) Bougainvillea b) Hibiscus

c) Rose d) Carnation

51. Thornless rose rootstock was developed at

a) IARI b) NBRI

c) IIHR d) Rose Garden, Chandigarh

52. First cultivar of rose released by Dr BP Pal in the year1962 was

a) Rose Sherbet b) Aruna

c) Rose Scented d) Mehak

53. International Bougainvillea registration centre is at

a) IIHR b) IARI

c) NBRI d) TNAU

54. Which of following is growing as a long stem cut rose in India?
    a) Mother Teressa b) Anurag
    c) Mehak d) Raktagandha
55. Name the floribunda type cultivar of rose which is also used as cut flower
    a) Banjaran b) Rose Sherbet
    c) Sindhoor d) Mohini
56. Banjaran cultivar of rose belongs to the category
    a) Hybrid Tea b) Polyantha
    c) Miniature d) Floribunda
57. Pusa Basanti an open pollinated cultivar belongs to
    a) Zinnia b) Chrysanthemum
    c) Bougainvillea d) Marigold
58. Bottom heating in case of ___________ cuttings enhances rooting percentage
    a) Hibiscus b) Rose
    c) Bougainvillea d) Dahlia
59. Queen Elizabeth is a common cultivar of
    a) Rose b) Carnation
    c) Chrysanthemum d) Marigold
60. In North Indian plains which of the following is a superior rootstock of rose?
    a) *Rosa bourboniana* b) *Rosa multiflora*
    c) *Rosa gallica* d) *Rosa indica*
61. Crocus is propagated successfully by
    a) Tuber b) Corm
    c) Bulb d) Rhizome
62. Birbal Sahani a cultivar developed at NBRI, Lucknow belongs to
    a) Tuberose b) Bougainvillea
    c) Marigold d) Chrysanthemum

63. Amar Shola is a cultivar of
    a) Marigold b) Rose
    c) Amaranthus d) Verbena
64. French marigold is a/an__________ in nature
    a) Diploid b) Tetraploid
    c) Aneuploid d) None of these
65. Diploid chromosome number of gladiolus is
    a) 60 b) 30
    c) 80 d) 40
66. Samrat is a tetraploid cultivar of
    a) Amaryllis b) Tuberose
    c) Rose d) Verbena
67. "The Rose in India" is a book written by
    a) RS Randhawa b) Vishnu Swarup
    c) MS Randhawa d) BP Pal
68. Most of the cultivars of chrysanthemum are
    a) Short day b) Long day
    c) Day neutral d) None of above
69. Major problem in breeding roses is/are
    a) Difficult pollination b) Poor seed setting
    c) Absence of rose trials d) All of these
70. Powdery mildew in roses is caused by
    a) *Diplodia* b) *Botrytis*
    c) *Diplocarpon* d) *Sphaerotheca*
71. Which cultivar of rose is/are resistant to powdery mildew?
    a) Spotless Yellow b) Spotless Pink
    c) Spotless Gold d) All of these

72. Which of following species is resistant to powdery mildew?

a) *moschata* b) *bourboniana*

c) *rugosa* d) *indica*

73. Mohini cultivar of rose is famous for its

a) Red colour b) White colour

c) Chocolate colour d) Yellow colour

74. Total area under protected cultivation in the world is nearly about _________ thousand hectares

a) 40 b) 50

c) 60 d) 90

75. The growth rate of global floriculture industry is ________ per cent per annum

a) 30 b) 15-20

c) 10-15 d) 20-25

76. Which one of following is number one foliage plant at global level?

a) *Ficus elastica* b) Cordyline

c) Aglaonema d) Dieffenbachia

77. The leading cut foliage exporter is

a) USA b) Netherlands

c) France d) Italy

78. The largest flowers exporter in Asia is

a) India b) Korea

c) China d) Japan

79. The largest flowering plant species family is

a) Asteraceae b) Rosaceae

c) Brassicaceae d) Orchidaceae

80. How many species of orchid are native to India?

a) 1600 b) 5000

c) 1000 d) 1800

81. Orchid species which grow on trees are known as
    a) Epiphyte b) Lithophytes
    c) Saprophyte d) Terrestrial
82. Orchid species which grow on moss covered rocks are known as
    a) Epiphyte b) Terrestrial
    c) Both a and b d) Lithophyte
83. Phaius orchids belongs to the group
    a) Saprophyte b) Terrestrial
    c) Epiphyte d) Lithophyte
84. Jewel orchids are valued for their beautiful
    a) Leaves b) Stamens
    c) Flowers d) All of these
85. Gynoecium in orchid flower is known as
    a) Stamens b) Tube
    c) Endosperm d) Column
86. Orchid seeds are devoid of
    a) Seed coat b) Cotyledon
    c) Endosperm d) All of these
87. Tissue culture industry in the world has revolutionized by
    a) Orchid b) Rose
    c) Tulip d) Carnation
88. Which of following flower has longest vase-life?
    a) Tulip b) Rose
    c) Chrysanthemum d) Paphiopedilum
89. Which of the following alkaloid is not present in orchids?
    a) Denrobine b) Pierardine
    c) Chysine d) Atrazine

90. A flat like projection between male and female parts in orchid flowers is known as
    - a) Rostellum
    - b) Column
    - c) Screen
    - d) None of these
91. Indian shot is the name given to seeds of
    - a) Dog flower
    - b) Rose
    - c) Orchid
    - d) Canna
92. Fruit of rose is known as
    - a) Hip
    - b) Indian shot
    - c) Nut
    - d) Berry
93. For getting large size flowers which of following operation is important?
    - a) Pinching
    - b) Disbudding
    - c) Puncturing
    - d) Disshooting
94. Which one of following is growth retardant?
    - a) IBA
    - b) IAA
    - c) B-Nine
    - d) NAA
95. Pigment responsible for blue colour in flowers is
    - a) Pelargolin
    - b) Delphilidin
    - c) Lycopene
    - d) None of these
96. Aspermy in chrysanthemum is caused by
    - a) Fungus
    - b) Bacteria
    - c) Virus
    - d) All of above
97. Gladiolus belongs to the family
    - a) Liliaceae
    - b) Rosaceae
    - c) Begoniaceae
    - d) Iridaceae
98. Which of the following is not a blue colour flowering annual?
    - a) Larkspur
    - b) Cosmos
    - c) Ageratum
    - d) Delphinium

99. Corm dormancy in gladiolus is broken by
    a) IAA b) GA_3
    c) SADH d) 2, 4-D
100. 'Liliput' is a variety of
    a) Rose b) Marigold
    c) Dahlia d) Chrysanthemum
101. The most serious fungus in gladiolus is
    a) Fusarium b) Alternaria
    c) Botrytis d) Curvularia
102. Canna is propagated commercially by
    a) Corms b) Rhizome
    c) Bulb d) Tuber
103. Soil sterilization is done by
    a) Formaldehyde b) Chloropicrin
    c) Methyl Bromide d) All of these
104. Shoot tip culture is practiced in which of following:
    a) Carnation b) Orchid
    c) Chrysanthemum d) All of these
105. Lt Governor of Himachal Pradesh Shri Bajrang Bahadur Singh Bahaduri has developed 160 cultivars of
    a) Rose b) Gladiolus
    c) Dahlia d) Chrysanthemum
106. Dioecy is very common in
    a) Asparagus b) Aster
    c) Tulip d) Petunia
107. Male sterility is common in
    a) Petunia b) Marigold
    c) Ageratum d) Aster

108. Self incompatibility is not common in

a) Ageratum b) English daisy

c) Petunia d) Rose

109. 'Yellow Rose' is a scented variety of

a) Rose b) Gladiolus

c) Tuberose d) Aster

110. Rose oil is primarily extracted from which of following species

a) *odorata* b) *damascena*

c) *indica* d) *gallica*

111. Bonsai culture has originated in which country

a) China b) Korea

c) India d) Japan

112. Which of following is most common rooting hormone?

a) IBA b) NAA

c) 2, 4-D d) GA

113. Air layering is commonly used to propagate

a) Rose b) Jasmine

c) Rubber plant d) Azalea

114. Mame bonsai are normally up to________feet

a) Two b) One

c) Half d) Three

115. Those cultivars of chrysanthemum which produce flower between 10-27°C temperature are grouped in

a) Thermo-zero b) Thermo-positive

c) Thermo-negative d) None of these

116. Which of following is not a primary colour?

a) Red b) Yellow

c) Blue d) Green

117. Which of following is softer or cooler colour?

a) Green b) Orange

c) Blue d) Violet

118. The basic colour is

a) Orange b) Red

c) Grey d) Violet

119. Which of following is not a neutral colour?

a) White b) Grey

c) Black d) Pink

120. Closely related colours are also known as

a) Contrasting colour b) Analogous colour

c) Complimentary colour d) All of these

121. Yellow colour is contrasting to

a) Orange b) Black

c) Blue d) Violet

122. Which country in Asia is the leading exporter of orchids?

a) Malaysia b) India

c) China d) Japan

123. Colours which are placed at opposite ends of triangles of colour wheel are known as

a) Complimentary colour b) Monochromatic

c) Analogous d) None of these

124. Which of flowering is most suitable for hanging baskets?

a) Rudbeckia b) Cosmos

c) Portulaca d) Rubber plant

125. Which annual can be grown more successfully in shade?

a) Pansy b) Stock

c) Cineraria d) Daisy

126. Which of the following is not a good loose flower?

a) Marigold
b) Gailardia
c) Zinnia
d) Sweat pea

127. Which of the following is not grown as foliage annual?

a) Kochia
b) Ageratum
c) Coleus
d) Celosia

128. In cryo-preservation, the seeds are immersed in liquid nitrogen at ________ ^{o}C temperature.

a) 100
b) -196
c) -100
d) 196

129. The seeds of ________ loose viability after drying

a) Mapple
b) Jasmine
c) Rose
d) Quercus

130. Which of the following is seed germination inhibitor?

a) ABA
b) GA
c) BA
d) PBA

131. Seed viability is determined by

a) Direct germination
b) Excised embryo
c) Tetrazolium test
d) All of these

132. Seeds of which of following can not germinate at any temperature?

a) Cupressus
b) Ailanthus
c) Casuarina
d) All of these

133. Scarification of seeds is done by

a) Hot water
b) Acid
c) High temperature
d) All of these

134. Seed priming is done by

a) Alcohol
b) Hot water
c) Infusion
d) Acid

135. Non-tunicated bulbs are common in

a) Lilium b) Narcissus

c) Nerine d) All of these

136. Scooping is very common practice in

a) Hyacinth b) Rose

c) Lilium d) Crocus

137. Pseudo-bulbs are commonly used to multiply

a) Tulip b) Orchids

c) Gladiolus d) Tuberose

138. Single or multiple node cuttings are taken in

a) Dieffenbachia b) Dracaena

c) Song of India d) All of these

139. Wintering of roses is very common in

a) Delhi b) Mumbai

c) Shimla c) Kolkatta

140. Which of the following is not a common loose flower in India?

a) Jasmine b) Tuberose

c) Marigold d) Carnation

141. Indian cut flowers can be sold through out the year in

a) Singapore b) South Korea

c) Japan d) China

142. Which of following is propagated by tuberous roots?

a) Eranthes b) Begonia

c) Iris d) Anemone

143. Among bulbous plants maximum area is under which flower

a) Gladiolus b) Tulip

c) Lilium d) All of these

144. Which country is largest exporter of bulbous plants?

a) China b) USA

c) Netherlands d) Israel

145. Aerial bulblets formed in the leaf axils are known as

a) Aerial bulb b) Corms

c) Cormlets d) Bulbils

146. Scoring is very common in

a) Gladiolus b) Begonia

c) Lilium d) Tulip

147. Which of the following is not propagated by rhizome?

a) Canna b) Hydechium

c) Iris d) Lilium

148. Spring flowering bulbous plants are planted during

a) August b) January

c) November d) March

149. Which of following is planted at maximum depth

a) Gladiolus b) Tulip

c) Lilium d) Tuberose

150. Which is most sensitive to temperature?

a) Clivia b) Gladiolus

c) Crocus d) Tulip

151. Which of the following cultivar of gladiolus is resistant to Fusarium wilt?

a) Sagar b) Sapna

c) Dhiraj d) Apsara

152. Which of the following is a hybrid of African marigold?

a) Pusa Shankar-I b) Pusa Narangi

c) Pusa Sweta d) Pusa Basanti

153. Which of the following is not a cultivar of China aster?

a) PG Purple b) Poornima

c) PG Violet d) None of these

154. Which of following is not a cultivar of Tuberose?

a) Shringar b) Suvashini

c) Rajat Rekha d) Swarna

155. Which is not a cultivar of *Jasminum auriculatum*?

a) Motia b) Large round

c) Long point d) Pari Mullai

156. Plants which complete their life cycle within one year are known as

a) Annual b) Biennial

c) Perennial d) None of above

157. Rainy season annuals are sown in nursery during

a) February b) June

c) August d) April

158. Which of following is foliage annual?

a) Aster b) Salvia

c) Kochia d) Cosmos

159. Which is not grown during summer season?

a) Kochia b) Portulaca

c) Gaillardia d) Pansy

160. Which of following is intermediate day flowering annual?

a) Coleus b) Petunia

c) Gaillardia d) Pansy

161. Which of following is long day annual?

a) Antirrhinum b) Rudbeckia

c) Petunia d) All of these

162. Which is most tender annual and can not be grown in open in high hills?

    a) Stock b) Pansy
    c) Statice d) Rudbeckia

163. Seeds of which of following can germinate in dark

    a) *Echium* b) *Lobelia*
    c) *Nicotiana* d) None of above

164. Seeds of which flower require stratification and scarification

    a) Sweat pea b) Nigella
    c) Clianthus d) Marigold

165. Direct seed sowing is not economical in

    a) Sweat pea b) Petunia
    c) Hollyhock d) Balsam

166. Kochia is having a plant form of

    a) Informal b) Globular
    c) Columnar d) Conical

167. Person made significant contribution in floriculture even being a non-professional

    a) MS Randhawa b) GS Randhawa
    c) KL Chadha d) BP Pal

168. Bhabha Atomic Research Institute, Bombay has mandate on floriculture especially

    a) Rose oil extraction
    b) Micro-propagation of ornamentals
    c) Landscaping for pollution control
    d) Breeding of bulbous ornamentals

169. Research on Nymphaea has been conducted at

    a) IIHR, Bangalore b) NBRI, Lucknow
    c) IARI, New Delhi d) BSI, Calcutta

170. Dr Foja Singh made significant contribution in breeding of

a) Chrysanthemum b) Gladiolus

c) Orchids d) Rose

171. In Himachal Pradesh, model floriculture centre is at

a) Chail b) Shimla

c) Rajgarh d) Kandaghat

172. In India, research work on Jasmine is being conducted at

a) IARI b) TNAU

c) IIHR d) None of these

173. *Dendranthema grandiflora* is botanical name of

a) Paper flower b) Chrysanthemum

c) Carnation d) China aster

174. Who is associated with Jasmine breeding?

a) S Muthuswami b) RS Malik

c) BP Pal d) TK Bose

175. Who is associated with Marigold breeding in India?

a) B Singh b) ML Chaudhary

c) RL Mishra d) SPS Raghawa

176. Who is associated with greenhouse cultivation of ornamentals?

a) NK Dahlani b) KR Bhandari

c) P Chandra d) All of above

177. The Temperate Horticulture Research Institute (THRI) is situated at

a) Srinagar b) Almora

c) Kullu d) Shimla

178. Monogenic recessive male sterility is common in

a) Marigold b) Zinnia

c) Calceolaria d) All of above

179. Heterostyly is a common feature in

a) Petunia b) Ageratum

c) Primula d) Gerbera

180. Cytoplasmic male sterility is found in

a) Antirrhinum b) Petunia

c) Ageratum d) Salvia

181. Which of following is not a self pollinated flowering annual?

a) Larkspur b) Sweat pea

c) Lupine d) None of these

182. Cypress in Persian gardens was used as a symbol of

a) Idea of heaven b) Death and Eternity

c) Persian Paradise d) Life and youth

183. Which of following is not often cross pollinated annual?

a) Ageratum b) Lineria

c) Pansy d) Antirrhinum

184. Self-pollination depends on the mechanism of

a) Chasmogamy b) Heterostyly

c) Dichogamy d) Decliny

185. Nugget is a hybrid cultivar of

a) Petunia b) Marigold

c) Zinnia d) Antirrhinum

186. First F-1 hybrid in petunia was developed in Japan during year

a) 1965 b) 1945

c) 1935 d) 1970

187. Marigold has originated in

a) South Africa b) Mexico

c) USA d) UK

188. Gladiolus has originated in

a) South Africa b) Mexico

c) Asia d) UK

189. Which of following tree is not of Indian origin?

a) *Cassia fistula* b) *Michelia champaca*

c) *Grevillea robusta* d) All of these

190. Which of following shrub is not originated in India?

a) *Barleria cristata* b) *Holmskoidia sanguine*

c) *Tecoma stans* d) *Jasminum sombac*

191. Which of following flowering pot plant has originated in India?

a) Azalea b) Crossandra

c) Gardenia d) All of these

192. Genetic male sterility is common in

a) China Aster b) Marigold

c) Gaillardia d) Dahlia

193. Which of following is most common type of sterility in ornamental plants?

a) Genetic b) Cytoplasmic genetic

c) Cytoplasmic d) All of above

194. Basic chromosome number (x=) of lotus is

a) 8 b) 10

c) 9 d) 7

195. Basic chromosome number (x=) of rose is

a) 8 b) 7

c) 11 d) 13

196. Basic chromosome number (x=) of orchids is

a) 18 b) 17

c) 20 d) 16

197. Basic chromosome number (x=) of gladiolus is

a) 15 b) 9

c) 8 d) 7

198. Basic chromosome number (x=) of carnation is

a) 9 b) 7

c) 8 d) 15

199. Basic chromosome number (x=) of chrysanthemum is

a) 9 b) 8

c) 7 d) Plenty

200. Basic chromosome number (x=) of jasmine is

a) 15 b) 25

c) 13 d) 9

201. Basic chromosome number (x=) tuberose is

a) 17 b) 15

c) 13 d) Plenty

202. Basic chromosome number (x=) of dahlia is

a) 13 b) 12

c) 15 d) 8

203. Basic chromosome number (x=) of amaryllis is

a) 7 b) 8

c) 11 d) 15

204. Basic chromosome number (x=) of gerbera is

a) 15 b) 13

c) 11 d) 25

205. Basic chromosome number (x=) of anthurium is

a) 15 b) 13

c) 11 d) 25

206. Basic chromosome number (x=) of china aster is

a) 12 b) 9

c) 15 d) 25

207. Basic chromosome number (x=) of marigold is

a) 9 b) 15

c) 12 d) 25

208. Basic chromosome number (x=) of Mentha is

a) 11 b) 12

c) 10 d) 6

209. Basic chromosome number (x=) of Scented geranium is

a) 9 b) 8

c) 12 d) 6

210. Basic chromosome number (x=) of Lavender is

a) 10 b) 8

c) 12 d) 6

211. Basic chromosome number (x=) of Citronella is

a) 6 b) 12

c) 10 d) 16

212. Basic chromosome number (x=) of Palmarosa is

a) 8 b) 6

c) 7 d) 10

213. Basic chromosome number (x=) of Lemongrass is

a) 7 b) 8

c) 10 d) 6

214. Basic chromosome number (x=) of Rosemerry is

a) 10 b) 9

c) 12 d) 8

215. Basic chromosome number (x=) of Patchouli is

a) 17 b) 9

c) 12 d) 8

216. Self-incompatibility is overcome by

a) Bud pollinatioin b) Surgical techniques

c) Irradiation d) All of above

217. Virus free plants can be produced from

a) Anther b) Meristem culture

c) Nodes d) All of these

218. Who designed landscaping of Chandigarh city?

a) MS Randhawa b) Corbusier

c) Maxwell d) Meyer

219. Which of following is most suitable for planting in Rajasthan?

a) Albizia lebbek b) Pongamia glabra

c) Butea monosperma d) Prosopis juliflora

220. Mohini, a well known cultivar of rose is __________ in nature

a) Diploid b) Triploid

c) Aneuploid d) Tetraploid

221. One gram seed of petunia contains how many seeds

a) 10000 b) 10

c) 1000 d) 100

222. Which garden is regarded as genesis of gardening?

a) Eden b) Brindavan

c) Hampshire d) Osaka

223. Osaka garden is located in

a) UK b) South Korea

c) China d) Japan

224. Vatsyayana did not describe which of following garden

a) Pramadodyan b) Nandanvana

c) Passage garden d) Vrikshavatika

225. Gardens at Nalanda and Takshshila were developed in the time of

a) Mughals b) Aryans

c) Budhists d) None of above

226. `Char Bagh' the paradise garden is situated in

a) India b) Iran

c) Pakistan d) Turkey

227. Taj Mahal was built by

a) Nur Jahan b) Shah Jahan

c) Jahangir d) Akbar

228. Dilkhush garden of Lahore was built by

a) Fadai Khan b) Jahangir

c) Akbar d) Shah Jahan

229. Moorish garden style was developed in

a) France b) Germany

c) Spain d) Iran

230. Baradari garden of Patiala was developed by

a) Fadai Khan b) Ranjeet Singh

d) Sansaar Chand d) Bhupinder Singh

231. Royal Botanic garden of Kew is located in

a) Germany b) England

c) USA d) Australia

232. First Botanical garden in the world was started at Venice during

a) 1621 b) 1543

c) 1840 d) 1759

233. Heart of garden is

a) Hedges b) Fountains
c) Rose d) Lawn

234. Baradari is a main feature of

a) Japanese garden b) Mughal garden
c) Italian garden d) English garden

235. Mughal style gardening was developed by

a) Shah Jahan b) Akbar
c) Babar d) None of these

236. Pagoda is a name of

a) Japanese monument b) Flowering tree
c) Rock statue d) Shrub shaping

237. Dry landscape is important feature of

a) Mughal garden b) Japanese garden
c) English garden d) Italian garden

238. Oldest botanical garden in Europe is at Leyden in

a) Germany b) Spain
c) Netherlands d) None of these

239. Budha Jayanti Park is situated at

a) New Delhi b) Chandigarh
c) Varanasi d) Mysore

240. Which of following is not a Japanese type garden?

a) Vertical garden b) Hill garden
c) Tea garden d) Flat garden

241. Who gives an idea about informal gardening through his paintings?

a) W Robinson b) Le Notre
c) C Lorain d) H Hoare

242. Which of the following symbolizes death and eternity?

a) Bougainvillea b) Kachnar

c) Chenar d) Cypress

243. ____________ introduced Indian style gardening in Japan.

a) Prof H Mori b) Chinese

c) English trackers d) Budhist Monks

244. Which of following is associated with life of Lord Budha?

a) *Saraca indica* b) *Butea monosperma*

c) *Shorea robusta* d) All of these

245. Mandor garden of Jodhpur was built by

a) Ranjeet Singh b) Abhai Singh

c) Fadai khan d) None of above

246. Mughal garden at Pinjore was laid out by

a) Fadai Khan b) Bajendra Singh

c) Aurangzeb d) Ranjeet Singh

247. Roshanara Park, in New Delhi was built by

a) Prof K Mori b) Heian

c) Nara d) Muromachi

248. Which park belongs to Japanese style?

a) Roshnara park b) Budha Jayanti park

c) PM House at Saldarjung d) All of these

249. Shalimar garden in Kashmir was built by

a) Jahangir b) Akbar

c) Nur Jahan d) Jafar Khan

250. Chasma-e-Shahi garden was built by

a) Fadai Khan b) Ali Mardan Khan

c) Ranbir Singh d) None of above

251. Sand garden is also know as

a) Soto-roji b) Roji-niwa

c) Ryoanji d) Rithai-seki

252. Which chemical is used for dehydration of flowers?

a) CaO b) CaC_2

c) Borax d) All of these

253. 'White Star' is a variety of

a) Dahlia b) Chrysanthemum

c) Rose d) Aster

254. Byrant Park is situated at

a) Coimbatore b) Trichy

c) Rameshwaram d) Kodaikanal

255. Lloyd botanic garden, Darjeeling was laid down by

a) Sir George King b) Dr N Wallich

c) William Llyod d) Dr CC Calder

256. Stone lanterns are important feature in

a) Japanese garden b) Persian garden

c) Mughal garden d) English garden

257. Which of following is/are not formal gardens?

a) English b) Italian

c) French d) All of these

258. Which of the following statement is incorrect?

a) Portulaca – Rose moss b) Kochia – Burning bush

c) Gompherena - Globe amaranthd) Gaillardia – Summer cypress

259. Which of the following is a winter annual?

a) Calendula b) Kochia

c) Balsam d) Portulaca

260. After whom the generic name Kochia has been given

a) SD Koch b) WDJ Koch

c) AD Koch d) BDC Koch

261. *Amaranthus caudatus* is commonly called as

a) Rose moss b) Sun plant

c) Love-lies-Bleeding d) Blanket flower

262. Wall flower belongs to the family

a) Crucifereae b) Solanaceae

c) Caryophyllaceae d) None of these

263. Wall flower is native to

a) Chile and Peru b) Europe

c) Mediterranean region d) Mexico

264. Phlox belongs to the family

a) Polemoniaceae b) Solanaceae

c) Violaceae d) Rosaceae

265. State which of the following pair is incorrect?

a) *Iberis amara*-Candytuft b) *Mathiola incana*-Ice plant

c) *Lythyrus odoratus*-Sweet Pea d) *Limonium sinuatum*- Statice

266. Amaranthus and Cock's Comb belongs to the family

a) Amaranthaceae b) Balsaminaceae

c) Asteraceae d) Chenopodiaceae

267. Balsam belongs to the family

a) Amaranthaceae b) Portulaceae

c) Balsaminaceae d) Asteraceae

268. Zinnia, Tithonia, Sunflower and Gaillardia belong to the family

a) Portulaceae b) Asteraceae

c) Chenopodiaceae d) Amaranthaceae

269. Kochia belongs to the family

a) Asteraceae b) Balsaminaceae

c) Portulaceae d) Chenopodiaceae

270. Gaillardia is commonly called as

a) Blanket flower b) Sun plant

c) Globe amaranth d) Rose moss

271. Which of following is a floating plant?

a) Azolla b) Water Hyacinth

c) Duckwood d) All of above

272. Which is/are the biggest formal garden in India?

a) Vrindhavan garden (Mysore) b) Rock garden (Chandigarh)

c) Both a and b d) None of these

273. Which flower is grown in all seasons?

a) Chrysanthemum b) Candytuft

c) Corn flower d) Marigold

274. Cutting from broad leaved evergreen trees are usually taken in

a) Early summer b) Early winter

c) Late summer d) None of the above

275. Herbaceous stem cuttings for propagation are used in

a) Carnation b) Begonia

c) Grape d) Holly

276. Leaf and leaf bud cuttings for propagation are used in

a) Jumpier b) Begonia

c) Carnation d) Grape

277. Soft wood cuttings for propagation are used in

a) Dogwood b) Wisteria

c) Begonia d) None of these

278. Hard wood cuttings for propagation are used in

a) Dogwood b) Wisteria

c) Fig d) Begonia

279. Tip, simple, trench and mound are the kinds of

a) Layering b) Rootage

c) Budding d) Grafting

280. Lawn in mughal garden is

a) Sloppy b) Star shape

c) Terraced d) Circular

281. Stone lantern was first designed by

a) San-chu-keu b) Josef

c) Oribe d) Ashoka

282. Mughal style of gardening was developed by

a) Shahjahan b) Akbar

c) Babar d) None of these

283. Shade loving annual flowering plant is

a) Salvia b) Forget-Me-Not

c) *Dianthus* d) Anchuja

284. Mucilage in cut flowers is responsible for

a) Improving flower life b) Decreasing transpiration

c) Bickering of vessels d) All of these

285. Hogarth course is also known as

a) Line of beauty b) Circular curve

c) Tangent arrangement d) None of these

286. Any one type of flowers has

a) Plane disc b) Curled petals

c) Doom shaped disc d) Ring around disc

287. Name of annual climber is

a) *Quisqalis indica* b) *Imqurea pentaphyla*

c) *Lathyrus odoratus* d) *Tecoma grandis*

288. Pagoda is a name of

a) Japanese flowering tree b) Japanese monument

c) Statue d) None of these

289. Botanical name of carnation is

a) *Celosia cristata* b) *Tagetes errecta*

c) *Dianthus caryophyllus* d) *Centuria cyathus*

290. Dahlia is best propagated by

a) Layering b) Rhizomes

c) Sucker d) None of these

291. Crescent is well known as

a) Flower arrangement b) Pigment

c) Type of jasmine scent d) English garden feature

292. Peony is a name for the class of

a) Marigold b) Sunflower

c) Chrysanthemum d) Dahlia

293. Which place among the following is known as ‘Heaven for orchids’?

a) Shillong b) Cherapunji

c) Kalimpong d) None of these

294. β-Hydroxy quinoline sulphate (HQS) is used in

a) Hormone preparation b) Cut flower solution

c) Micro-nutrient spray d) Weed control

295. Shalimar garden is situated at

a) Bangalore b) Kashmir

c) Hyderabad d) Delhi

296. Which of the following is known retardant

a) Alar b) Kinetin

c) GA_3 d) IBA

297. Persian style of gardening was introduced in India by

a) Shahjahan b) Babur

c) Akbar d) Noorjahan

298. Which of the following are the kinds of branch pruning?

a) Heading back b) Thinning

c) Branch tipping d) All of these

299. Which of the following plants are used for boundary tall hedge?

a) Allysum b) Fresine

c) *Tecoma stans* d) Allocasia

300. Fairy ring is a disease noticed commonly in

a) Calendula b) Chrusanthemum

c) Lawn grasses d) Rose

301. Acacia is planted as

a) Hedge b) Fruits

c) Ornamentals d) None of these

302. Carissa carandus is used as

a) Ornamental b) Hedge

c) Fruit d) Fence

303. The term scion and root-stock are used in

a) Layering b) Budding

c) Grafting d) Cutting

304. Bougainvillea is propagated by

a) Budding b) Layering

c) Cutting d) All of these

305. Roses are grown for

a) Perfume or rose oil b) Cut flower

c) Rose water, gulkand d) All of these

306. Chrysanthemum is propagated by means of

a) Suckers b) Cuttings

c) Budding d) Inarching

307. Floral bangles and crowns are made from flowers of

a) Jasmine b) Tuberose

c) Chandni d) All of above

308. Which of following are not commonly seen in painting of Ram and Sita?

a) Garlands b) Bangles

c) Buttonhole d) Bajubandhs

309. Flowers of *Albizia lebbek* are used for decorating

a) Ears b) Neck

c) Hairs d) Wrist

310. Which of following is not used for making gajra?

a) Marigold b) Barieria

c) Michelia d) Crossandra

311. Veni popular in South India is made from

a) Jasmine b) Tuberose

c) Crossandra c) All of above

312. Bouquets are not presented for

a) Birthday b) Welcoming a guest

c) Departed soul d) Marriage function

313. Which of following is a free type flower arrangement?

a) Jiyubana b) Moribana

c) Zenei-ka d) None of above

314. In Japanese language fillers are known as

a) Shin b) Soe

c) Jushi d) Hikae

315. Japanese flower arrangement is based on

a) Religious theme b) Artistic theme

c) Spiritual theme d) Social theme

316. English flower arrangement is based on

a) Artistic theme b) Imaginary theme

c) Spiritual theme d) All of above

317. Floral clock is important feature at which garden?

a) Pinjore Bagh b) Lal bagh

c) Nishat Garden d) None of above

318. Which of the *Jasminum species* contains maximum oil?

a) *grandiflorum* b) *auriculatum*

c) *narcissus* d) *humile*

319. Maximum refineries of oil extraction of Jasmine are located in

a) Kerala b) Tamil Nadu

c) Karnataka d) West Bengal

320. Oldest botanical garden in Europe is at Leyden in

a) Germany b) Spain

c) Netherland d) None of these

321. Which of the following literature mentions the lotus symbol?

a) Jainism b) Buddhist

c) Hinduism d) All of these

322. Which of following is a symbol of self-esteem?

a) Narcissus b) Stock

c) Irish d) Carnation

323. Which of the following is a symbol of purity?

a) Tulip b) Tuberose

c) Lily d) Daffodil

324. Die back, a serious disease of rose indicates

a) Dark brown spot on leaves

b) Raddish orange pustules on petiole

c) Death of plant from top to down

d) Powdery growth on leaves lower sides

325. Die back in rose is due to

a) Virus b) MLO

c) *Diplodia rosarum* d) *Diplocarpon rosae*

326. Rose cultivars resistant to die back is/are

a) White Christmas b) Royal Ascot

c) Blue Moon d) All of these

327. The powdery mildew of rose appears when

a) Days are warm and nights are cool

b) Days are rainy and nights are cool

c) Days are rainy and nights are warm

d) Both days & nights are cool

328. 'Pankhuri' prepared from

a) Rose b) Gladiolus

c) Carnation d) None of these

329. Which of the following is a temperate aromatic crop?

a) Palmarosa b) Lemon grass

c) Lavender d) Citronella

330. The terms Padma, Kamala and Pankaja relate to

a) Rose b) Lotus

c) Marigold d) Jasmine

331. Aquatic flower resembling with lotus is

a) Day lilly b) Tiger lilly

c) Water lilly d) Blue African lilly

332. Brahma (the creator), Vishnu (the protector) and Shiva (the destroyer) are associated with

a) Lotus b) Tuberose

c) Carnation d) Jasmine

333. Lotus is the symbol of the God/Goddess.

a) Lakshmi b) Ganesh

c) Shiva d) Vishnu

334. For which of the following the `Golden Lotus Prize" is given?

a) Best feature film b) Best sportsman

c) Best social worker d) Best Horticulturist

335. Stalks of which of flower are used to make necklace and bracelets in West Bengal.

a) Gladiolus b) Lotus

c) Carnation d) Chrysanthemum

336. Optimum temperature for storing gladiolus corms is _______

a) 5-7°C b) 10-12°C

c) 15-20°C d) 1-5°C

337. Which of the following is not a fragrant variety of gladiolus?

a) Lucky star b) Sagar

c) Jimmy Boy d) None of these

338. Punjab Gold is a variety of

a) Chrysanthemum b) Tuberose

c) Rose d) Marigold

339. Fluorine injury is very common in

a) Tulip b) Rose

c) Iris d) Gladiolus

340. Negative geotropism a disorder occur during transportation of

a) Tulip b) Rose
c) Carnation d) Gladiolus

341. Storage corm rot in gladiolus is caused by

a) Fusarium b) Rhizoctonia
c) Penicillium d) All of the above

342. Sleepiness a disorder occurs in

a) Gladiolus b) Carnation
c) Chrysanthemum d) Tulip

343. Basic chromosome number of carnation is

a) 20 b) 26
c) 60 d) 15

344. Arthur Sim carnation is highly resistant to

a) Fusarium wilt b) Rust
c) Stem Rot d) Blight

345. The best time of rose pruning in North Indian plains is

a) September-October b) October-November
c) November-December d) June-July

346. Pruning in roses is done twice during November and June at

a) Shimla b) Bangalore
c) Delhi d) Both b and c

347. Which of following is not a Sympodial orchid?

a) Cymbidium b) Vanda
c) Dendrobium d) None of these

348. Who started tissue culture in orchids for first time?

a) Morel b) Kundson
c) Chang d) None of above

349. Which of following is commonly known as sword lily?

a) Crocus b) Gladiolus

c) Daffodil d) Irish

350. In carnation, calyx splitting is a problem due to

a) Genetic factors b) Nutritional factors

c) Environmental factors d) All of above

351. In carnation, sleepiness is a problem because of

a) Ethylene b) CO_2

c) High temperature d) All of above

352. In carnation, curly tip a disorder is due to

a) Low light b) Low temperature

c) Nitrogen deficiency d) All of above

353. ____________ is the most serious pest in carnation.

a) Red spider mite b) Aphid

c) Thrips d) Moth

354. *Nelumbo lutea* is commonly known as

a) American lotus b) Kamala

c) Indian lotus d) None of these

355. Silver thio-sulphate enhances flower longevity in

a) Rose b) Tulip

c) Lily d) Carnation

356. __________ tons of roses produces one kg oil.

a) 10 b) 3-4

c) 10-15 d) 1-15

357. Gulkand is a processed product prepared by mixing rose petals and sugar in ratio of

a) 1 : 1 b) 2 : 1

c) 1 : 2 d) 1 : 3

358. Chemical defoliation in roses is done by
   a) GA b) Urea
   c) Auxin d) Copper sulphate
359. _______ coloured roses are most popular
   a) Red b) White
   c) Pink d) Yellow
360. Which flower is universally acclaimed as the queen of flowers?
   a) Lotus b) Rose
   c) Orchid d) Tulip
361. Which type of chrysanthemum looks globular?
   a) Incurve b) Pompon
   c) Anemone d) Decorative
362. Grey mould in chrysanthemum is caused by
   a) *Alternaria* b) *Fusarium*
   c) *Botrytis* d) None of these
363. Dahlia is native to
   a) Canada b) USA
   c) Mexico d) Asia
364. Removal of undesirable auxillary buds at initial flowering stage is known as
   a) Notching b) Clipping
   c) Deblossoming d) Topiary
365. Bougainvillea belongs to the plant family
   a) Nyctaginaceae b) Rosaceae
   c) Apocynaceae d) Asteraceae
366. Which of following is bi-coloured cultivar?
   a) Splendens b) Lasbenos
   c) Snow Queen d) Sonnet

367. CO_2 concentration (ppm) in greenhouse for rose growing should be

a) Upto 500
b) 4000-6000
c) 1000-3000
d) 10000-30000

368. Coals and bark are important constituents of potting media for growing

a) Rose
b) Orchid
c) Tulip
d) Rubber plant

369. Suitable green house covering material used in hills is

a) Glass
b) Polythene
c) Fibber glass
d) All of these

370. Most favourable green house structure for hilly areas is

a) Tunnel
b) Quonset
c) Ground to ground
d) Gable

371. Normal humidity in greenhouses should be

a) 40-50%
b) 60-65%
c) 70-80%
d) 80-100%

372. The optimum night temperature of chrysanthemum at bud initiation stage should be

a) 10-12°C
b) 15.5-16.5°C
c) 13.5-15.5 °C
d) 18-20 °C

373. Which of following is not common name of Gerbera?

a) Transvaal daisy
b) Barberton daisy
c) African daisy
d) French daisy

374. Gerbera belongs to the family

a) Asteraceae
b) Euphorbiaceae
c) Liliaceae
d) Rosaceae

375. Air drying of flowers is common in

a) Helichrysum
b) Aster
c) Dahlia
d) Daisy

376. Which of the following is not a double bract cultivar of bougainvillea?

a) Archana b) Mrs HC Buck

c) Cherry blossom d) None of these

377. Which of the following is variegated bract cultivar of bougainvillea?

a) Archana b) Dr BP Pal

c) Partha d) Shubhra

378. Bougainvillea is propagated by

a) Softwood cutting b) Partially mature cuttings

c) Hardwood cutting d) None of above

379. Which of the following is not a growth retardant

a) SADH b) B-Nine

c) Cycocel d) 2, 4-D

380. The first hybrid tea rose was developed by

a) BP Pal b) Guillot

c) McMillan d) Dhall

381. The source of blue pigmentation in roses are found in the cultivar

a) Blue moon b) Sonia

c) Samba d) Bhim

382. Pigment responsible for blue colour is

a) Pelargolin b) Delphilidin

c) Lycopene d) Roseline

383. Nicki is a hybrid of ______

a) Petunia b) Rose

c) Nicotiana d) Primula

384. Who gave the name Dahlia in 1791?

a) Abbe Cavanilles b) Andreas Dehl

c) Willis d) Pizetti

385. What is the scientific name of Gerbera?

a) *Gerbera viridifolia* b) *G jamesonii*

c) *G aurantiaea* d) *Dendrenthema grandiflora*

386. Common name of *Hemerocallis fulva* is

a) Torch lily b) Water lily

c) Day lily d) Tiger lily

387. Botanical name of bird of paradise is

a) *Sterlitzia reginae* b) *Sterlitzia aungusta*

c) *Sterlitzia kwensis* d) *Sterlitzia nicolai*

388. Bird of paradise is native to

a) India b) Peru

c) China d) South Africa

389. Bird of paradise belongs to family

a) Cannaceae b) Musaceae

c) Iridaceae d) None of above

390. Botanical name of China aster is

a) *Aster chinensis* b) *Callistephus chinensis*

c) *Callistephus hortensis* d) None of above

391. Basic chromosome number of China aster is

a) 10 b) 9

c) 13 d) 18

392. Stock belongs to the family

a) Scrophularaceae b) Brassicaceae

c) Leguminaceae d) None of above

393. Which of the following is known as blanket flower?

a) Limonium b) Gomphrena

c) Gaillardia d) None of these

394. Native place of Gomphrena is

a) Mexico b) India
c) China d) USA

395. Gomphrena belongs to family

a) Gaillardiaceae b) Amaranthaceae
c) Solanaceae d) Compositae

396. Solidago is also known as

a) Amaranths b) Blanket Flower
c) Golden Rod d) Stock

397. Native place of solidago is

a) India b) China
c) America d) Japan

398. Pin and thrum type of flowers are found in

a) Petunia b) Primula
c) Cyclamen d) Gompherina

399. Which of the following is not a true species of bougainvillea?

a) *peruviana* b) *buttiana*
c) *speciabilis* d) None of these

400. Designing and beautification of a place with definite use of plant to serve certain aesthetic or utility purpose is known as

a) Landscape b) Landscaping
c) Garden d) All of above

401. Representation of the structure of any surface is known as

a) Texture b) Canopy
c) Design d) Floriculture

402. Which of the following is not an element of landscaping?

a) Line b) Texture
c) Canopy d) Rhythm

403. Rhythm in a garden is created through

a) Repetition of shapes b) Progression of sizes

c) Continuous line movement d) All of above

404. Which of following have drooping growth habit?

a) *Salix babylonica* b) Bottle brush

c) *Pinus peptula* d) All of these

405. Area of the home which is viewable from the street is known as ______ area.

a) Public b) Front

c) Approach d) All of these

406. Part of home landscape which provide room for necessities is known as ___ area.

a) Service b) Family

c) Approach d) All of above

407. Mobility in garden is created by use of _______

a) Different size b) Evergreen trees

c) Deciduous trees d) Evergreen shrubs

408. Shrubbery borders in home garden are kept around ______%

a) 10-15 b) 20-30

c) 15-20 d) 30-40

409. Accent draws attention of human being through ______

a) Colour b) Shape

c) Texture d) All of these

410. Which of the following is not a part of texture?

a) Fine b) Large

c) Medium d) Coarse

411. Selection of garden style depends upon its

a) Topography b) Location

c) Space d) All of these

412. Largest importer of houseplants is

a) India b) Italy

c) USA d) Germany

413. Optimum water holding capacity of potting medium should be

a) 50-60% b) 40-50%

c) 60-70% d) 20-30%

414. Poor aeration in potting medium is due to

a) Compactation b) Inadequate pore space

c) Over watering d) All of above

415. Which of the following type of containers are cheapest?

a) Earthern b) Concrete

c) Plastic d) Copper

416. For growing cacti, which type of pots is preferred?

a) Earthern b) Copper

c) Concrete d) Plastic

417. Corts are commonly used to multiply

a) Ivy b) Araucaria

c) Chlorophytum d) Maranta

418. Came baskets are suitable for growing _________

a) Ferns b) Orchids

c) Succulents d) Begonias

419. Which of the following is most suitable to dark corner of the house?

a) Aspidistra b) Acalypha

c) Hoya d) Marinate

420. Plants suitable for growing in sunny areas require _______ hours light in winter.

a) 1-2 b) More than 5

c) 2-3 d) Upto 5

421. Optimum temperature during day for house plants should be ______ °C.

a) 15-20 b) 20-30

c) 10-15 d) 0-2

422. Optimum soil temperature of potting medium should be _____°C

a) 10-15 b) 20-25

c) 18-21 d) 15-25

423. Optimum relative humidity in room growing house plants should be

a) 30-40% b) 50-60%

c) 70-80% d) 100%

424. Application of fertilizer along with watering is known as ______

a) Fertilizer application b) Liquid fertilization

c) Fertigation d) None of above

425. Which is not commonly propagated by seed?

a) Araucarai b) Aralia

c) Deacaena d) Palm

426. Tip cutting having 1-2 nodes is very common in _______

a) Coleus b) Aglaonema

c) Dracaina d) All of above

427. Leaf lamina cutting is very common in ________

a) Rex begonia b) Peperonia

c) Ivy d) Coleus

428. Cane cutting is very common in _______

a) Dieffenbachia b) Araucaria

c) Both a and b d) Philodendron

429. Air layering is not common in _______

a) Dracaena b) Crotion

c) Begonia d) Aglaonema

430. Saddle grafting is very common in

a) Hydrangea b) Rhododendron

c) Rosewood d) Bougainvillea

431. Mound layering is common in

a) Hydrangea b) Cestrum

c) Agave d) Cactus

432. Which of the following is acommon rooting hormone

a) IBA b) NAA

c) IAA d) GA

433. Offsets are commonly used to propagate

a) Agave b) Aloe

c) Pandanus d) All of these

434. Treatment of cut flowers with high concentration of sugar is known as

a) Pulsing b) Hardening

c) Loading d) a & b

435. Optimum pH of holding solution should be

a) 7-10 b) 4-5

c) 6-7 d) 2-3

436. Name the flower which is less ethylene sensitive

a) Gerbera b) Snapdragon

c) Orchids d) Carnation

437. Which of following is most important ethylene inhibitor?

a) Silver thiosulphate b) Sugar

c) Citric acid d) Nickel chloride

438. The most commonly used germicide is

a) Salt of Hydroxy quinoline b) Silver nitrate

c) Aluminium sulphate d) Silver thiosulphate

439. Which of the following is not ethylene inhibitor?

a) AVG	b) MVC

c) NAA	d) AOA

440. The strongest senescence stimulators is

a) ABA	b) BA

c) PBA	d) AOA

441. Which of following is used as a wetting agent?

a) Tween 20	b) Soap

c) Washing powder	d) None of these

442. Impregnation of cut flower is very common in _______

a) Aster	b) Gerbera

c) Carnation	d) All of these

443. Which of following is highly ethylene sensitive pot plant?

a) Euphorbia	b) Scindapsus

c) Nephrolepis	d) None of these

444. Which of following is not highly sensitive to ethylene?

a) Archimedes	b) Fuchsia

c) Hibiscus	d) Primula

445. Which of following is less sensitive to ethylene?

a) Chrysanthemum	b) Kalanchoe

c) Begonia	d) All of these

446. Flower highly sensitive to chilling injury is

a) Tulip	b) Anthurium

c) Freesia	d) Lily

447. Name the flower less sensitive to chilling injury

a) Rose	b) Cattleya

c) Poinsettia	d) Bird of paradise

448. Optimum light in cold storage is ______ Lux.

a) 2000-5000 b) 100-200

c) 500-1000 d) 1000-15000

449. In home, which of following is used to increase vase-life?

a) Sugar b) Salt

c) Glucose d) All of these

450. Bird of paradise flowers are stored at ________ °C

a) 10-15 b) 8-10

c) 1-2 d) 4-5

451. Water disinfection is done by ________

a) Sodium chloride b) Sodium hypochloride

c) Potassium chloride d) Tween 20

452. Which of following is not commonly used as water disinfection?

a) UV rays b) Aluminium sulphate

c) Sodium hypochloride d) Copper sulphate

453. Optimum dose of gamma radiation for prolonging vase life is _____ K rad.

a) 10-15 b) 1-2

c) 50-100 d) 30-40

454. In low pressure storage (LPS), the pressure in storage room is reduced to ___ atm.

a) 1 b) 10

c) 5 d) 0.1

455. Which is not suitable for dry transportation?

a) Carnation b) Chrysanthemum

c) Lily d) Iris

456. Geotropic bending during transportation is common in_______

a) Gladiolus b) Snapdragon

c) Lupin d) All of these

457. Flower stems of the following should be normally kept in boiling water for seconds.

a) Rose b) Poinsettia

c) Lily d) Tulip

458. 8-Hydroxy Quinoline Citrate works as preservative, it normally

a) Acidify water b) Improve water balance

c) acts as germicide d) All of above

459. 'Bull head' roses are produced due to ______

a) Thrips infestation b) Hard pruning

c) Insufficient carbohydrates d) All of these

460. Yellow rose cultivars are harvested at

a) Half open stage b) Slightly loose stage

c) Tight bud stage d) None of these

461. Which of following is not serious fungus in cut roses?

a) Pythium b) Botrytis

c) Penicillium d) Alternaria

462. Which of following accelerate senescence in cut carnation?

a) Abscissic acid b) Ethylene

c) High temperature d) All of above

463. Quilling of florets is common disorder in

a) Chrysanthemum b) Carnation

c) Dahlia d) Tulip

464. Petal burn in chrysanthemum is due to deficiency of _____

a) Copper b) Boron

c) Calcium d) Potassium

465. Optimum temperature for long term holding of chrysanthemum is _____ ^{o}C

a) 0-1 b) 2.5

c) 5-9 d) 10-12

466. A lip opposite to odd sepal in orchid flower is known as

a) Column b) Labellum

c) Keel d) None of these

467. Orchids under normal conditions can be stored up to 2 weeks at _____ °C.

a) 5-7 b) 2-5

c) 0-2 d) 10-12

468. Short days at 1-2 leaf stages in gladiolus leads to _______

a) Bud blasting b) Blind shoot

c) Poor spike d) Multiple spike

469. Topple disorder in gladiolus is due to deficiency of

a) Potassium b) Calcium

c) Nitrogen d) Boron

470. Bud blasting in Iris is caused by

a) Poor light b) High temperature

c) Water stress d) All of above

471. Which of the following preservative show phyto-toxicity in daffodil?

a) 8-HQC b) STS

c) Both a and b d) Citric acid

472. Epinasty in poinsettia can be controlled by

a) Sugar b) Silver Nitrate

c) Salt d) Ancymidol

473. Ground cover of perennial grass which persist under continuous mowing is called as

a) Turf b) Paving

c) Lawn d) All of above

474. Lawn can be established perfectly by

a) Plastering b) Seed

c) Dibbling d) All of these

475. Rolling, an important operation in lawn is done to

a) Level the ground b) Touch nodes with ground

c) Break grass d) All of above

476. Which of following is effective weedicide in *Zoysia* grass?

a) 2, 4-D b) Sylvex

c) Glyphosate d) All of above

477. Fairy ring spot is a problem in lawns might be due to

a) Fungus b) Bacteria

c) Nutrient deficiency d) Both a and c

478. Which of the following is highly cold tolerant?

a) Rough blue b) Zoysia

c) Creeping bent d) All of these

479. Which of the following is least heat tolerant?

a) Rough blue b) Carpet

c) Zoysia d) Creeping bent

480. Which of the following is highly tolerant to salinity?

a) Creeping bent b) Rough blue

c) Carpet d) Red top

481. Which type of grass has the fastest establishing rate?

a) Kentucky blue b) Manilla grass

c) Both a and b d) Bermuda

482. Which of following grasses has medium establishment rate?

a) Creeping bent b) Red fescue

c) Bahia d) All of these

483. *Amhersita nobilis* a flowering tree has ________ flowers.

a) Yellow b) Red

c) White d) Violet

484. *Ailanthus excelsa* is native to.

a) China b) India

c) Africa d) Iran

485. *Peltophorum ferrugenium* a flowering tree has _____ flowers.

a) Pink b) Red

c) Yellow d) White

486. *Delonix regia* is commonly known as

a) Gulmohar b) Yellow Gulmohar

c) Lal Gulmohar d) None of these

487. Which of the following has beautiful fruits?

a) *Kigellia* b) *Delonix*

c) Gulmohar d) *Bauhinia*

488. *Azadirachata indica* belongs to the family

a) Meliaceae b) Caselpiniaceae

c) Sapindaceae d) None of above

489. Which of following yield nectar?

a) Bottle brush b) Neem

c) Horse chestnut d) All of above

490. Which of following have drooping branches?

a) *Salix bodylonica* b) Bottle brush

c) *Australian acacia* d) All of above

491. Which of following is suitable for planting alongside of canals?

a) Bottle brush b) Jacaranda

c) Silver oak d) All of above

492. Which of following has beautiful trunk?

a) *Chorisia* b) *Araucaria*

c) *Bauhinia* d) *Acacia*

493. Which of following has fragrant flowers?

a) Devil's tree b) Michelia

c) Magnolia d) All of above

494. Which of following tree have blotched bark?

a) Pride of India b) Platanus

c) Eucalyptus d) All of above

495. Which of following tree has bark with prickles?

a) *Erythrina* b) *Bombax*

c) *Chorisia* d) All of above

496. Botanical name of coral tree is

a) *Erythrina indica* b) *Erythrina suberosa*

c) *Erythrina cristagalli* d) None of these

497. Which of the following tree is associated with Sita in Ramayana?

a) *Polyalthia longifolia* b) *Salix* spp

c) *Cedrus deodara* d) *Saraca indica*

498. Which of the following flower during November?

a) *Bauhinia variegata* b) *Bauhinia purpurea*

c) *Bauhinia vahli* d) None of above

499. Which of the following has white flower?

a) *Dillenia indica* b) *Bauhinia purpurea*

c) *Tecomella undulata* d) *Ceiba pentandra*

500. Which of the following is most suitable flowering tree for high hills?

a) *Cedrus deodara* b) *Rhododendron arborerum*

c) *Tecomella undulata* d) *Ceiba pentandra*

501. Which of following tree is/are grown for cut foliages?

a) Podocarpus b) Cupressus

c) Thuja d) All of these

502. To check air pollution the planted foliage should be

a) Fine b) Thick and shining

c) Glabrous d) Pubescent

503. Which of following is suitable for alkaline and saline soils?

a) *Casuarina equisetifolia* b) *Pinus roxburghii*

c) *Salix babylonica* d) *Grevillea robusta*

504. *Ficus* species grown for religious purpose is

a) *infectoria* b) *retusa*

c) *religiosa* d) *benghalensis*

505. Which of following is a quick growing tree?

a) Eucalyptus hybrid b) *Ficus benjamina*

c) *Erythrina suberosa* d) *Parkinsonia aculeata*

506. Which of following is used as climber, shrub as well as pot plant?

a) Silver oak b) Bougainvillea

c) Begonia d) All of these

507. Which of the following climb by means of tendrils?

a) *Jasminum grandiflorum* b) *Ficus repens*

c) *Ipomoea* sp d) *Antigonon leptopus*

508. Which of following is a rambler?

a) *Jasminum grandiflora* b) *Antigonon leptopus*

c) *Quisqualis indica* d) *Pyrostegia venusta*

509. Which of the following *Tecoma* species is not a climber?

a) *Grandiflora* b) *Stans*

c) *Capensis* d) *Jasminoides*

510. Which of following species of *Jasminum* is not a climber?

a) *Grandiflorum* b) *Dispermum*

c) *Humile* d) *Officinale*

511. Which of following has coarse texture foliage?

a) *Tecoma grandiflora* b) *Pyrostegia venusta*

c) *Quisqualis indica* d) *Thumbergia grandiflora*

512. Name any climber which is commonly used as hedge.

a) *Clitoria ternatea* b) *Clerodendron splendens*

c) *Clemata paniculata* d) *Ipomoea* sp

513. Which of following is a foliage climber?

a) *Monstera deliciosa* b) *Hedera helix*

c) *Scindapsus aureus* d) All of these

514. Which of following has fragrant flowers?

a) *Lonicera japonica* b) *Tecoma grandiflora*

c) *Jasminum dispermum* d) All of above

515. Which of following has Watch shaped flower?

a) *Passiflora caerulea* b) *Aristolochia elegans*

c) *Ipomoea purpurea* d) *Tecoma grandiflora*

516. Which of following is not a member of family Bignoniaceae?

a) *Pyrostegia venusta* b) *Tecoma grandiflora*

c) *Bignona unguiscati* d) *Begonia sempervirens*

517. *Hiptage benghalensis* belongs to the family

a) Hiptageaceae b) Malphigiaceae

c) Saxifragaceae d) Moraceae

518. Which of following has beautiful fruits?

a) *Pyrostegia venusta* b) *Tecoma jasminoides*

c) *Smilax aspera* d) *Lonicera japonica*

519. Which of the following has duck shaped flowers?

a) *Aristolochia elegans* b) *Bignonia unguiscate*

c) *Bauhinia* spp d) *Beaumontia grandiflora*

520. Which of following has orange coloured flowers?

a) *Jasminum grandiflorum* b) *Beaumon sterlitzia*

c) *Bignonia unguiscun* d) *Pyrostegia venusta*

521. Which of following produces white coloured flowers?

a) *Clematis paniculata* b) *Jasminum grandiflorum*

c) *Beaumontia grandiflora* d) All of above

522. Which of following is used for screening walls?

a) *Pyrostegia venusta* b) *Lonicera japonica*

c) *Ficus repens* d) All of above

523. Which of following Ipomoea species is known as Railway creeper?

a) *Alba* b) *Purpurea*

c) *Tuberosa* d) None of these

524. Which of following has shining foliage?

a) *Tecoma jasminoides* b) *Thunbergia grandiflora*

c) *Lonicera japonica* d) *Pyrostegia venusta*

525. Climber suitable for pots.

a) Golden shower b) Passion flower

c) Cat's claw d) Bougainvillea

526. Which of following *Solanum* species is known as potato creeper?

a) *Wendlandii* b) *Seaforthianum*

c) *Jasminoides* d) *Tuberosum*

527. Which of the following does not belong to family Leguminosae?

a) *Derris scandens* b) *Wisteria sinensis*

c) *Clematis paniculata* d) None of these

528. Which of the following is classified as light climber?

a) *Solanum wendlandii* b) *Cobaea scandens*

c) *Petrea volubilis* d) *Thumbergia grandiflora*

529. Which of following is cool season climber?

a) *Derris scandens* b) *Quisqualis indica*

c) *Pyrostegia venusta* d) *Tecoma grandiflora*

530. Which of following has blue flower?

a) *Clitoria ternatea* b) *Ipomoea violacea*

c) *Wisteria sinensis* d) All of above

531. Which of following *Bignonia* species is known as cut's claw?

a) *Purpurea* b) *Graclis*

c) *Unguiscan* d) *Speciosa*

532. Duck flower a climber is native to

a) South America b) Brazil

c) India d) Japan

533. Which of following climb by secreting sticky substance?

a) *Clitoria temata* b) *Ficus repens*

c) *Clematis paniculata* d) None of above

534. Which of following is suitable for porches?

a) *Pyrostegia venusta* b) *Ipomoea horsfalliae*

c) *Clerodendron splendens* d) All of above

535. Which of following *Solanum* species is known as potato creeper?

a) *Wendiandii* b) *Seaforthianum*

c) *Jasminoides* d) *Tuberosum*

536. A perennial plant having distinct trunk and crown at top is known as

a) Shrub b) Tree

c) Climber d) Herb

537. A low growing woody or semi-woody perennial plant with little or no trunk having height almost 4 m is known as

a) Climber b) Shrub

c) Tree d) Herb

538. Which of the following has mild odour in flowers and foliage?

a) *Hamiltonia suaveolens* b) *Duranta repens*

c) *Acalypha hispida* d) All of above.

539. Which of the following is night blooming?

a) *Nerium oleander* b) *Hamelia patens*

c) *Nyctanthes arbortritis* d) *Acer palmatum*

540. Which coloured shrubs are grown in night garden?

a) Red b) Blue

c) White d) Yellow

541. Area of garden devoted exclusively to shrubs is known as

a) Border b) Shrubbery

c) Hedge d) None of above

542. Which of the following has bicoloured foliage?

a) Excoecuria b) Nandina

c) Gynura d) All of above

543. Which of the following has beautiful bracts?

a) Bougainvillea b) Mussandra

c) Poinsettia d) All of above

544. In double faced shrubbery tall shrubs are planted in

a) Corner b) Under tree

c) Near wall d) Centre

545. Shrubs when planted at regular interval to form a thick screen is known as

a) Edge b) Shrubbery

c) Hedge d) All of these

546. For making good hedge any shrub should have ______

a) Edge b) Topiary

c) Shrubbery d) None of these

547. For rockeries shrubs should be________

a) Moisture loving b) Drought loving

c) Deciduous d) Any of above

548. Which of the following is good tall protective hedge?

a) Popular ciliata b) *Cuphea milvillea*

c) *Acacia farnensiana* d) All of above

549. Which of the following is not good dwarf protective hedge?

a) *Agave americana* b) *Jasminum humile*

c) *Euphorbia tetragoria* d) All of above

550. Which is planted as tall ornamental hedge?

a) *Polyalthia longifolia* b) *Putranjiva roxburghii*

c) *Thuja orientalis* d) All of above

551. Formal edging is made off with which one of the following.

a) Tiles b) Bricks

c) Stones d) All of above

552. Informal edging is made from

a) Stones b) Plants

c) Concrete d) All of above

553. Art of training plants into shapes of different statues, birds or animals is known as

a) Edge b) Hedge

c) Topiary d) None of above

554. For making topiary plants should be

a) Quick growing b) Dense branching

c) Small foliage d) All of above

555. Which of the following is used for making topiary?

a) *Thuja orientalis* b) *Cuperssus torulosa*

c) *Clerodendron inerme* d) All of above

556. Which of following is a popular pot plant in international market?

a) Ixora b) Poinsettia

c) Crossandra d) Hibiscus

557. Cycads belong to the family

a) Cycadaceae b) Cupressaseae

c) Conifereae d) Palmaceae

558. Which is grown for cut greens?

a) *Breynia nivosa* b) Bongainvillea

c) *Lantana depressa* d) *Vinca rosea*

559. Which of following has red flowers?

a) *Punica granatum* b) *Lagerstroemia indica*

c) *Acucuba japonica* d) All of above

560. Which of following has dark green branches and red flowers?

a) *Hibiscus rosasinensis* b) *Malvabiscus arboreus*

c) Russelia juncea d) All of these

561. Which of following is not a member of Malvaceae?

a) *Hibiscus syriacus* b) *Malvabiscus arboreus*

c) *Dombeya spectabilis* d) All of above.

562. Which of following is native to India?

a) *Russelia juncea* b) *Hibiscus mutabilis*

c) *Cassia glanca* d) *Hamelia patens*

563. Which of following has black fruits?

a) *Pentas lanceolata* b) *Ochna jabotapita*

c) *Nerium oleander* d) *Punica granatum*

564. Botanical name of Din-ka-raja is

a) *Cestrum diurnum* b) *Cestrum pargui*

c) *Cestrum nocturnum* d) None of these

565. Palms belong to family

a) Palmeae
b) Palmaceae
c) Palmideae
d) None of these

566. *Hydrangea macrophylla* produces blue flowers in which soil

a) Neutral
b) Acidic
c) Alkaline
d) All of above

567. *Hydrangea macrophylla* produces pink/red flowers in which soils

a) Acidic
b) Neutral
c) Alkaline
d) All of these

568. Which is not a cool flowering shrub?

a) *Barleria cristata*
b) *Plumbago rosea*
c) *Cassia alata*
d) All of above

569. Which of following has not yellow flowers?

a) *Bauhinia tomentosa*
b) *Pentas lanceolata*
c) *Ochna squarrosa*
d) All of these

570. Botanical name of China shoe flower is

a) *Hibiscus mutabilis*
b) *Hibiscus syriacus*
c) *Hibiscus rosa sinensis*
d) *Malvabiscus arborcus*

571. Din ka raja is a local name of

a) *Cestrum diurnum*
b) *Cestrum parqui*
c) *Cestrum nocturnum*
d) None of above

572. How many genera are included a palm group?

a) 100
b) 500
c) 150
d) 50

573. Botanical name of China shoe flower is

a) *Hibiscus syriacus*
b) *Malva biscus arborcus*
c) *Hibiscus rosa sinensis*
d) *Hibiscus mutabilis*

574. Which of following is not a feather leaved palm.

a) Areca b) Caryota

c) Phoenix d) Livistonia

575. Which is a fan-leaved palm?

a) *Rhapis excelsa* b) *Livistonia chinensis*

c) *Thrinas argentea* d) All of above

576. Which of the following plant has beautiful trunk?

a) Rhapis b) Roystonea

c) Zamia d) Cyeas

577. Most of palms are propagated by

a) Seed b) Suckers

c) Cutting d) Layering

578. The conventional method of propagation in tuberose is

a) Radial cutting of bulbs b) Seeds

c) Callus of scale stem d) Bulbs

579. Which of the following statement is incorrect?

a) Banjaran – 1969 b) Raktagandha – 1975

c) Rose sherbet – 1962 d) Swati – 1960

580. Dr Homi Bhabha, a rose cultivar belongs to class

a) Hybrid teas b) Floribunda

c) Miniatures d) Climbers

581. Chrysanthemum cultivars Apsara, Birbal Sahni, Jayanti and Kundan were developed at

a) IARI b) NBRI

c) IIHR d) TNAU

582. 'No Pinch No Stake' relates to

a) Chrysanthemum b) Rose

c) Carnation d) Lotus

583. Rakhee is an open pollinated seedling of

a) Flirt b) Lord Doonex

c) Indira d) Red Gold

584. Red Gold, a hybrid of gladiolus is cross between

a) Flirt × Valentine b) Indira × Rakhee

c) Flirt × Rakhee d) Indira × Valentine

585. Apsara, Meera, Nazrana, Poonam, Sapna and Shoba are cultivars of

a) Lotus b) Gladiolus

c) Carnation d) Tuberose

586. Apsara is a cross between

a) Green wood pecker × Friendship b) GPI × Friendship

c) Shoba × Sapna d) Black Jack × Friendship

587. Shoba is a mutant of

a) Sapna b) Wild Rose

c) Poonam d) Meera

588. Meera is a cross between

a) GPI × Friendship b) Poonam × Sapna

c) Shoba × Wild Rose d) Sapna × Shoba

589. Mirage, a small flower variety of gladiolus was introduced from

a) USA b) Mexico

c) Japan d) Germany

590. Sapna is a cross between

a) Poonam × Sapna b) Black jack × Meera

c) Black jack × Friendship d) Green wood packer × Frienship

591. Zakariana, Jawahar Lal Nehru, Purple wonder, Sholay, Usha and Dr HB Singh are varieties of

a) Rose b) Tuberose

c) Bougainvillea d) China aster

592. Dr HB Singh is hybrid between

a) Trinidad × Formosa b) Formosa × Trinidad
c) Lalbagh × Red Glory d) Sholay × Purple Wonder

593. Usha is seedling selection of

a) Red Glory b) Lady Hope
c) Chitravati d) Formosa

594. Jawahar Lal Nehru is a spontaneous mutant of

a) Lal Bagh b) Trinidad
c) Red Glory d) Lady Hope

595. Flower yield in Rose cv Queen Elizabeth can be increased by application of

a) GA (10-100 ppm) b) GA (500 ppm)
c) GA (400 ppm) d) Cycocel (200 ppm)

596. Chemical used for enhancing shelf-life of chrysanthemum is

a) Cycocel 50 ppm b) 8-HQC 200 ppm
c) Both (a) & (b) d) None of these

597. Growth regulator used to reduce plant height in carnation is

a) Etheral 1500 ppm b) Etherel (500-1000 ppm)
c) ABA d) NAA

598. Palm seeds are treated for quick germination with treatment called

a) Scarification b) Water soaking
c) Mechanical treatment d) Stratification

599. Sago palm is a species of genus *Cycas*.

a) *Revoluta* b) *Rumphii*
c) *Cercinalis* d) None of these

600. Selaginella belongs to the family

a) Selaginelleae b) Lycopodiaceae
c) Selaginellaceae d) None of above

601. Selaginellas are commonly known as

a) Club moss
b) Lycopodium
c) Moss
d) None of above

602. Which of following is known as Royal fern?

a) *Osmunda regalis*
b) *Asplemium nidus*
c) *Pteris multifida*
d) *Polystichum aristatum*

603. Drooping cactus is

a) *Echinocereus pentalophus*
b) *Chamaecereus silvestris*
c) *Aporocactus*
d) All of above

604. *Cephalocereus albispinus* is a root stock for which of following.

a) Cleistocactus
b) Notocactus
c) Aporocactus
d) All of above

605. *Echinocactus grusonii* is commonly known as

a) Golden Barrel
b) Rainbow cactus
c) China cactus
d) Tom thumb

606. Which species of *Opuntia* is known as Bunny Ears'?

a) *tetracantha*
b) *tunicata*
c) *microdosys*
d) *mulgaris*

607. Which of following cactus grown luxuriantly in moist locations?

a) *rhipsalis*
b) *opuntia*
c) *notocactus*
d) *parodia*

608. Which of following is commonly known as 'century plant'?

a) Aloe
b) Agave
c) Echeveria
d) Lobivia

609. Which of following is known as climbing onion?

a) *Stapelia variegata*
b) *Adenium obesum*
c) *Bowiea volubilis*
d) *Gasteria hybrida*

610. Which of following is known as Slipper plant?

a) *paphiopedilum* b) *pedilanthus*

c) *pachyveria* d) *greenovia*

611. Which is commonly known as Song of India?

a) *Dracaena sanderiana* b) *Dracaena fragrans*

c) *Pleomele reflexa* d) *Pleomele reflexa vuriegata*

612. Cacti and succulents are also grouped as

a) Mesophytes b) Xerophytes

c) Lithophytes d) Saprophytes

613. Silver dollar is the name of *Crassula*

a) *Arborescens* b) *Tricolor*

c) Both a and b d) None of these

614. Botanical genus of rat tail cactus is

a) *Ariocarpus* b) *Aporocactus*

c) *Zygocactus* d) *Ferocactus*

615. Which of following is propagated by leaf cuttings?

a) Agave b) Aloe

c) Kalanchoe d) Cereus

616. Which of following is propagated by offsets.

a) Agave b) Notocactus

c) Howonhia d) All of above

617. Which species of *Opuntia* is known as India fig?

a) *Falcate* b) *Ficus-indica*

c) *Rufida* d) *Vitis*

618. Which species of Crassula is known as Silver dollar.

a) *Arborescens* b) *Falcata*

c) *Tricolor* d) None of above

619. Inflorescence of which grass is used as cut flower.

a) *Cynodon dactylon* b) *Agrostis nebulosa*

c) *Ophiopogon intermedius* d) All of above

620. Which of following medicinal plants are used as ornamental plant?

a) Anise b) Indian dill

c) Bladderdock d) All of above

621. Heliconia belongs to the family

a) Bromeliadaceae b) Musaceae

c) Cannaceae d) None of above

622. Palms prefers luxuriantly climate as

a) Cool-humid b) Warm-dry

c) Both a and b d) Warm-humid

623. Which of following methods are used to identify viral diseases?

a) ELISA b) DIBA

c) DAS d) All of these

624. Cultivar (s) of *Rosa damascena* developed at IHBT Palampur is/are

a) Rose Sherbet b) Damascena selection

c) Himroz d) All of these

625. Name the flower(s) suitable for air drying.

a) Helichrysum b) Statice

c) Acroclinum d) All of these

626. Which of the following is most suitable flower for press drying?

a) Gladiolus b) Rose

c) Pansy d) Helichrysum

627. Which of the following desssicant is used for flowers drying?

a) Silica gel b) Borax

c) River sand d) All of these

628. Biggest market for dry flowers is in

a) Germany b) UK

c) Japan d) USA

629. Bleaching of petals during drying is due to

a) Sand b) Silica gel

c) Borax d) Saw dust

630. Which of the following insects damage flowers seriously in greenhouse?

a) Aphids b) Thrips

c) Nematodes d) White fly

631. Nematodes can be controlled by

a) Malathion b) Phorate

c) Chlorpyriphos d) All of these

632. Which of following cultivar of chrysanthemum flowers during July-August?

a) Meghdoot b) Birbal Sahni

c) Punjab Gold d) All of these

633. Name the chrysanthemum cultivar flowers during February-March.

a) Sharad Mala b) Maghi

c) Jwala d) None of these

634. Pollen sterility in roses is checked by using

a) Potassium Iodide b) Acetocarmine

c) Ethyl alcohol d) All of these

635. Which of following is not used for making garlands?

a) Orchids b) Crossandra

c) Chrysanthemum d) Marigold

636. The beauty of trees planted along water canals get enhanced due to

a) Reflection b) Refraction

c) Dispersion d) Colourful stem and leaves

637. The native place of rose is

a) England b) USA

c) India d) China

638. Hybrid 77 is a variety of

a) Japanese mint b) Lavender

c) Cetronella d) Jasmine

639. Siwalik is a variety of

a) Lemongrass b) Citronella

c) Lavender d) Japanese mint

640. Mandakani is a variety of

a) Palmarosa b) Citronella

c) Lavender d) Patchauli

641. Noor-Jahan is a variety of

a) *Rosa demascena* b) *Rosa moschata*

c) *Pogostemon cablin* d) *Pelargonium graveolens*

642. Jasmine belongs to the sub-family

a) Jasminoideae b) Pomoideae

c) Prunoideae d) None of these

643. Botanically, the Jasmine fruit is

a) Pome b) Berry

c) Nut d) Drupe

644. How many species of Jasmine are known in India?

a) 30 b) 25

c) 50 d) 42

645. CO1 Pitchi, a variety of Jasmine is released by

a) IIHR b) TNAU

c) IARI d) CIMAP

646. *Jasminum grandiflorum* is commonly known as

a) French Jasmine b) Spanish Jasmine
c) Chameli d) All of these

647. Surabhi is a highly fragrant species released at IIHR belongs to

a) Jasmine b) Tuberose
c) Rose d) Carnation

648. Jasmine plant starts flowering after

a) 3 years b) 4 years
c) 2 years d) 5 years

649. In North India, flowering period in jasmine crop is

a) October-January b) June-September
c) November-March d) December-March

650. Which of the following types of medium is best to plant jasmine cutting?

a) Vermiculite b) Sand
c) Clay d) Moss

651. In Egypt, jasmine is mostly propagated by

a) Layering b) Grafting
c) Cutting d) Seeds

652. Jasmine can be propagated by

a) Layering b) Stem cutting
c) Grafting d) All of these

653. Which of the following flower is universally acclaimed as "Queen of flowers"?

a) Lotus b) Rose
c) Gladiolus d) Carnation

654. Which of the following is National flower of England?

a) Rose b) Lotus
c) Chrysanthemum d) Carnation

655. Rosa species only having four petals and sepals

a) *Serica* b) *Persica*

c) *Damascena* d) *Gallica*

656. The term `hip' in rose refers to

a) Petals b) Sepals

c) Thalamus d) Ripe fruits

657. Scented geranium needs

a) Moderate rainfall b) Heavy rainfall

c) Hot summers d) High humidity and moderate rainfall

658. Black spot is a serious problem in temperate areas having

a) Dull climate

b) High temperature & low rainfall

c) Low temperature & heady rainfall

d) Low temperature & low rainfall

659. Warm and humid climate is considered serious for

a) Stem blight b) Black spot

c) Rose rust d) Die back

660. Which of following is not correctly matched?

a) Die back (*Diplodia rosarum*)

b) Powdery mildew (*Sphaerotheca pannosa var Roseae*)

c) Black spot (*Diplocarpon roseae*)

d) Rose Rust (*Alternaria alternata*)

661. Which of the following is the favourable reason for occurrence of Rose rust?

a) Warm days and cool night

b) Dull cold climate of temperate region

c) Warm and humid areas

d) Improper pruning

662. Among the following diseases, which is caused by *Alternaria alternata*?

a) Die back b) Powdery mildew

c) Black spot d) Leaf spot

663. Rose fruits are rich in

a) Ascorbic acid b) Vitamin-C

c) Vitamin-A d) Both (a) and (b)

664. Miniature roses are propagated by

a) Cutting b) Seed

c) Grafting d) Layering

665. *Nelumbo lutea* is a native of

a) Mexico b) Africa

c) America d) India

666. *Nelumbo nucifera* is synonymous to

a) *Nelumbiun nelumbo* b) *Nymphea spp*

c) *Nelumbo lutea* d) None of these

667. In lotus, carpel's maturing into nut like achene's are called

a) Spores b) Spongy receptacle

c) Filaments d) Seeds

668. Lotus is propagated by

a) Rhizome b) Division

c) Seed d) All of these

669. Quantity of seeds (kg per hectare) required to produce lotus seedlings

a) 5-6 b) 7-8

c) 10-12 d) 8-10

670. Lal bagh is at

a) Bangalore b) Delhi

c) Mysore d) Ootacamund

671. Java citronella is native to

a) Pakistan b) Japan

c) India d) Sri Lanka

672. Manjusha and Mandakini are clonal selection of

a) Citronella b) Lavender

c) Jasmine d) Palmarosa

673. Citronella is vegetatively propagated by

a) Cutting b) Grafting

c) Clumps d) Mound layering

674. Citronella is a

a) Diploid b) Tetraploid

c) Hexaploid d) Aneuploid

675. In citronella, leaves are harvested __________ cm above ground.

a) 30 b) 25

c) 5 d) 15

676. The major lavender oil producing country in the world is

a) USSR b) Bulgaria

c) India d) Sri Lanka

677. Lavender is native to

a) USSR b) Europe

c) Bulgaria d) India

678. Lotus belongs to the family

a) Nymphaceae b) Irridaceae

c) Asteraceae d) Oleaceae

679. Orchids belong to the family

a) Oleaceae b) Irridaceae

c) Orchidaceae d) Nymphaceae

680. Gladiolus belongs to the family

a) Irridaceae b) Oleaceae
c) Asteraceae d) Araceae

681. Carnation belongs to the family

a) Oleaceae b) Irridaceae
c) Carryophyllaceae d) Asteraceae

682. Chrysanthemum belongs to the family

a) Irridaceae b) Asteraceae
c) Oleaceae d) Rosaceae

683. Jasmine belongs to the family

a) Oleaceae b) Asteraceae
c) Irridaceae d) Rosaceae

684. Tuberose belongs to the family

a) Irridaceae b) Amaryllidaceae
c) Rosaceae d) Nymphaceae

685. Amaryllis belongs to the family

a) Rosaceae b) Asteraceae
c) Amaryllidaceae d) Oleaceae

686. Gerbera belongs to the family

a) Oleaceae b) Asteraceae
c) Irridaceae d) Rosaceae

687. Anthurium belongs to the family

a) Araceae b) Asteraceae
c) Irridaceae d) Carryophyllaceae

688. China aster belongs to the family

a) Irridaceae b) Oleaceae
c) Araceae d) Asteraceae

689. Origin place of gladiolus is

a) South Africa
b) Mexico
c) Southern France
d) Columbia

690. Origin place of carnation is

a) South Africa
b) Southern France
c) Asia
d) China

691. Origin place of dahlia is

a) Southern France
b) India
c) Mexico
d) Columbia

692. Origin place of anthurium is

a) Colombia
b) Mexico
c) India
d) apan

693. Origin of marigold is

a) India
b) Mexico
c) China
d) Japan

694. Botanically, tuberose fruit is a

a) Capsule
b) Pome
c) Berry
d) ggregate

695. The name 'Tuberose' is derived from

a) Tuberosus
b) Tube-rose
c) Tuberosa
d) Tuber-ose

696. The 'gardener's dictionary' was written by

a) Phillip miller
b) Clusius
c) Linnaeus
d) None of these

697. Who among the following kept tuberose under genus *Polyanthus* and species *tuberose*

a) Miller
b) Carlos Clusius
c) Palmer
d) Linnaeus

698. Which of the following statement about tuberose is incorrect?

a) Gulchari-Hindi b) Rajanigandha-Bengali

c) Sugandhraja-Kannada d) Nilasampangi-Telugu

699. In Hindi, tuberose is known as

a) Rajanigandha b) Gulshabbo

c) Sukandaraji d) Nilasampangi

700. Rajat Rekha and Swarna Rekha are the cultivars of tuberose released at

a) NBRI b) IARI

c) TNAU c) IIHR

701. For a very rapid multiplication, the tuberose is propagated through

a) Bulbs b) Tissue culture

c) Division of bulb d) Seeds

702. Tuberose is mainly propagated by

a) Bulbs b) Seeds

c) Division of bulbs d) Tissue culture

703. Banjaran- a Floribunda rose was released in

a) 1965 b) 1967

c) 1969 d) 1970

704. Madhosh is a mutant of

a) Gulzar b) Kiss of fire

c) Abhisarica d) Banjaran

705. Which of the following rose cultivar has won many prizes in USA?

a) Jantar-Mantar b) Mohini

c) Banjaran d) Rose Sherbet

706. Research on floriculture started at IARI in

a) Late Sixties b) Late Seventies

c) Late Fifties d) Early Fifties

707. The author of book 'Rose in India' is

a) Dr MS Randhawa b) Dr SD Mookherji

c) Dr Homibhaba d) Dr B P Pal

708. 'Rose growing in Tropics' was written by

a) BS Bhattacharji b) Dr B P Pal

c) Dr M S Randhawa d) Dr S D Mookherji

709. 'Rose Sherbet' a variety of floribunda Rose was released in

a) 1965 b) 1962

c) 1960 d) 1975

710. Mohini, floribunda rose is a cross between

a) Akash Sundari x Granda b) Shola x Sea Pearl

c) Super Star x Granda d) Sea Pearl x Shola

711. Shubra is a bud sprout of

a) Sweta b) Mary Palmer

c) Archana d) Shubra

712. Which of the following is sensitive to geotropic bending?

a) Freesia b) Lotus

c) Carnation d) Chrysanthemum

713. Basil is name given to aromatic plants belonging to genus

a) *Ocimum* b) *Cymbopogon*

c) *Basilicum* d) *Rosemarinus*

714. Basil is pollinated by

a) Wind b) Insects

c) Housefly d) Air

715. Trishna and Jamrosa are cultivars of

a) Palmarosa b) Citronella

c) Japanese nut d) Patchouli

716. Basil thrives well under

a) Fair to high rainfall and humid condition

b) Humid conditions

c) High temperature and heavy rainfall

d) Low temp. & heavy rainfall

717. Victoria, Comet, Giant California asters and Branching asters refers to

a) Varieties of asters

b) Classification of asters

c) Dwarf varieties of asters

d) Tall varieties of asters

718. The word `Dianthus' is derived from Greek word meaning

a) Devil flower

b) God flower

c) Divine flower

d) All of these

719. Which of the following species of Jasmine is the chief source of essential oil?

a) *J. grandiflorum*

b) *J. sambac*

c) *J. humile*

d) *J. auriculatum*

720. Most suitable spacing for *J auriculatum*

a) 2.5 x 2.5 meters

b) 1.8 x 1.8 meter

c) 1.2 x 1.2 meters

d) 3.0 x 3.0 meters

721. The term 'Phylloidy' is related with

a) Carnation

b) Rose

c) Tuberose

d) Jasmine

722. The best rooting hormone in jasmine is

a) IBA 4000 ppm

b) GA_3

c) CA

d) IBA 100 ppm

723. Fossils of roses on USA have been reported ________ million year oil.

a) 10

b) 1

c) 30

d) 100

724. Diploid chromosome no. of roses is

a) 10 b) 28

c) 14 d) 20

725. Which of the Rosa species is resistant to cold?

a) *centiflora* b) *rugosa*

c) *foetida* d) *chinensis*

726. *Pelargonidin enthocyanidin* is present in _______ colour.

a) Blue b) Orange – Red

c) Yellow d) White

727. Cyandin anthocyanidin is present in _______ colour

a) Black b) Pink

c) Bluish-Red d) Yellowish-white

728. Inheritance of pigments is controlled by ______ gene action.

a) Additive b) Dominance

c) Epistasis d) None of above

729. Fragrance is controlled by _________ gene.

a) Mono b) Oligo

c) Poly d) None of these

730. Chemical defoliatioin in roses is done by.

a) Urea b) Copper sulphate

c) Auxin d) GA

731. Which fragrant cultivar of roses is grown in greenhouses?

a) Kontetti b) Cocktail

c) Jacaranda d) All of above

732. Which is most popular variety of roses in protected cultivation in India?

a) Grand gala b) First Red

c) Konfetti d) All of above

733. The layout of Lalbagh was designed by

a) Sim b) Hyder Ali

c) Sir George King d) Akbar

734. Which of the following is botanical garden of Karnataka state?

a) Sim's park b) Brindavan garden

c) Lal bagh d) Rock garden

735. Lal bagh is the seat of the Directorate of Horticulture of which state of India?

a) Maharashtra b) Karnataka

c) Kerala d) Tamil Nadu

736. Government Botanic garden is situated in the

a) Shivalik hills b) Nilgiri hills

c) Aravalli hills d) Satpura hills

737. Which of the following is popularly known as `Sikander Bagh?'

a) NBRI, Lucknow b) Government botanic garden

c) Botanic garden, Coimbatore d) The Indian Botanic garden, Sibpur

738. The most interesting plant popularly known as "Living Fossil tree" in Llyod botanic garden is

a) Dawn Red Wood b) Araucaria

c) Chinar d) Cupressus

739. Which of the following gardens is connected with dal lake?

a) Rose garden, Chandigarh b) Shalimar garden, Kashmir

c) Mandor garden, Jodhpur d) Botanic garden, Coimbatore

740. Diwan-e-Aam and Diwan-e-Khas are concerned with

a) Shalimar bagh b) Roshanara park

c) Nishant bagh d) Mandoor garden

741. The Sim's park located at Coonoor was established by

a) D.K. Sim b) A.S. sim

c) A.K. Sim d) J.D. Sim

742. The Sim's park was established in the year

a) 1774 b) 1874

c) 1674 d) 1974

743. The Royal botanic garden has been renamed as

a) Indian Botanic garden b) Government botanic garden

c) Botanic garden d) None of these

744. The Byrant Park, Kodaikanal is a centre to supply

a) Fruit plants b) Ornamental plants

c) Nursery plant d) Rootstocks

745. The Roshanara Park designed by Dr MS Randhawa and Prof K Mori in 1958 is at

a) Chandigarh b) Mysore

c) Delhi d) Dehradun

746. State which of the following pairs is incorrect

a) 1st Japanese style garden - Roshanara Park, Delhi

b) Prof K Mori - Famous Japanese landscape architect

c) The Byrant Park - Darjeeling (West Bengal)

d) The Indian Botanic garden - Sibpur (Calcutta)

747. Which of the following is correctly matched?

a) The Byrant park-Kodaikanal (Tamil Nadu)

b) Lal Bagh-Ootacamond

c) Botanic garden- Bangalore

d) Sim's Park- Coimbatore

748. In which State the Satyaji park is situated?

a) Haryana b) Gujarat

c) Kashmir d) Uttar Pradesh

749. Which of the following garden were not laid out by Fidai Khan?

a) Mandoor garden b) Rose garden

c) Llyod botanic garden d) All of these

750. The credit for developing Mughal gardens in Kashmir goes to

a) Akbar b) Jahangir

c) Shah Jahan d) All of these

751. Which of the following is not a Japanese style garden?

a) Nishat Bagh b) Chasma-e-Shahi

c) Roshanara park d) None of these

752. The Sayaji Park is named in honour of

a) Maharaja Sayaji Rao III b) Sayaji Rao II

c) Soayaji Satya Rao d) None of these

753. The Baroda museum situated in the 'Sayaji Park' was opened in the year

a) 1979 b) 1880

c) 1894 d) 1881

754. Raja Abhai Singh is associated with

a) Mandor garden b) Rose garden

c) Rock garden d) Mughal garden, Pinjore

755. Where is Queen Marry rose garden situated?

a) Paris b) London

c) Spain d) Chandigarh

756. Which of the following Mughal garden of Kashmir is/are correctly matched

1) Shalimar garden-Jahangir and Zafar Khan

2) Nishat bagh- Asaf Jah

3) Chasma-e-Shahi-Ali-mardan Khan

4) Achabal-Nur Jahan

a) 1 only b) 2 & 3

c) 2, 3 & 4 d) All of these

757. The Shish Mehal, Rang Mahal and Jal Mahal are magnificent building of

a) Mandoor Garden, Jodhpur b) Mughal garden, Pinjore

c) Rose garden, Chandigarh d) Sayaji Park, Baroda

758. Ornamental plants collection in the Mughal garden, Pinjore goes in the credit of

a) Fidai Khan b) Dara Shikoh

c) Yadvindra Singh d) Abhai Singh

759. The Indian Botanic garden sibpur was established on advice of Robert kyad, he was

a) A farmer b) A confectioner

c) An army men d) A scientist

760. The 1st Indian to occupy the post of superintendent of Indian Botanic garden, Sibpur.

a) Dr K Biswas b) Dr M K Randhawa

c) Dr K L Chadha d) Dr J N Kaul

761. Flower vase should not be kept near _____ in room.

a) Oven b) Fan

c) Heater d) All of these

762. Which of following is commonly used to increase vase-life?

a) Salt b) Oil

c) Sugar d) Glucose

763. The period for which flowers remains in presentable form is known as _____ of particular flowers.

a) Vase life b) Shelf life

c) Display life d) All of these

764. In vase solution, which of following acts as bactericide

a) DICA b) DDMH

c) 8-Hydroxy quinoline d) All of these

765. Hypobaric storage is also known as

a) Modified atmospheric storage b) Low pressure storage

c) Controlled atmospheric storaged) All of these

766. Preservative that shows toxicity in Daffodil.

a) 8-HQC b) STS

c) Citric acid d) Silver nitrate

767. Which of following flowers is/ are suitable for air drying

a) Helichrysum b) Acraclinum

c) Statice d) All of these

768. Which of following flowers is/ are suitable for press drying

a) Gladiolus b) Rose

c) Pansy d) All of these

769. Medium used in drying of flowers is/ are

a) Silica gel b) Borax

c) River sand d) All of these

770. In oven drying most of flowers are dried for _____ hours.

a) 10-20 b) 20-30

c) 48-72 d) 72-90

771. Terrarium is

a) Plant grown on terraces b) Transparent race for keeping flowers

c) Solution for using in flowers d) Pot for raising plants

772. Plant part of saffron used as spice

a) Bark b) Rhizome

c) Seed d) Flower

773. Chemical content of Safed Musali is

a) Saponins b) Morphine

c) Nicotine d) Reserpine

774. Which medicinal plant is used to cure heart disease?

a) Foxglove b) Henbane

c) Belladona d) Isabgol

775. Medicine to check high blood pressure is obtained from

a) Cinchona spp. b) Rauwolfia serpentina

c) Digitalis purpurea d) All of these

776. Medicinal plant used to reduce cholesterol content in blood

a) Guggal b) Isabgol

c) Neem d) None of these

777. Major flowers dried by freeze drying

a) Rose b) Carnation

c) Both (a) & (b) d) None of these

778. Most suitable flowers subjected to glycerin drying

a) Magnolia b) Oak

c) Eucalyptus d) All of these

779. Process of converting ice directly into water vapour

a) Sublimation b) Evaporation

c) Drying d) Dehydration

780. The best drying agent for Anemone, Aster, larkspur flowers

a) White sand b) Silica gel

c) Sand d) Borax

781. Basic steps involved in dry flower production

a) Drying b) Bleaching

c) Dying d) All the above

782. In an ideal preserving mixture to treat the foliage the glycerine and water ratio should be

a) 1 : 2 b) 2 : 2

c) 1 : 1 d) 1 : 4

783. Glycernizing is most suitable special preservation technique for

a) Eucalyptus b) Hydrangia

c) Magnolia d) All of these

784. Floral preservative used as pretreatment to improve the quality of dry flowers

a) Citric acid b) Hydrogen peroxide

c) Sodium hydroxide d) None of these

785. The optimum conditions for hypochlorite bleaching

a) Low temperature b) Low concentration

c) pH d) All of these

786. The best bleaching agent for plant foliage

a) Hydrogen Peroxide b) Sodium chlorite

c) Hypochlorite d) None of these

787. The European Economic Community standard and grades for Carnation flower are based on

a) Stem length b) Stem strength

c) Flower diameter d) Flower colour

788. Bull head in roses is caused due to

a) Insufficient carbohydrate supply to buds

b) High light intensity

c) Excessive fertilizer application

d) High humidity

789. Senescence in rose flowers is associated with

a) Blueing of red petals b) Decreases in protein content

c) Increase in Ribonuclease activity d) All of these

790. Exposure of carnation flowers to ethylene causes

a) Sleepiness b) Calyx splitting

c) Uneven opening of flower d) Shedding of flowers

791. Calyx splitting in carnation is a common disorder of

a) warmer areas b) temperate areas

c) dry temperate areas d) None of these

792. A plant hormone having significant role in regulation of senescence in flowers

a) Gibberellic acid b) Abscissic acid

c) Cytokinin d) None of these

793. Calyx splitting & uneven opening of carnation flowers are due to

a) High temperature

b) Nutritional deficiencies

c) Sudden fluctuation in day and night temperature

d) All the above

794. The best harvest stage in tulip

a) Tight bud stage b) Paint brush stage

c) Pink bud stage d) Green bud stage

795. The optimum temperature for long term storage of cut gladiolus

a) 1.7 to 4.4°C b) below 1.0°C

c) 0°C d) 5.8°C

796. TBZ stands for

a) Thiobenzene b) Thiobendize

c) Thiobengene d) Thiobendazole

797. STS stands for

a) Sulphuric-tri-sulphide b) Sulforated-tri-sulphide

c) Silver-Tri-Sulphate d) Silver Thio-sulphate

798. QAS stands for

a) Quarterly Ammonium salt b) Quarternary Amino Salt

c) Quarternary Amino Salt d) None of these

799. HQS stands for

a) Butylated Hydroxy Quinino Sulphide

b) ß-Hydroxy Quinoline Sulphate

c) ß-Hydroxy Quinine Sulphate

d) ß-Hydroxy Quinoline Sulphide

800. BHQC stands for

a) Butylated Hydroxy Quinaline Chlorine

b) ß-Hydroxy Quinoline Chlorate

c) ß-Hydroxy Quinoline Citrate

d) ß-Hydroxy Quick Cis Citride

801. One kg oil is obtained from _______ rose petals

a) 10 ton b) 10-15 tones

c) 3-4 tones d) 0.1-10 tones

802. Pelargonidin anthocyanidin pigment is responsible for which of following colour

a) Orange-Red b) Blue

c) Yellow d) White

803. Which of the following methods are used to extract rose oil

a) Steam stills b) Old fashioned field stills

c) Modern direct fire stills d) All of these

804. Oil percentage in *Rosa damascena*

a) 0.3 b) 0.2

c) 0.03 d) 0.02

805. A treatment given to flowers after harvesting by using water to restore turgidity is

a) Loading b) Hardening

c) Pulsing d) Both (b) & (c)

806. Treatment of cut flowers after harvesting by using high concentration of sugar is known as

a) Hardening
b) Loading
c) Pulsing
d) Both (a) & (c)

807. Optimum pH of holding solution should be

a) 2-3
b) 6-7
c) 5-6
d) 4-5

808. Ethylene in cold storage is removed by

a) Ventilation
b) Low pressure
c) UV light
d) All of these

809. Optimum cold storage temperature for carnation storage is _____°C

a) 0-1
b) 1-2
c) 3-5
d) 10-12

810. Flower vase should not be kept near _____ in room.

a) Oven
b) Fan
c) Heater
d) All of these

811. Which of following is commonly used to increase vase life?

a) Salt
b) Oil
c) Sugar
d) Glucose

812. The period for which flowers remains in presentable form is known as _____ of particular flowers.

a) Vase life
b) Shelf life
c) Display life
d) All of these

813. The country having highest Rose oil production

a) Bulgaria
b) Italy
c) China
d) India

814. Rose oil is primarily extracted from which *Rosa species*

a) *odorata*
b) *damascena*
c) *indica*
d) *gallica*

815. In cryo-preservation seeds are preserved in liquid nitrogen at ______°C

a) 100 b) -96

c) -196 d) 0

816. Air drying of flowers is common in

a) Aster b) Dahlia

c) Daisy d) Helichrysum

817. In roses, blue pigmentation source is found in cultivar

a) Blue moon b) Bhim

c) Samba d) Sonia

818. Blue colour pigment is

a) Lycopene b) Delphilidin

c) Pelargolin d) Reseline

819. Lilium bulbs are stored in moist sand at a temperature of

a) 5°C b) 10°C

c) -2°C d) -5°C

820. Sweet pea is a __________ winter annual.

a) Tall b) Medium

c) Dwarf d) Climber

821. Hollyhock is a __________ winter annual.

a) Tall b) Medium

c) Dwarf d) Climber

822. Portulaca is a __________ summer annual.

a) Tall b) Medium

c) Dwarf d) All of these

823. Summer annuals are planted in month of

a) Oct.-November b) Dec.-January

c) February- March d) July-August

824. Winter annuals are planted in month of

a) November-December b) October-November

c) April-May d) July-August

825. Rainy season annuals are planted in month of

a) September-October b) December-January

c) March- April d) June- July

826. Chrysanthemum is planted in the month of

a) July-August b) November-December

c) February- March d) May-June

827. Rose is planted in the month of

a) June-July b) End of Sept. to Oct. 1st fortnight

c) April- May d) May-June

828. Brachycome is a ____________ winter annual.

a) Tall b) Medium

c) Dwarf d) All of these

829. Pot plants need relative humidity (%) of

a) 60-80 b) 40-70

c) 20-40 d) 80-100

830. Most common disease of pot plant is

a) Black rust b) Botrytis

c) Black spot d) Die back

831. Yellowing in lawns might be due to

a) Water logging b) Insect attack

c) Fungus attack d) Snow-fall

832. Dahlia is a

a) Bulbous plant b) Tuberous plant

c) Corm d) Rhizome

833. Daffodil is a

a) Bulbous plant
b) Tuberous plant
c) Corm
d) Rhizome

834. Narcissus is a modified

a) Root
b) Stem
c) Leaf
d) Flower

835. Formal style gardens were originated in

a) Persia
b) India
c) Japan
d) England

836. Informal style gardens were originated in

a) Persia
b) India
c) Japan
d) England

837. Herbaceous border concept was originated in

a) Italy
b) India
c) Japan
d) England

838. Cottage gardens were originated in

a) Italy
b) England
c) Japan
d) India

839. Which of following is most suitable for hedge making?

a) *Duranta plumieri*
b) *Poinsettia pulcherima*
c) *Cassia glauca*
d) *Clerodendron inerme*

840. Which of following is most suitable for topiary making?

a) *Duranta plumieri*
b) *Nyctanthus arbortristis*
c) *Cestrum nocturnum*
d) *Clerodendron inerme*

841. Dibbling method of lawn plantation should be practiced during

a) July-August
b) December-January
c) February-March
d) May-June

842. Top dressing of lawn is usually done in month of

a) July b) December

c) February d) April

843. Raking in lawn is practiced for

a) Killing weeds b) Aeration

c) Mixing fertilizer d) Hoeing

844. Fairy ring disease of lawn is caused by

a) Nematodes b) Parasites

c) Fungus d) All of these

845. Roses are wintered in month of

a) April-May

b) December-January

c) End of Sept. to Oct. 1st fortnight

d) June-July

846. *Butea monosperma* produces flower in the month of

a) September-October b) February-March

c) December-January d) June-July

847. *Casssia fistula* produces ___________ colour flowers.

a) Yellow b) White

c) Blue d) Red

848. *Jasminum grandiflorum* produces ___________ colour flowers.

a) Yellow b) White

c) Blue d) Red

849. *Canna indica* is planted in the month of__________.

a) April-May b) February-March

c) November-December d) July-August

850. Money plant is also known as

a) *Hedera halix* b) *Irish ivy*

c) *Scindapsis aureus* d) *Ficus repens*

Answer Key of Multiple Choice Questions

1. (c)	2. (a)	3 (c)	4 (d)	5 (b)	6. (b)
7. (b)	8. (a)	9 (c)	10 (b)	11 (a)	12. (d)
13. (a)	14. (d)	15. (b)	16 (d)	17 (a)	18. (a)
19. (b)	20. (c)	21. (b)	22 (c)	23 (b)	24. (a)
25. (b)	26. (b)	27. (c)	28 (b)	29 (b)	30. (a)
31. (a)	32. (b)	33. (a)	34 (d)	35 (b)	36. (d)
37. (c)	38. (a)	39. (c)	40 (b)	41 (a)	42. (a)
43. (d)	44. (b)	45. (c)	46 (b)	47 (c)	48. (b)
49. (a)	50. (b)	51. (c)	52 (a)	53 (b)	54. (d)
55. (c)	56. (d)	57. (d)	58 (c)	59 (a)	60. (d)
61. (b)	62. (d)	63. (c)	64 (b)	65 (a)	66. (a)
67. (d)	68. (a)	69. (b)	70 (d)	71 (d)	72. (c)
73. (c)	74. (c)	75. (c)	76 (d)	77 (a)	78. (d)
79. (d)	80. (a)	81. (a)	82 (d)	83 (b)	84. (a)
85. (d)	86. (c)	87. (a)	88 (d)	89 (d)	90. (a)
91. (d)	92. (a)	93. (b)	94 (c)	95 (b)	96. (c)
97. (d)	98. (b)	99. (b)	100. (d)	101. (a)	102. (b)
103. (d)	104. (d)	105. (b)	106. (a)	107. (d)	108. (d)
109. (a)	110. (b)	111. (a)	112. (a)	113. (c)	114. (c)
115. (a)	116. (d)	117. (c)	118. (b)	119. (d)	120. (b)
121. (d)	122. (a)	123. (a)	124. (c)	125. (c)	126. (d)
127. (b)	128. (b)	129. (d)	130. (a)	131. (d)	132. (b)
133. (d)	134. (c)	135. (a)	136. (a)	137. (b)	138. (d)
139. (b)	140. (d)	141. (c)	142. (a)	143. (b)	144. (c)
145. (d)	146. (a)	147. (d)	148. (c)	149. (b)	150. (d)
151. (c)	152. (a)	153. (b)	154. (d)	155. (a)	156. (a)
157. (b)	158. (c)	159. (d)	160. (a)	161. (d)	162. (a)
163. (d)	164. (c)	165. (b)	166. (c)	167. (a)	168. (b)
169. (d)	170. (c)	171. (a)	172. (b)	173. (b)	174. (a)
175. (d)	176. (d)	177. (a)	178. (d)	179. (c)	180. (b)
181. (a)	182. (b)	183. (a)	184. (a)	185. (b)	186. (b)
187. (b)	188. (a)	189. (c)	190. (c)	191. (b)	192. (b)
193. (c)	194. (a)	195. (c)	196. (c)	197. (a)	198. (d)
199. (a)	200. (c)	201.(b)	202. (d)	203. (c)	204. (d)
205. (a)	206. (b)	207. (c)	208. (b)	209. (a)	210. (d)
211. (c)	212. (d)	213. (c)	214. (c)	215. (a)	216. (d)
217. (b)	218. (b)	219. (d)	220. (c)	221. (a)	222. (a)
223. (d)	224. (b)	225. (c)	226. (b)	227. (b)	228. (b)
229. (a)	230. (d)	231. (b)	232. (b)	233. (d)	234. (b)
235. (c)	236. (a)	237. (b)	238. (c)	239. (a)	240. (a)
241. (c)	242. (d)	243. (d)	244. (a)	245. (b)	246. (a)

247. (a)	248. (d)	249. (a)	250. (b)	251. (c)	252. (c)
253. (a)	254. (d)	255. (a)	256. (a)	257. (a)	258. (d)
259. (a)	260. (b)	261. (c)	262. (a)	263. (b)	264. (a)
265. (b)	266. (a)	267. (c)	268. (b)	269. (d)	270. (a)
271. (d)	272. (a)	273. (d)	274. (c)	275. (a)	276. (b)
277. (a)	278. (b)	279. (a)	280. (c)	281. (c)	282. (c)
283. (c)	284. (c)	285. (a)	286. (c)	287. (c)	288. (b)
289. (c)	290. (d)	291. (a)	292. (d)	293. (c)	294. (b)
295. (b)	296. (a)	297. (b)	298. (d)	299. (d)	300. (c)
301. (a)	302. (b)	303. (c)	304. (d)	305. (d)	306. (a)
307. (d)	308. (c)	309. (a)	310. (a)	311. (c)	312. (c)
313. (a)	314. (c)	315. (c)	316. (d)	317. (c)	318. (a)
319. (b)	320. (c)	321. (d)	322. (a)	323. (c)	324. (c)
325. (c)	326. (d)	327. (a)	328. (a)	329. (c)	330. (b)
331. (c)	332. (a)	333. (a)	334. (a)	335. (b)	336. (a)
337. (b)	338. (a)	339. (d)	340. (d)	341. (c)	342. (b)
343. (d)	344. (b)	345. (b)	346. (b)	347. (b)	348. (a)
349. (b)	350. (d)	351. (a)	352. (d)	353. (a)	354. (a)
355 (d)	356. (b)	357. (a)	358. (c)	359. (a)	360. (b)
361 (b)	362. (c)	363. (c)	364. (b)	365. (a)	366. (c)
367 (c)	368. (b)	369. (a)	370. (d)	371. (b)	372. (b)
373 (d)	374. (a)	375. (a)	376. (b)	377. (c)	378. (c)
379 (d)	380. (b)	381. (c)	382. (b)	383. (c)	384. (a)
385 (b)	386. (c)	387. (a)	388. (d)	389. (b)	390. (b)
391 (b)	392. (b)	393. (c)	394. (b)	395. (b)	396. (c)
397 (c)	398. (b)	399. (b)	400. (b)	401. (a)	402. (d)
403 (d)	404. (d)	405. (d)	406. (a)	407. (c)	408. (c)
409 (d)	410. (b)	411. (d)	412. (d)	413. (a)	414. (d)
415 (a)	416. (b)	417. (c)	418. (b)	419. (a)	420. (b)
421 (b)	422. (c)	423. (b)	424. (c)	425. (c)	426. (d)
427 (a)	428. (a)	429. (c)	430. (b)	431. (b)	432. (a)
433 (d)	434. (a)	435. (b)	436. (a)	437. (a)	438. (a)
439 (c)	440. (a)	441. (a)	442. (d)	443. (a)	444. (d)
445 (a)	446. (b)	447. (a)	448. (c)	449. (a)	450. (b)
451 (b)	452. (d)	453. (a)	454. (d)	455. (d)	456. (d)
457 (b)	458. (d)	459 (d)	460. (c)	461. (a)	462. (d)
463 (a)	464. (b)	465. (b)	466. (b)	467. (a)	468. (b)
469 (b)	470. (d)	471. (a)	472. (b)	473. (a)	474. (c)
475 (b)	476. (b)	477. (a)	478. (d)	479. (a)	480. (a)
481 (d)	482. (d)	483. (b)	484. (b)	485. (c)	486. (c)
487 (a)	488. (a)	489. (d)	490. (d)	491. (a)	492. (a)
493 (d)	494. (d)	495. (d)	496. (a)	497. (d)	498. (b)
499 (a)	500. (b)	501. (d)	502. (b)	503. (a)	504. (c)

505 (a)	506. (b)	507. (b)	508. (c)	509. (b)	510. (c)
511 (d)	512. (b)	513. (d)	514.(d)	515.(a)	516. (d)
517 (b)	518. (b)	519. (a)	520. (d)	521. (d)	522. (c)
523 (a)	524. (a)	525. (d)	526. (b)	527. (c)	528. (b)
529 (c)	530. (d)	531. (c)	532. (a)	533. (b)	534. (d)
535 (b)	536. (b)	537. (b)	538. (a)	539. (c)	540. (c)
541 (b)	542. (a)	543. (d)	544. (d)	545. (c)	546. (d)
547 (b)	548. (c)	549. (b)	550. (d)	551. (d)	552. (b)
553 (c)	554. (d)	555. (d)	556. (b)	557. (a)	558. (a)
559 (a)	560. (b)	561. (c)	562. (a)	563. (b)	564. (a)
565 (b)	566. (b)	567. (c)	568. (d)	569. (b)	570. (c)
571 (a)	572. (c)	573. (c)	574. (d)	575. (a)	576. (b)
577 (a)	578. (b)	579. (d)	580. (d)	581. (b)	582. (a)
583 (b)	584. (a)	585. (b)	586. (d)	587. (b)	588. (a)
589 (a)	590. (d)	591. (c)	592. (a)	593. (b)	594. (d)
595 (a)	596. (c)	597. (b)	598. (d)	599. (a)	600. (c)
601 (b)	602. (a)	603. (d)	604. (d)	605. (a)	606. (c)
607 (a)	608. (b)	609. (c)	610. (b)	611. (d)	612. (b)
613 (a)	614. (b)	615. (c)	616. (d)	617. (b)	618. (a)
619 (b)	620. (d)	621. (b)	622. (d)	623. (d)	624. (c)
625 (d)	626. (c)	627. (d)	628. (b)	629. (c)	630. (d)
631 (b)	632. (a)	633. (b)	634. (b)	635. (c)	636. (a)
637 (a)	638. (a)	639. (d)	640. (b)	641. (a)	642. (a)
643 (b)	644. (d)	645. (b)	646. (d)	647. (a)	648. (c)
649 (b)	650. (a)	651. (a)	652. (d)	653. (b)	654. (a)
655 (a)	656. (d)	657. (a)	658. (a)	659. (c)	660. (d)
661 (c)	662. (d)	663. (d)	664. (a)	665. (c)	666. (a)
667 (d)	668. (d)	669. (c)	670. (a)	671. (d)	672. (a)
673 (c)	674. (a)	675. (d)	676. (a)	677. (b)	678. (a)
679 (c)	680. (a)	681. (c)	682. (b)	683. (a)	684. (b)
685 (c)	686. (b)	687. (a)	688. (d)	689. (a)	690. (b)
691 (c)	692. (a)	693. (b)	694. (a)	695. (c)	696. (a)
697 (b)	698. (d)	699. (b)	700. (a)	701. (b)	702. (a)
703 (c)	704. (a)	705. (b)	706. (c)	707. (d)	708. (a)
709 (b)	710. (d)	711. (b)	712. (a)	713. (a)	714. (b)
715 (a)	716. (a)	717. (b)	718. (c)	719. (a)	720. (b)
721 (d)	722. (a)	723. (c)	724. (c)	725. (b)	726. (b)
727 (c)	728. (a)	729. (c)	730. (c)	731. (d)	732. (b)
733 (b)	734. (c)	735. (b)	736. (b)	737. (a)	738. (a)
739 (b)	740. (a)	741. (d)	742. (b)	743. (a)	744. (b)
745 (c)	746. (c)	747. (a)	748. (b)	749. (d)	750. (d)
751 (d)	752. (a)	753. (c)	754. (a)	755. (b)	756. (d)
757 (b)	758. (c)	759. (c)	760. (a)	761. (d)	762. (c)

763 (a)	764. (d)	765. (b)	766. (a)	767. (d)	768. (c)
769 (d)	770. (c)	771. (b)	772. (d)	773. (a)	774. (a)
775 (b)	776. (a)	777. (c)	778. (d)	779. (a)	780. (b)
781 (d)	782. (a)	783. (d)	784. (a)	785. (d)	786. (b)
787 (a)	788. (a)	789. (d)	790. (a)	791. (a)	792. (b)
793 (d)	794. (d)	795. (a)	796. (d)	797. (d)	798. (a)
799 (b)	800. (c)	801. (c)	802. (a)	803. (d)	804. (c)
805 (b)	806. (c)	807. (d)	808. (d)	809. (a)	810. (d)
811 (c)	812. (a)	813. (a)	814. (b)	815. (c)	816. (d)
817 (c)	818. (b)	819. (c)	820. (d)	821. (a)	822. (c)
823 (c)	824. (b)	825. (d)	826. (a)	827. (b)	828. (c)
829 (a)	830. (b)	831. (a)	832. (b)	833. (a)	834. (c)
835 (a)	836. (c)	837. (d)	838. (b)	839. (a)	840. (d)
841 (a)	842. (c)	843. (b)	844. (c)	845. (c)	846. (b)
847 (a)	848. (b)	849. (d)	850. (c)		

5

Important Cultivars of Ornamental Crops

Plant name	Cultivars
Amaranthus tricolor	NBRI, Lucknow: Amar Kiran, Amar Mosaic, Amar Parvarti, Amar Prithu, Amar Raktabhy, Amar Suikiran, Amar Summer King, Amar Summer Queen, Amar Tarang
Amaranthus caudatus	NBRI, Lucknow: Amar Shola
Bougainvillea	Dr BP Pal, New Delhi: Dr RR Pal, Sonnet, Spring Festival, Summer Time, Stanza. Agri-Horticultural Society, Calcutta:- Dr BP Pal IARI, New Delhi: Vishakha, Dr RR Pal, Spring Festival, Stanza. Lalbagh-Bangalore: Bhabha, Lalbagh, Trinidad, Thimma. NBRI, Lucknow: Archana, Begam Sikander, Chitra, Dr BP Pal, Los Benos Beauty Variegata, Mahtma Variegata, Many Palmer Special, Nirmal, Pallavi Parthasarthy, Shubhra, Tetra Mrs McCleans, Wazid Ali Shah. Soundaraya Nursery, Madras: Vericolour, Sensation, Flame. IIHR, Bangalore: Purple Wonder, Gopal Jaylakshmi and Mahatma Gandhi. Chitravati (1979): Lalbagh × Red glory (Hybrid) Jawahar Lal Nehru (1975): Spontaneous mutant of Lalbagh Purple Wonder: Formosa × Trinidad Sholey(1977): Seedling selection of Red Glory Usha (1977): Seedling selection of Lady Hope DR HB Singh (1977): Trinidad × Formosa (Hybrid).
Chrysanthemum	Atma Sahay, Allahabad: Mahatma Gandhi, Modinagar, Mr KB Srivastava, KN Modi.
	Barin Gupta, Jamshedpur: Jamshedji, Jamshedpur Glory, Pride of Jamshedpur, Red Carpet, Steel City Beauty, Sri Ganga.
	Chandra Nursery, Sikkim: Anokha, Chandra's Choice, Rang Mahal.
	IIHR, Bangalore: Chanderkant, Chandrika, Kirti, Nilima, Pankaj, Ravikiran, Yellow Gold and Yellow Star.
	Indira (1980): Hybrid between open pollinated seedlings of Lord Doonex and a hybrid seedling of Flirt × Valentine
	Rakhee (1980): open pollinated seeding of cv Lord Doonex
	Red Gold: Flirt × Valentine
	NBRI, Lucknow

Plant name	Cultivars
	Large Flowered Mutant: Aruna, Asha, Basant, Kanak, Kum Kum, Nirbhaya, Pingal, Pitaka, Pitamber, Rohit, Shefali, Shukla, Shweta, Swarnim, Tamra and Taruni.
	Small Flowered Induced Mutant: Agnishikha, Alankar, Anamika, Basanti, Hemanti, Lohit, Manbhavan, Sharad Har, Sheela, Sonali, Subarna, Surekha Yellow.
	Mutant with change in form: Ashankit, Cosmonaut, Jhalar, Kunchit, Shabnam, Tulika.
	Pompon type: Apsara, Birbal Sahni, Jayanti, Jubilee, Kundan.
	No pinch No stake type: Appu, Apurva, Arun Kumar, Arun Singar, Guldasta, Haldi Ghati, Hemant Singar, Shard Singar, and Suhag Singar.
	Off-season blooming cultivars: Ajaya, Himanshu, Haldi Ghati, Jaya, Jwala, Jyoti, Maghi, Meghdoot, Phuhar, Sarada, SardMala, Sarad Singar, Tushar, Usha, Vasantika.
	PAU, Ludhiana: Basanti, Gul-e-Shair, Punjab Gold, Shanti. TNAU, Coimbatore: MDU-1 Chrysanthemum, CO-1, CO-2.
	Large flowered varieties: Sonar Bangla, Redwest field, Cresta, City beauty, Day Dream, Peach Blossom, Sweet Heart, Green Sensation, Rupsi Bangla, Kirti, Chandarkant, Kasturba Gandhi.
	Small flowered varieties: Gul-a-Sahir, Birbal Shani, King Fisher, Red Star, Stella, Sharad Kumar: No staking or pinching
	Off season blooming varieties: Haldi Ghati, Himanshi, Jwala, Maghi, Meghdoot.
	Export varieties:
	A) Standard: Dignity, Wild Fire, Detroit News
	B) Spray: Parliament, Dazzler Florida, Marble
	C) Pot mums: Fantasy, Albert, Alpine.
Cooperanthus	Percy Lancaster, Agri-Horticultural Society, Calcutta: Alipore Beauty, King Emperor, Lancastrian Percy, Sunset, Sydney, The Governor, The President, The Viceroy.
China Aster	IIHR, Bangalore: Kamini, Poornima, AST-1, AST-2 and Sashank.
	MPKV, Rahuri: Phule Ganesh Pink, Phule Ganesh Purple, Phule Ganesh Violet, Phule Ganesh White.
Coreopsis	IARI, New Delhi: Pusa Tara Croton
Dahlia	IARI, New Delhi: Kenya Blue, Kenya White, Kenya Yellow, Manali, Manjushri.
	Swami Vinayananda: Bhikhus Mother, Bhikhus Vivek, Jyotsana, Lord Budha, Sarada Devi, Swami Gauri Swarananda, Swami Madhavananda.
	LN Singh Thakur: Chitchor, Zail Singh
	R Mitra: Manjushri
	SC Dey: Disco, Swami Vinayananda.
Carnation	Perpetual: Winter Cheer, Britania, Jokar, Mr. Thomas Lawson, Day Break, Willium Sim, Lipstick, Pink Dona.

Plant name	Cultivars
	Standard or Sim: Corleone, Empire, Dark Tempo, Regina, Gold Rush, Peterson Red, Scania Red, White Sim, red Diamond. Malmaison: Princess of Wales, Mr Martin Smith
	Royal: Royal Fancy, White Perfection
	Modern: Pico
Gladiolus	IARI, New Delhi: Agnirekha, Anjali, Archana, Bindiya, Chandani, Chirag, Dhanvantari, Mayur, Neelam, Neelkanth, Noopur, Pusa Suhagin, Sanjeevni, Sarang, Shweta, Suchitra, Sunayana, Vandana.
	NBRI, Lucknow: Archana, Arun, Basant Bahar, Hans, Indrani, Jwala, Kajal, Kalima, Kohra, Manhar, Manisha, Manmohan, Manohar, Monaka, Mohini, Mridula, Mukta, Priyadarshini, Tabassum, Rim Jhim, Sada Bahar, Sanyukta, Sumita, Triloki, Usha.
	Lt Gov Shri Bajrang Bahadur Singh Bhadari, Himachal Pradesh: Bhadri Blue Beauty, Bhadri Bright Red, Bhadri Fortune, Bhadri Lemon Queen, Bhadri Little White, Bhadri Pearl, Bhadri Purple Queen, Bhadri Rose Glory, Bhadri's Simla Sunset, Bhadri Tricolour, Bhadri Yellow Beauty, May Blossom, Raj Niwas Pride, Rose of Heaven, Sakir Hussain. IHBT (CSIR), Palampur, Himachal Pradesh: Anurag, Brick Beauty, Palampur Queen, Palampur Princess, Tushar Mauli.
	IIHR, Bangalore: Aarti (1981): Shiley × Melody,
	Apsara (1981): Black jack × Friendship
	Poonam (1979) – Gelliber Herald × RN 121
	Sapna (1979) - Green Woodpecker × Friendship
	Shoba (1981) - Mutant of wild rose
	Gladiolus (IARI-New Delhi): Agni Rekha, Mayur, Suchitra, Apple Blossom, Melody and Sylvia.
	Aarti, Darshan, Dhiraj (Resistant to Fusarium), KumKum, Meera, Nazrana, Poonam, Sagar, Shakti, Sindhoor, Jwala, Gazal, Priyadarshani, Melody, Suchitra, Friendship (2n=60), Prabha, Oscar, Hunting Song, Her Majesty, Blue sky, Agni Rekha.
	Mutant varieties: Shobha, Pusa Swasini- mutant of wildrose variety
	Export varieties: Cartago, Priscilla, American Beauty, Mayur.
Hibiscus	IIHR, Bangalore: Aikta, Anuradha, Arunodaya, Ashirwad, Basant, Benazeer, Bharat Sundari, Chitralekha, Geetanjali, Jogan, Nartaki, Nazneen, Neelofer, Parkeejah, Phulkari, Priya, Queen of Hesarghatta, Ratna, Red Gold, Red Saturn, Shanti, Smt Indira Gandhi, Smt Kamla Nehru, Tribal Queen.
	Lalbagh, Bangalore: Bangalore-22.
	NBRI, Lucknow: Anjali.
	TNAU, Combatore: Punnagai, Thilagum
Hippeastrum	IARI, New Delhi: Suryakiran
	BCKV, Nadia, West Bengal: Anjali

Plant name	Cultivars
	NBRI, Lucknow: Apollo, Apurb, Charm, Charon, Chitwan, Coquette, Deepali, Diana, Emperor, Garima, Goergeous, Hannibal, Jyoti, Kiran, Lady Lancaster, Man Bhavan, Man Mayur, Minerva, Nizam, Percy Lancaster, Phoenix, Poonam, Raktamanjari (Mutant), Samrat, Saturn, Snow White, Sydney
Hollyhock	IARI, New Delhi: Deepika, Dulhan, Gouri, Pusa Gulabi, Pusa Krishna, Pusa Lalima, Pusa Pastel Pink, Pusa Pink Beauty, Pusa Yellow Beauty, Pusa Sweta
Jasmines	Jasminum auriculatum: CO 1, CO-2, Parimullai, Large Round, Large Point, Short Point, Medium Point, Long Round.
	Jasminum grandiflorum: CO 1 Pichi, CO 2 Pitchi, Arka Surabhi
	Jasminum sambac: Adukkaumalli, Irubachi, Gungumali, Ramabanam, Virupakshi, Motia, Single Mogra, Double Mogra, Mohra, Sujimalli, Madanban, Arka Aradhana.
Marigold	IARI, New Delhi: Pusa Basanti Gainda, Pusa Narangi Gainda, Pusa Sankar-I.
	TNAU Coimbatore: MDU-1 Marigold
	African marigold: Alaska, Giant Sunset, Golden Age, Honey Comb, Cracker jack, Climax, Golden Age, Crown of Gold, Chrysanthemum Charm, Star Gold, Pusa Narangi Gainda, Pusa Basanti Gainda, Snowbird, Texas, Yellow Climax and Yellow Fluffy.
	F1 hybrids: Apollo, Climax, First Lady, Moon Light, Orange Lady.
	French marigold: Melody, Orange Flame, Primrose Climax, Rusty Red, Spun Gold, Tangerine Yellow, Butter Scotch, Valencia.
Portulaca	NBRI, Lucknow: Jhumka, Lalita, Mukta, atnam, Vibhuti.
Roses	IARI, New Delhi: Abhisarika (1975), Anurag (1980), Arjun, Bhim, Chitwan, Dr BP Pal, Gang, Jawahar, Mother Teressa, Mridula, Mrinalini, Nurjahan, Priyadarshini, Pusa Sonia, Raj Kumari, Raktagandha, Rangasala, Surabhi (Hybrid Tea); Floribunda type: Arunima, Chandrama, Deepshikha, Himangini, Mohini (1970), Nav Sadabahar, Neelambri, Prema, Sadabahar, Shabanum, Sindhoor, suchitra, Suryodaya. Miniature: Delhi Scarlet (1963).
	Polyantha: Swati (1974).
	NBRI, Lucknow: Light Pink Prize, Mrinalini Stripe, Pink Montezuma, Summer Holiday Mutant, Winter Holiday Mutant (Hybrid Tea).
	Floribunda type: Angara, Curio, Pink Contempo, Pink Imperator, Sharada, Sukumari, Twinkle, Yellow Contempo, Zorina Pink (Miniature).
	Dr B P Pal: Akash Sundari, Apsara, Aravali Princess, Ashirwad, Dilruba, Dr Homi Bhabha, Dr MS Randhawa, Dr RR Pal, Hasina, Indian Princess, Kanakangi, Lalima, Lal Makhmal, Mehak, Maharani, Nayika, Nishada, Pahadi Dhun, Poornima, Raat ki Rani, Raja Surendra Singh of Nalagarh, Rajhans, Ranjana, Sandeepani, Surkhab and Uma Rao (Hybrid Tea); Akash Nartaki, Banjaran, Chitchor, Delhi Brightness, Delhi Princess, Deepak, Jantar Mantar, Madhura, Paharan, Parwana, Rangini, Rupali, Suryakiran, (Floribunda type).

Plant name	Cultivars
	MN Hardikar: Cynosure, First Rose Convention, Flying Tata.
	YK Hande: Ajanta Caves, Gauri, Good Morning, Indian Pearl, Perfumer, Pink Wave.
	MS Viraraghavan: Kanchi, Nefertiti, Priyatama, Rajni, Tamrabarani, Vamsadhara (Hybrid Tea), Amarpali, Bhagmati, First Offering, Mahadev, Vanamali (Floribunda); Kanyakumari (Climber type).
	Raja Surendra Singh of Nalagarh: Ghajal, Nazar-e-Nazar, Yamini Krishnamurthy (Hybrid Tea); Gopika (Floribunda). Braham Dutt: Don Nielson, Gond Beauty, Indian Festival, KK Thakur, Price of Nagpur, Soft Touch (Hybrid Tea).
	Rose cultivars developed by nurserymen in India:
	BK Roychowdhary: Bagha Jatin, Dr P Banerjee, Dr S D Mukherjee and Muzibar.
	BS Bhattacharji: Kalima, President Radhakrishnan, Raja Ram Mohan Roy, Ramkrishna Dev, Sugandha (Hybrid Tea); Jai Hind, Menaka, Mukttadhara, Pandit Nehru, Peetmanjari, Sir Jagdish Bose, Urbashi (Floribunda); Rishi Bankim, Tarapunja (Poliantha).
	JP Agarwal: Kasturi Rangan (Hybrid Tea); City of Lucknow (Floribunda).
	PL Arun: Divine Light, Golden Days, Mahak (Floribunda); Dark Beauty (Miniature); Tata Centenary (TELCO Nursery); Pioneering Pilot, Suvarnarekha (TISCO Nursery).
Tuberose	IIHR, Bangalore: Shringar (Single), Suvasini (Double); NBRI, Lucknow: Rajat Rekha (Single), Swarna Rekha (Double)
Lotus	Alba Striata, Alba White, Angel Wings, Perry Superstar, Alba Grandiflora, Shiroman, Baby Doll, Ben Gibson.
	Nelumbo lutea: Yellow Bird, Carolina Queen, Patricia Garrett, Flavescens.
	Hybrid cultivars: Embolene, Alexander the Great, Big Ben, Bonnie Clyde.
Orchids	IIHR, Bangalore: IIHR-164 (Vanda group), IIHR-38 (Dendrobium group).
	Scorpion orchids: Maggie Oei Yellow, Catherine, Ishbel.
	Renanthera: Brokkie Chandler, Kilauea, Poipu, Tom Thumb.
	Sympodial Cattelya: Bow Bells, Diane Salo, Empress Bells, Estelle.
	Dendrobium: Sonia-17, Sonia-28, Earsakul, Kasem Gold, Snow White, Jurie Red, Tongchai Blue.

Rose Cultivars Developed at IARI New Delhi

Hybrid Teas	Abhisarika (1975) - Mutant of Kiss of fire Anurag (1980) - Hybrid seedling of Sweet Afton × Gulzar Arjun (1980) - Blithe Spirit × Montezuma Bhim (1970) - Charles Mallerin × Delhi Princess Chitwan (1971) - Western Sun × Golden Splendour Ganga (1970) - A seedling of Sabina Jawahar (1980) - Sweet Afton × Delhi Princess Mridula (1975) - Queen Elizabeth × Sir Henry Segrave Mrinalini (1972) - Pink Perfact × Christian Dior Nur Jahan (1980) - Sweet Afton × Crimson glory Pusa Sonia (1968) - A seedling of MC grey yellow Raj Kumari (1969)- Charles Mallerin × Delhi Princess Raktagandha (1975)- Christian Dior × Seedling of Carrousel Surabhi (1975) - Oklahoma × Delhi Princess Vasant (1980) - Sweet Afton × Delhi Princess
Floribunda	Arunira (1976) - A seedling of Frolic Chandrama (1980) - A hybrid seedling white bouquet × Virgo Himangini (1968) - A seedling of Saratoga Mohini (1970) - A hybrid seedling of Sea Pearl × Shola Nav Sadabahar - Mutant of Sadabahar Neelambari - Blue Moon × African Star Preema - A hybrid seedling of Sea Pearl × Shola Sada bahar (1975) - A seedling of Baby Sylvia Sindoor (1980) - Sea Pearl × Suryodaya Suchitra (1972) - A hybrid seedling of Lady Frost × Swati
Polyantha	Swati (1968) - A seedling of Winifred Coulter

6

Hints for Self-Confidence

- Harmony is the principle of landscaping.
- Texture is an important element of landscaping.
- Blue is a primary colour.
- Green in a secondary colour.
- Garden furniture is a tangible item.
- Sound of waterfall is a intangible item.
- Pinjore garden was developed by Fadai Khan.
- Roshnara park is of Japanese style.
- Pilkhan is suitable for bonsai.
- *Delonix regia* is a flowering tree.
- Ikebana is a Japanese style flower arrangement.
- Sweet pea is a climbing annual.
- Acalypha is a foliage shrub.
- Gardenia is a flowering shrub
- *Lonicera japonica* is a climber.
- *Agrostis palustris* is a lawn grass.
- Marigold is used for making garlands.
- Veni is made from Jasmine flowers.
- Gladiolus flowers are used for making bouquets.
- Ikebana is an oriental flower arrangement.
- The book 'Ornamental Horticulture' is written by Vishnu Swarup.
- The book 'Planting Design' is written by Brian Hackett.
- The book 'Flower Trees' is written by MS Randhawa.

- Form is an element of landscaping.
- Balance is a principle of landscaping.
- *Lawsonia innermis* is used for edge.
- Cupressus is suitable for topiary.
- Blue colour is due to Delphidin.
- *Haemanthus multiflorus* is called football lily.
- J W Robinson is associated with wild garden.
- Le-Notre is associated with French garden.
- International flower market is situated at Alsmeer in the Netherlands
- HQ of International cut flowers grower association: USA
- HQ of International Society for Horticulture Science: Belgium
- International Registration authority for Rose : USA
- International Registration Authority for Bouganvillia : New Delhi
- No one foliage plant at global level : Diffenbachia
- No of one cut flowr at global level: Rose
- Total area under floriculture in India : 1 lakh lac (Approximately)
- State having maximum area under floriculture in India : Karnataka
- State having max production under floriculture in India : Tamil Nadu
- Largest importer of floriculture product from India : USA (27%)
- Share of dry flower product in India's total export : 60%
- Maximum cut flower production in India : West Bengal
- Division of ornamental crops started at IIHR in: 1989
- Division of floriculture and landscaping started at IARI in : 1983
- In AICRP on floriculture started in 1971.
- Flower crop covering maximum area in India: Jasmine
- Leading Bulbous plant producing country: Netherlands
- Leading Bulbous plant importing country: USA
- India is largest producer of loose flower in the world

- `Hedra' – No one pot plant in global flower market
- Helichrysum – 1st rank in dried ornamental in global flower market
- Flower capital of world: California, USA
- Foliage capital of the world : Apokka, Florida, USA
- Aspargus rank 1st in cut green in global flower market
- Leading flower seed producing states (i) Punjab (50%) (ii) Haryana (iii) HP
- Area under seed production in India: 800 hectare
- Annual having maximum number of seed/ gram: Petunia and Portulaca (over 10,000)
- Annual having minimum number of seed/ gram: Sweet pea and Sunflower (15-20)
- Bold seed: Holyhock, morning glory, lupin, Nasturtium
- Stevia - `Wonder Plant' (Sweteners of future)
- `Beautiful garden' book is written by M S Randhawa
- `Garden flowers' book is written by V Swarup
- `Garden through age' book is written by MS Randhawa
- Complete gardening in India is published by Hoseli Press
- Introductory ornamental horticulture is published by Kalyani Publishers
- Hogarth course is also known as line of beauty
- Biggest formal garden : Vrindavan Garden, Mysore
- Heaven of Man – Italian Garden
- Kadam tree is associated with Lord Krishna
- Semal tree is associated with Shiva
- Bauhinia tree is associated with Sarswati
- Amaranthus tree is associated with Kali
- Yellow Amaltas tree is associated with prosperity in trade
- Ashoka, Sal and Palash tree is associated with Buddha

- Babar was 1st Mougul emperor who started gardening in India and established Aram Bagh at Agra
- Akbar: Garden in Fatehpur Sikri (Agra), Tomb Garden is Sikandara (Agra)
- Jhangir – Shalimar Garden (Kashmir), Dilkhush Garden (Lahore)
- Shah-Jhan: Chasma-a-shahi (Sri Nagar) Shalimar Garden (Lahore)
- Taj Mahal Garden (Agra): Redfort (Agra & Delhi)
- Fadai Khan: Pinjore Garden
- King Hyder Ali: Lalbagh Garden (Bangalore)
- Maharaja Ranjit Singh: Garden at Amritsar
- King Bhupinder Singh: Baradari Garden at Patiala
- Peet Kalidas mentioned plant in the play Shkuntla: Madhvi
- Noorjahan discovered otto of rose while taking bath
- Garden which is considered as genesis of gardening: Garden of Eden (UD)
- Moorish Garden were developed in Spain
- Famous French garden designer: Le Notre
- Bulgeria is largest producer of rose perfume
- Egypt is largest producer of Jasmine perfume
- France is largest produce of tuberose perfume
- France is largest producer of carnatioin perfume
- Non purified form of essential oil obtained by solvent extraction method is known Concrete that contains 45-55% absolute.
- Total duration from the harvest to wilting of cut flowers is called. **Longevity.**
- Gladiolus spikes should be held in **Vertical** position during transportation
- Pre-cooling is done to **Remove field heat**
- Most effective way to remove field heat from the flowers is **Forced air cooling**
- Tropical orchids and anthurium should be stored at **10-13** °C

- Geotropism is common in Gladiolus, Freesia and Snapdragon
- Time of harvest, Method of harvest and Stage of harvest are the factors that determine the potential longevity of cut flowers
- A holding solution having **3-4.5** pH is most beneficial
- **Anthurium** flower is highly sensitive to chilling injury
- **Sucrose** is used to increase vase life of cut flower
- STS, 1-MCP and 8-HQC are used as preservatives in enhancing shelf life of flowers
- Stem break is a major problem of **Gerbera**
- Sleepiness is a disorder associated with. **Carnation**
- Flower senescence is often associated with increased **Ethylene**
- Generally loose flowers are packed in Gunny bags, Bamboo baskets and Corrugated card board boxes
- In normal air 3-**5 ppb** ethylene is present
- Bent neck is a physiological disorder of **Rose** and it occurs at **low** light intensity.
- **BA** is used to improve the shelf life of loose flowers
- Luitein is commercially extracted from **Marigold** Flower
- Pulsing is related to **Cut flowers**
- In pre-cooling heat is mainly removed by **Conduction**
- Paint brush stage of flower harvesting is related to **Carnation**
- Treating of flowers with high concentration of $CoCl_2$, $AgNO_3$ and $NiCl_2$ is Impregnation
- Hypobaric storage is also called as **Low pressure storage**
- Gladiolus spikes are harvested for long distance when **Basal florets show colour**
- Cut flowers are generally harvested during Early **morning**
- Leaf scorching and bud blast are disorders of **Lilium**
- Calyx splitting is major problem in **Carnation**
- Leaf scorching in lily is due to excess of **Fluorine**

- Gladiolus is highly sensitive to **Fluorine**
- Bacteria, Yeast and Moulds are responsible for blockage of xylem in cut flowers
- Quilling of florets is common disorder of **Chrysanthemum**
- **Carnation** is most sensitive to Ethylene
- **8-HQC** is used as germicide
- Pre-cooling temperature of gladiolus and alstromeria is **4** ^{0}C
- Pre-cooling should be done **Immediately after harvest**
- Pre-cooling temperature of anthurium **13** 0C
- The purpose of conditioning is **to restore turgidity**
- Sorting of flowers can be done according to Cultivar, Stage of maturity and Extent of damage
- Market distance, Cultivar and Purpose determine the correct harvest stage of cut flowers
- Shattering of florets of snapdragon is due to **Ethylene**
- Bluing of rose petals is due to **Accumulation of ammonia**
- **Gerbera** is less sensitive to ethylene
- **STS** is the most important ethylene inhibitor
- **Chlorhexidine** is not a germicide
- Purpose of preservatives is Keep water acidic, Counter act ethylene affect and Provide sugars
- Hard wood stems of rose should always be given **Slanting cut**
- Ethylene is commonly known as **Ripening** hormone
- A short term treatment given to the cut flower before packing is known as **Pulsing**
- Storage in gas tight chambers under decreased O_2 and increased CO_2 levels is called **Modified atmospheric** storage
- Bull head physiological disorder of rose is due to **Low carbohydrate level**
- Orchids and Anthurium are suitable for wet packing

- **Tinting** is not associated with improving vase life of cut flower
- Cut flowers should be kept at **90-95** % RH to maintain turbidity
- The term pulsing is related to **Cut flower**
- **Sucrose** is used enhance the shelf life of cut flow
- Red colour of rose is due to **Anthocyanin**
- Blue colour of larkspur is due to **Delphidin**
- **KNO_3** is not a flower preservative
- Loose flower of rose should be harvested at Fully **opened stage**
- Harvesting of rose for cut flower purposeshould be at **Tight bud stage**
- Controlled atmosphere storage is invented by **Kidd and West**
- Queen Elizabeth and Banjaran are popular varieties belongs to **Floribunda** rose group
- Pseudo- bulb is commercial propagation method for **Orchids**
- Minimum number of florets in fancy grade gladiolus spike is **16**
- Insufficient hardening commonly results **Bent neck** in roses
- The vase life of roses is best when the plants are cultivated at **20-21** ^{0}C
- Excessive **Nitrogen** fertilization decreases the vase life of cut flowers and increases the susceptibility to pests and diseases
- Harvesting of flowers at **Morning** is recommended which loose water quickly after harvesting
- Flowers originating in tropical conditions can be stored at **8-15** ^{0}C
- In a normal, non contaminated atmosphere, ethylene content fluctuates between **3-5** ppb changing with the season
- The precursor of ethylene is **Metionine**
- **Cytokinin** growth regulator is antagonistic to ethylene
- AVG , MVG and AOA are the ethylene inhibitors
- Freesia, Gladiolus and Gerber are highly susceptible to fluoride ions
- Lilacs, Cymbidiums and Daffodils are resistant to fluoride ions
- Ethylene can be removed from the cold storage room by $Co_{2,}$ UV rays and $KMnO_4$

- Low pressure storage principle was developed by **S.P Burg**
- Most widely used fumigant in fumigation of cut flowers is **Methylbromide**
- Carnation, Gerbera and Lily flowers are suited for dry storage and transportation
- Freesia Iris and Narcissus flowers are suited for wet storage and transportation
- **Ctokinins** growth regulator is used to protect leaves from yellowing and to protect against chilling injury in *Anthurium andreanum*
- **Packing** Should protect flowers against physical damage, water loss and external conditions detrimental to the transported flowers.
- Total vent size for a packing box should equal to**4-5%** of the area of the end wall of the box.
- **Goose neck** is harvesting stage of daffodil
- **Bio fertilizers:** certain strains of micorganisms that enhance the productivity of the soil, whether by fixing atmospheric nitrogen or by dissolving soil phosphorus, or by stimulating plant growth through the synthesis of growth promoting substances.
- **Bonsai:** Literally meaning ‘ a plant in a tray’, . refers to a tree or a plant whose typical growth in nature has been copied exactly in a miniature style within the confines of a container.
- **Compost:** Manure formed by the decomposition of organic matter by a mixed population of microorganisms in a warm, moist, and aerobic environment over a period of time.
- **Deciduous:** Trees and shrubs that shed their leaves periodically.
- **Deck:** An exterior platform of wooden planks or wood covered iron frames adjoining an interior living area. It may be used as a sit-out or a space for sunbathing. The term is also used interchangeably with ‘patio’.
- **Evergreens:** Trees and shrubs that keep their leaves all the year round.
- **Groundcover:** Grass or low-growing plants spread over a large area to ‘carpet’ the ground.
- **Hardscape:** The non-living structures and materials incorporated in a planned landscape.

- **Horticulture** : The science of growing plants or of gardening.
- **Landscaped area** : An area where trees, plants, turf, decks, walks, ponds, and so on have been used to create a natural looking outdoor space that is functional and visually appealing.
- **Manure** : Any substance, natural or artificial, to be spread over or mixed with soil to fertilize it.
- **Patio** : An exterior, paved, usually roofless area adjoining interior living areas. The term is also used interchangeably with 'deck'.
- **Perennials** : Plants that flower throuhout the year.
- **Succulents** : Plants that have thick, fleshy stems and leaves due to their high water content.
- **Trellis** : Metal grilles or cane or bamboo frameworks used in the garden to train climbers or to hang ots from.
- **Turf** : Grass together with the surface layer of soil held together by their roots.
- **Vermicompost / Vermicasts** : A natural organic manure consisting of the excreta of earthworms fed on decomposed organic wastes such as the dung of cattle and other animals, coir pith, farm wastes, urban garbage such as paper and rags, and various agro-industrial wastes.

7

Descriptive Notes

7.1 Annuals and their management

Annuals arc thc group of plants that complete their life cycle in one season or in one year during which they grow, flower and produce seed; and after this they wither out. A true annual (like zinnia) is a plant that will grow from seeds, flower, produce seeds and die in one season. Zinnias provide a succession of flowers for summer colour in any sunny location with good soil drainage

The term annual when applied to herbaceous ornamentals refers to plants that are grown for only one season. A true annual completes its life cycle (bears seed) in one season and has an extended bloom span lasting (in most cases) throughout the summer. Some plants that we use like annuals in the garden actually are herbaceous perennial plants that bloom the first season but are unable to survive the winter climate.

Some varieties will self-sow or naturally reseed themselves. This may be undesirable in many flowers because the parents of this seed are unknown and hybrid characteristics get lost. Plants will scatter everywhere instead of growing in their designated spot. Examples are Alyssum, Petunias, and Impatiens. Impatiens flowers are currently the most popular annuals and are unsurpassed for abundant flowers in a shady garden. Some perennials, which are plants that live from year to year are classed with annuals because they are not winter-hardy and must be set out every year. Examples are begonias and snapdragons.

Typically, the annuals are known as loving the heat of summer, but there are some popular annual plants that prefer the cool of spring and fall. Examples are pansies, snapdragons, ornamental cabbage and kale. These plants actually grow more lush and vigorous when the weather is cool not hot and dry; therefore, they are often offered for sale in early spring.

Classification of annuals according to hardiness

Hardy	Plants that tolerate cool temperatures and freezing conditions are termed hardy annuals. Examples are Pansy and Snapdragon. Such annuals may be planted for early spring colour well before the frost-free date, or planted late in the summer for fall colour.
Semi-hardy	This group of annuals (petunia and calendula) can tolerate cool temperatures and a moderate frost (28°F). These annuals may be planted slightly before the frost and will give extended colour into the cooler days.
Tender	Plants in this group do not tolerate cool weather and should not be planted until the danger of frost has past and the soil has warmed in spring. Examples are vinca, marigold and zinnia

Classification of annuals according to growing season

Summer	Grow luxuriantly and produce flower under high temperature. Sowing of seeds during end of February or beginning of March and seedlings are transplanted in end of march-april. Examples are zinnia, kochia, portulaca, gaillardia, petunia, venidium, celosia/cocks comb.
Rainy season	Withstand heavy rains and high humidity in air as compared to other annuals. Seeds are sown in June and transplanted in july. Examples are amaranthus (princess feather), balsam, gomphrena, marigold, sunflower, cleome (spider plant).
Winter	Tolerate comparatively low temperature and bloom best during this season, sown in september and transplanted in October in plains and in hills planted in February-March and july-August. Examples are ageratum, sweet alyssum, hollyhock, forget me not, antirrhinum, African daisy, Adonis agrostema, bartonia (golden star), begonia, daisy, English daisy, China aster, pot marigold, calceolaria (pouch flower), wall flower, clianthus, chrysanthemum, cigar plant, clarkia, cosmos, coreopsis, campanula, corn flower, sweet sultan, Chinese forget me not, Sweet William, Indian pink, larkspur, California poopy, blanket flower. Gazania (treasure flower), gerbera, ,gypsophylla, acroclinium, candytuft, sweat pea, linaria, lupin, linum, statice, stock, marigold, monkey flower, nigella, nemasia, ornamental tobaco, evening primrose, poppy, ladys lace, phlox, salvia, nasturtium, lace flower, ursinia, verbena, pansy etc

Classification of annuals according to their use

Selection of annual flower can be made according to their use/purpose:

Bedding purpose	Dahlia, Marigold, Phlox, Verbena, Pansy, Carnation, Sweet William, sweet Sultan, Petunia, Ice Plant, Candytuft, Zinnia, Balsam, Portulaca, Gompherina, Gaillardia
For fragrant flowers	Carnation, Sweet Pea, Sweet Sultan, Sweet Alyssum, Stock
For cut flowers	Carnation, Sweet pea, Sweet William, Aster, Larkspur, Lupin, Helichrysum, Sweet sultan, Corn flower, Stock, Sweet pea
For loose flowers	Marigold, Annual chrysanthem, Aster, Zinnia, Gaillardia
For hanging basket	Daisy, Verbena, Nasturtium, Phlox, Sweet alyssum, Portulaca, Petunia
For shady location	Salvia, cineraria
For foliage	Amaranthus, Caladium, Canna, Coleus, Dusty miller
For rock garden	Ice plant, Nasturtium, Gamolepis, Phlox
For peculiar purposes	Clianthus
For pots	Carnation, Aster, Petunia, Antirrhinum
For dry flowers	Statice, Helichrysum, Acroclinum, Lady's lace
Drought tolerant	Amaranthus, Gaillardia, Gazania, Melampodium, Mexican heather, Plume celosia,, Rose moss, and Zinnia
Shade tolerant	Begonia, Browalia, Caladium, Coleus, Fuchsia, Impatiens
Heat tolerant	Canna, Hibiscus, Lantana, Mandevilla, Marigold, Melampodium, Plume, celosia, Rose moss, Salvia, Sunflower, Zinnia

Advantages of annuals

1. Annuals are easily grown plants.
2. They vary widely in form, habit of growth, flower colour and flower size.
3. Versatile, sturdy and relatively cheap.
4. Plant breeders have produced many new and improved varieties.
5. They bloom for most of the growing season.
6. Able to thrive without the need of grooming due to their "self-cleaning" ability.

Disadvantages of annuals

1. They need to be planted from seed every year, which involves some effort and expense.
2. For some annuals, removal of bloomed flower heads, on a weekly basis is necessary to "clean" the plant and promote continuous bloom.

3. If they are not removed, the plants will produce seed, complete their life cycle, and die.
4. Some annuals, such as petunias and snapdragons, begin to look disreputable by late summer and need to be cut back for re-growth or replaced

Germinating capacity of annuals	
1 Year	Larkspur, Candytufft
2 year	Aster, Straw flower, Cupressus
3 year	Centuria, Candiduca, Verbena, Phlox
4 year	Icebern, Antirrhinum
5 year	Hollyhock, Alysum, African daisy, Calendula, Caleopsis, cosmos, California poppy, Sweet pea, Nigella, Petunia, Nastursiun, Pansy, Marigold

Location and Establishment of Annual Flowers Beds

Site Selection: Major aspects like light, soil characteristics and topography should be taken into consideration during site selection. The slope of the site will affect temperature and drainage. Soil texture, drainage, fertility, and pH also influence plant performance. There is no "stressless" environment and no totally stress-resistant annuals are available. However, to reduce or avoid stress in the landscape before selecting plants to use, temperature averages for the flowering season, amount of sunlight received daily, rainfall averages and average intervals between rains and soil characteristics (drainage and moisture retention) are to be accurately analyzed.

Temperature: The temperature is the most important factor for flowers cultivation and the flowers can be classified according to season. Management of temperature is an important factor during cultivation of annual flowers. *Cool-season flowers* such as dianthus, snapdragons, and pansies can be used early in the season. It is possible to extend the flowering season of cool-season annuals by placing them in a protected location, shaded from direct sunlight from about 12:00 noon to 4:00 pm. *Heat-loving flowers* like gaillardia, portulaca and garden verbena do not begin to flower until early summer and are used for summer colour and high temperature situations. *Frost tolerance*-avoids early planting of tender plants to prevent frost damage. Tender species also will be the first to be killed from frost in the fall.

Light: Light and temperature are closely related and plants preferring lower light may tolerate more sun if temperatures are moderate. When evaluating light exposure, the duration and intensity of light, the site receivers are to be recorded. Four hours of full sun during the morning is much different than four hours of afternoon sun. In general, if the site receives more than 3 hours of unfiltered mid-day sun, it should be treated as a "full sun" site, with respect to plant selection. "Partial shade" can be defined as receiving unfiltered morning sun with either shade during the afternoon hours or moderate shading throughout the entire day. A ''heavily shaded" site would receive very little direct mid-day light and less than 60% of the sun's intensity during the remainder of the day. A mismatch of plant and light can lead to reduced flowering, leggy growth habit, burning of plants, or stunting of growth.

Water: Water stress covers both extremities of the spectrum, even for the same landscape site. Bed preparation is essential for avoiding both moisture excess and drought conditions. For most situations, supplemental irrigation will be required at some point during the growing season. For minimal irrigation sites, select species that are drought tolerant. The best protection against excessive moisture is proper bed preparation and sufficient drainage. Keep in mind that the majority of watering problems, assuming a well-prepared site, occur from too frequent irrigations rather than too much water applied at anyone time. Annuals require about 1-12 inches of water per week during the height of the growing season. Infrequent but thorough watering is much preferred over light yet frequent watering. If overhead irrigation is practiced, water as early in the morning as possible to all foliage to dry quickly. Wet foliage promotes disease infestation.

Soil characteristics: Plants depend on the soil for water, anchorage and nutrients. Frequent heavy rains in combination with poorly drained beds will reduce plant performance and increase the chances of root rot problems. On the other hand, beds with excellent drainage combined with little water holding capacity could require irrigation as frequently as every other day. Nutrient efficiencies and toxicities are common in the landscape, although they are easily avoided if roper steps are taken. Stress prevention and avoidance is much easier than relying on stress tolerance. An important issue concerning irrigation is how long it takes for the water to drain from the soil, allowing oxygen to return. Without adequate drainage between irrigations, there will be little oxygen in the soil. A clay soil will take longer to drain and re-aerate than a sandy soil. Bedding plants grown in a clay soil that has been properly watered may not have to be watered more than once a week. This will vary with time of year, amount of sun or shade, plant growth, and other environmental factors. However, bedding plants grown in a sandy soil may have to be watered 2 to 3 times a week. Subsoil compaction or the presence of a hard pan beneath the bed can also affect water drainage and soil aeration. It may be necessary to deep till beds to break up the subsoil and increase drainage rate.

Air Pollutant: Landscape sites, especially those in highly urbanized areas, are subjected to significant levels of air pollution. The most damaging pollutants are sulfur dioxide (SO_2), ozone (O_3), and peroxy acetyl nitrate. Symptoms of SO_2 injury include necrotic (dead) spots between the major veins, where the tissue turns light tan and papery in texture. The most common symptom of exposure to ozone is the formation of tiny, light-coloured flecks or spots on the upper surfaces of affected leaves, similar to spider mite damage peroxy acetyl nitrate injury is expressed as silvering, glazing, bronzing and sometimes death of the lower leaf surfaces. **Remedy**: Bedding plants do exhibit relative sensitivity and tolerance to these materials and if pollutants are a problem, plants should be selected accordingly.

Soil Preparation: Proper preparation of soil will enhance success in growing annuals. The soil testing is the first and most important step. Soil testing will indicate how much lime or acidifier needs to be added during preparation, how much fertilizer needs to be added in the spring and the pH level should be adjusted; if needed. Check and adjust drainage by digging a hole about 10 inches deep and fill with water. The next day, fill with water again and see how long it remains (should not exceed 8 hours). If drainage is poor, plan to plant in raised beds. The next step is to dig the bed. Add 4 to 6 inches organic matter (OM) to heavy clay to improve soil texture. Dig to a depth of 12 or 18 inches and leave "rough" in fall or early spring. (2 to 3" of OM should be applied if bed can only be turned 6 to 8" deep.) Finally, in spring, add fertilizer, spade again, and rake the surface smooth.

Seed Selection: To get a good start toward raising vigorous plants, buy good seed packaged for the current year. Seed of previous years usually loses its vigour and tends to germinate slowly and erratically and produce poor seedlings. Keep seed dry and cool until planted. If seed must be stored, place in an air-tight container with something absorbent to absorb excess moisture and refrigerate. When buying seed, look for new varieties listed as hybrids. Plants from hybrid seed are more uniform in size and more vigorous than plants of open-pollinated varieties. They are usually more vigorous and produce more flowers.

Seed Sowing: The best media for starting seeds is loose, well-drained, fine-textured, low in nutrients and free of disease causing fungi, bacteria, and unwanted seeds. Many commercial products meet these requirements. Fill clean containers about 2/3 full with potting medium. Level the medium and moisten it evenly throughout. It should be damp but not soggy. Make a furrow 1/4 inch deep. Sow large seed directly in the bottom of the furrow. Before sowing small seed, fill the furrow with vermiculite and sow small seed on the surface of the vermiculite. Seed may be sown in flats following seed package directions or directly in individual peat pots or pellets, two seeds to the pot. After seed is sown, cover all furrows with a thin layer of vermiculite, then water with a fine mist. Place a sheet of plastic over seeded containers and set them in an area away from sunlight where the temperature is between 60° and 75°F. Bottom heat is helpful for germination. As soon as seeds have germinated, remove plastic sheeting and place seedlings in the light. If natural light is poor, fluorescent tubes can be used. Place seedlings close to the tubes. After the plastic is removed from the container, the new plants need watering and fertilizing, since most planting material contains little or no plant food. Use a mild fertilizer solution after plants have been watered. When seedlings develop to two true leaves, thin plants in individual pots to one seedling per pot. Transplant those in flats to other flats, spacing 11 inches apart, or to individual pots.

Sowing Seed Outdoors: Annuals seeded in the garden frequently fail to germinate properly because the surface of the soil cakes and prevents entry of water. To avoid this, sow seed in vermiculite-filled furrows. Make furrows in soil about 112 inch deep. If soil is dry, water the furrow, then fill it with fine vermiculite and sprinkle with water. Then make another shallow furrow in the vermiculite and sow the seed in this furrow. Cover the seed with a layer of vermiculite, and using a nozzle adjusted for a fine mist, water the seeded area thoroughly. Keep the seed bed well-watered or cover with mulch, such as newspaper, to prevent excess evaporation of water. Remove mulch promptly after germination starts, so that young seedlings will receive adequate sunlight.

Planting Time: Do not be in a rush to start seeds outdoors or to set out started plants. As a general rule, delay sowing seed of warm-weather annuals outdoors or setting out started plants until after the last frost date. Most such seeds will not germinate well in soils below 60°F. If the soil is too cold when seed is sown, seeds will remain dormant until the soil warms, and may rot instead of germinating. Some cold-loving annuals, like larkspur or Shirley poppies, should be sown in late fall or very early spring.

Setting out Transplants: By setting started plants in the garden you can have a display of flowers several weeks earlier than if you sow seeds of the plants. This is especially useful for annuals (Verbena and Scarlet Sage) which germinate slowly or need several months to bloom. Before setting out transplants, harden them off by exposing them to outside conditions during the day which will provide more light and cooler temperatures than they received inside. After the last frost date, annual plants may be set out. Dig a hole for each plant large enough to accept its root system comfortably. Lift out each plant from its flat with a block of soil surrounding its roots. Set the soil block in a planting hole and backfill it so the plant sits at the same level. Irrigate each hole with a starter solution of high phosphate fertilizer which is water-soluble. Follow package directions.

If plants are in fiber pots, remove the paper from the out-side of the root mass and set the plant in a prepared planting hole. When setting out plants in peat pots, set the entire pot in the planting hole, but remove the upper edges of the pot so that all of the peat pot is covered when soil is firmed around the transplant. If a lip of the peat pot is exposed above the soil level, it may produce a wick effect, pulling water away from the plant and into the air. After setting the plants, water them with a starter solution as described above. Provide protection against excessive sun, wind, or cold while the plants are getting settled in their new locations. Inverted pots, newspaper, tunnels, or cloches can be used.

Thinning: Outdoor-grown annuals start developing the first pair of true leaves; they should be thinned to the recommended spacing. This spacing allows plants enough light, water, nutrients, and space for them to develop fully above and below the ground. If they have been seeded in vermiculite-filled furrows, excess seedlings can be transplanted to another spot without injury.

Maintenance of Flower Beds

Watering: Do not rely on summer rainfall to keep flower beds watered. Plan to irrigate them from the beginning. Moisten the entire bed thoroughly during watering but do not water so heavily that the soil becomes soggy. After watering, allow the soil to dry moderately before watering again. A canvas soaker hose is excellent for watering beds. Water from the soaker hose seeps directly into the soil without waste and without splashing leaves and flowers. The slow-moving water does not disturb the soil or reduce its capacity to absorb water. Sprinklers are not as effective as soaker hoses. Water from sprinklers wets the flowers and foliage, making them susceptible to diseases. Soil structure may be destroyed by the impact of water drops falling on its surface; the soil may puddle or crust, preventing free entry of water and air. The least effective method for watering is with a hand-held nozzle. Watering with a nozzle has all the objections of watering with a sprinkler.

Mulching: Mulching helps to keep the soil surface moist and aid in preventing growth of weeds. Organic mulches can also add humus to the soil. More common mulches are Pine needles, bark- readily available in bags or bulk, pine, cypress or hardwood trees. It is resistant to decomposition. Wind blown seeds often germinate in bark mulches and necessitate cultivation or herbicide application. The use of mulch or hand-cultivation can be effective in controlling weed populations and is the first line of defense against this problem. Organic mulches are especially beneficial in that they tend to enrich the soil as they break down over the summer. Mulches also help to curb water loss through evaporation from exposed soil.

Weeding: Cultivate only to break crusts on the surface of the soil. When the plants begin to grow, stop cultivating and pull weeds by hand. As annual plants grow, feeder roots spread between the plants; cultivation is likely to injure these roots. In addition, cultivation stirs the soil and uncovers weed seeds that then germinate. Mulching is preferred for weed control, since it makes conditions unfavorable for germination of weed seeds and provides a physical barrier for emerging weeds. A good mulch layer can save many hours of laborious weeding. Weed control is essential for attractive displays of annual flowering plants. Most herbicides labeled for use in annuals are pre-emergence in action. They should be applied after the annuals have been set but before any weed.

De-dheading (removing old flowers): To maintain vigorous growth of plants and assure neatness, remove spent flowers and seed pods. This step is particularly desirable for growing ageratum, calendula, cosmos, marigold, pansy, or zinnia.

Staking: Tall-growing annuals, like larkspur or tall varieties of marigold or cosmos, need support to protect them from strong winds and rain. Tall plants are supported by stakes of wood, bamboo, or reed large enough to hold the plants upright but not large enough to be conspicuous. Stakes should be about 6 inches shorter than the mature plant so their presence will not interfere with the beauty of the bloom. Begin staking when plants are about 1/3 their mature size. Place stakes close to the plant, but take care not to damage the root system. Plants with delicate sterns (like cosmos) can be supported by a framework of stakes and strings in criss-cross patterns.

Fertilizing: Fertilizers are added according to recommendations given by soil sample analysis, or derived from observation of plants that have grown on the site. Lime may also be needed if the soil test results indicate the requirement. Use dolomitic limestone rather than hydrated lime. Ideally, lime should be added in the fall so it will have time to change the pH. Fertilizer should be added in the spring so it will not leach out before plants can benefit from it.

Once annuals have germinated and begin to grow, additional fertilizers may be needed. This is especially true if organic mulches are added because micro-organisms decomposing the mulch take up available nitrogen. Thus a fertilizer high in nitrogen should be used in these situations. Be sure to apply the fertilizer around the plants in such a way as to avoid direct contact between the stems and the fertilizer. Apply fertilizers to damp soil. In mid summer, when plants are flowering well, many annual species (e.g., petunia) benefit from a side-dressing of a fertilizer high in nitrogen. Sprinkle the fertilizer lightly along the row, and water or gently incorporate it into the soil. If mulch is used, scatter the nitrogen fertilizer on the mulch and water it. Avoid applying excess nitrogen to annuals, especially those that are not flowering. The result is likely to be lush vegetative growth and poor, delayed flowering.

Pests and disease management: Do not apply an insecticide unless it is necessary to pre vent damage to flowers or shrubs. Most insect pests in the garden will not cause appreciable damage if their predators and parasites are protected by avoiding unnecessary applications of insecticides. However, if there is a pest that usually causes serious damage unless an insecticide is used, apply the insecticide as soon as the infestation appears and begins to increase. Spider mites, aphids, Japanese beetles and other beetles, lacebugs, and thrips; are some of the pests most likely to need prompt treatment with insecticides (or miticide for spider mites). Do not treat the soil for insects unless you find large numbers of cutworms, white grubs or wireworms when preparing the soil for planting. Aphid, spider mite and insects with chewing mouthparts for e.g; grass hoppers, are the most problematic. Prompt action with a good general purpose insecticide or fungicide should remedy the condition.

Since annuals only grow only for one season, diseases are not as serious as they are in case of perennials. Select varieties of plants that are resistant to disease, follow recommended practices for planting and maintaining annuals will avoid most disease problems. The incidence of diseases also depends on weather conditions which are highly favorable for diseases. Read and follow all directions given for use of insecticides as well as pesticides/chemicals on the label, including all precautions. If pesticides are handled, applied or disposed off improperly, they may be injurious to human beings, animals and as well as for plants and beneficial insects. Vigorous plants, well spaced for good air circulation, with good drainage and minimum shade usually have fewer disease problem.

Important tips for maintaining annuals

1. Seedlings indoors require good light, proper temperature, disease-free growing medium and adequate care. The gardeners who does not have these conditions or who has limited time are advised to purchase started plants from the local nursery/garden centre.

2. Healthy young plants grown in greenhouse provide a quick display of colour. Cultivar selection usually is quite good at most progressive nurseries.
3. Look for plants that do not appear overly mature and pot-bound. The latter condition can delay new transplants from becoming established rapidly and lead to disappointing results.
4. Soil destined for growing annuals should be dug or tilled deeply. Liberal amounts (up to 4 inches) of manure, compost or other organic matter should be added into the soil at the time of tillage. A complete fertilizer may be scattered over the surface at a maintenance rate of about 1 to 2 pounds per 100 square feet before preparation.
5. When soil fertility and acidity is unknown, a soil test is made to determine need for lime and fertilizer.
6. If seeds are to be planted in the bed, the surface should be raked until lumps are broken up and a fine level seedbed is developed.
7. If started plants are to be placed directly into the soil, small lumps may be allowed to remain. Always make sure that the surface is level, or slightly sloped toward the sides.
8. Low spots permit the development of disease because they remain too wet. If drainage is generally poor, the bed should be raised.
9. After the seedbed has been prepared, make a shallow trench, scatter seeds thinly into it and cover very lightly. In heavy soils, cover small seeds with vermiculite or some other light material to prevent crusting.
10. After planting, water the bed with a fine spray to avoid washing. The surface of the seedbed should be kept moist with light watering daily until germination is complete. Cover the rows with a thin layer of mulch or floating row cover. These covers must be removed promptly when germination begins. Seedlings should be thinned before they become crowded; the final plant density varies according to species.
11. Annual plants that have been purchased or started indoors may be planted outdoors when the season has reached the temperature preference for the species in question. Most avid gardeners are eager to start planting as early in the season as possible. While this is fine for some species of annuals that can tolerate cool temperatures, it is not suitable for others.
12. Never try to "rush the season" by planting species before their desired date. Plants should be well watered at the time of planting and set at the

same level that they were growing in the pots. A cloudy day is best for transplanting.

13. Tall, spindly plants are pruned back to about one-half their original height before transplanting.

14. Spacing of flowering annuals in the bed or border is based upon the mature size of the species

Description of Annuals: Summer and Rainy Season

Annual	Description
Amaranthus	The scientific name of Amaranthus is *Amaranthus sp.* and it belongs to the Amranthaceae family. The generic name consists of two greek words, A meaning not and maraino meaning fading. Amaranthus is considered to be a native of tropical asia and tropical America.
	The plant attains a height of about 90-120 cm and starts flowering in 40-60 days. Amaranthus is also known by names like princess feather, love lies bleeding.
	Plants are very ornamental due to colourful foliage. Therefore, it is grown in groups or in rows, but it is not mixed with other annuals.The flower has many species grown in gardens as rainy season viz; *A. caudatus*, *A. hybridus*, *A.tricolour*, *A.salicifolius*.
	A. caudatus : commonly called Love-lies bleeding, produces graceful long drooping catkins having purple, crimson, pale green or white flowers.
	A. tricolour ruber: produces rich scarlet foliage.
	A. salicifolius: popular in garden due to its undulating and drooping foliage of bright orange colour
	A. bicolour: It is commonly called as Molten Fire, produces deep foliage and crimson top.
	Amranthus requires full sun,frost free annual,available in coloured foliage, Suitable for poor soils,Heat and drought tolerant., Also grown in pots for indoor decoration
	Plant to plant distances :20-30 cm and row to row 45cm
	Planting is done in sunny situation where foliage develops rich colour.
	Propagated by seeds
Balsam	The scientific name of Balsam is *Impatiens balsamina* and it belongs to the Balsaminaceae family. Balsam, a very showy annual attains a height of nearly 25-75 cm and starts flowering after 60-70 days of planting . It is considered to be a native of India. Balsam is commonly known as Touch-me- not.
	Balsam produces many branches along with the main stem.Leaves are simple, having slightly serrated margin. Flowering continue upto 20-30 days.

	The flowers of Balsam are spurred, nearly 5-6 cm across and borne in leaf axils like camellia. The flowers are single or double in pure or variegated colours. red, pink, blue, lavender, violet, rose and purple white are dominating colours.
	I. holstii and *I. sultanii* are two perennial species which have been used to evolve evolve new types. Double camellia flowered mixed, rose flowered royal Balsam mixed, tall double mixed are important varieties grown in the garden. Tom thumb is dwarf variety that is uniform, bushy and compact.
	• Balsam plant being delicate requires much care • Proper training of plant by removing side shoots and only main shoot be kept for display • Early flowering and short duration • Pods should be harvested before scattering • Plant requires full sun, frost free, like abundant moisture and rich soil. • Tends to reseed itself each year • Pink baby, blaze scarlet, Bright rose, Holstic hybrid are examples of new types of important varieties. • Plants are grown at a spacing of 30-45 cm.
Cock's Comb	The scientific name of cock's Comb is *Celosia sp.* and it belongs to the family Amrantaceae. The generic name derived from Greek word kelos meaning burnt.
	Cock' Comb is considered to be a native of Tropical Asia, Africa and America.
	Thc plant attains a height of nearly 30-45 cm and starts flowering after 80-120 days of planting.
	Leaves are simple, having variation in light red or crimson colour. Celosia is popular in garden for their flower.
	Flowers are available in deep crimson, deep pink cardinal red to deep orange, colours.
	C. argentea var cristata, C. *plumosa* and *C. childsii* are species that are dominating in the garden. *C. argentea* variety cristata is commonly known as Cock's comb. It produces large compact head of dia. about 25 or 30 cm.
	C. childsi called Chinese woo-flower, produces wooly globular flowers which are 7-10 cm.across
	C. plumose (plume celosia): produces flowers like plumes resembling ostrich plume,
	• Plants are tall and dwarf and are also suitable for pot culture. And beds
	• Spacing of plants 15 cm (plant to plant)and30cm row to row
	• Tall varieties:– Gilbert celosia, toreador Royal velvet.
	• Dwarf varieties – Golden king, Lilliput, jewel box, Aurea, Flame of fire, Thompson magnific
	• Flower in clusters and appears on top
	• Plant requires fullsun ,frost free,easily grown,tolerantof heat and poor soils.

Gaillardia	The scientific name of gaillardia is *Gaillardia pulchella* and it belongs to the Asteraceae family. Gaillardia is commonly called as blanket flower and is considered to be a native of North America. The plant attains a height of nearly 30-45 cm and starts flowering after 100-120 days of planting.
	The plants are bushy. Single to double flowers measuring 5-7 cm are present on long thin stems.
	Available in yellow, orange, scarlet, brown coffee colours or in combinations of these.
	Picta (*G. pulchella* var picta) and Lorenziana (*G. pulchella* var. lorenziana) are two common varietiesof gaillardia. The flowers of picta group are large and single whereas flowers of lorenziana are double having quilled petals with split tips.
	G. grandiflora: very popular in garden, produces large flowers of yellow orange and red flowers. It is perennial sp. Important variety in this group is Goblin.
	Plant can resist dry conditions and can be grown as perennial also., Under Indian condition, the plant is grown throughout the year and seeds are sown in all the three sowing times, Spacing of plants 30-40 cm
	Varieties:
	Picta group:Indian chief red and pecta mixed are important varieties of
	Lorenziana group:Sunshine, gaity doubl mixed. Double tetra Fiesta – a tetraploid variety, Suitability: Good cut flower
Gomphrena	The scientific name of Gomphrena is *Gomphrena globosa* and it belongs to the amarantaceae family. Gaillardia is commonly called as globe amaranth and is considered to be a native of North America The plant attains a height of nearly 30-45 cm and starts flowering after 60-80days of planting
	The round flowers , measuring about 2 cm across, are present in white, purple, magenta, pink and rose colour. Profuse flowering can be seen in months of September – October. Common varieties are Alba (White) Rubra (Purple-red), aurea superba (golden yellow) Planting distance:30 cm plant to plant and 45cm row to row
	Important varieties are Lilliput, Buddy, globosa mixed, Cissy etc.
	Remarks: Require full sun, Frost free,Good heat and drought tolerance,Unique clover like flowers dries well,.
	Suitability: lasts for long duration
Kochia	The scientific name of Kochia is *kochia scoparia variety trichophylla* and it belongs to the chenopodiaceae family. The generic name has been given after Prof. W.D.J Koch. The Kochia is commonly called as summer cypress or burning Bush. The plant attains nearly a height of 60-120 cm.
	• Only annual provide bush green foliage during summer
	• Very popular due to its uniform ovoid conical or globular shape that looks naturally trimmed.

	• Mostly grown for foliage beauty
	• Plant is uniform, well shaped and bushy
	• Plant does not produce colourful flowers
	• Sunny situation for healthy growth
	• Plantingdistance: 30cm x45c
Portulaca	The scientific name of portulaca is *Portulaca grandiflora and it belongs to the* Portulaceae family. It is considered is a native of south America and known as sun plant or rose moss The flowers open in morning and close by afternoon. The plant attains a height of nearly 20-30cm and starts flowering after 70-100days of planting
	Plants are dwarf and have trailing growth habit. Branches are round and succulent. Leaves are thick, fleshy, small and pointed. Flowers are about 3 cm across In some varieties, flower petals have stripes of contrasting colours. The perennial form producing bright deep rose coloured single or double flowers is also commonly found growing.
	*portulaca oleracea:*Excellent heat and drought tolerance
	Portulaca grandiflor:Require full sun ,frost free,
	Suitability: It is most ideal for beds, pots and hanging baskets and small boxes
	Remarks:easily propagated by cutting
	Colour range: white, yellow, red, orange, pink, lavender, crimson, purple,
	Important varieties : Grandiflora single mixed, Double mixed and Magic carpet.
Sun Flower	The scientific name of sun flower is *Helianthus annus* and it belongs to the Asteraceae family. It is considered to be a native of of western parts of United States of AmericaThe generic name is composed of two Greek words *i.e. Helios-sun* and *anthos-flower.* The plant attains a height of nearly 75-150 cm and starts flowering after 70-80 days of planting
	In tall varieties flower rotates with the sun movement.
	The tall growing varieties (150-180 cm) are: Tall Single Yellow-huge (20-25 cm) Yellow Single Flowers and Tall Double chrysanthemum-Yellow chrysanthemum like flowers which is dominating now in the gardens. Sun Gold and Yellow Pigmy are double dwarf varieties which produce medium golden orange flowers.
	Now-a-days the hybrids of H.annus and *H. cucumerifolius* which are known as Sultan's autumn Beautyare available. They are well branched with small flowers on long stems of yellow, orange-yellow, chestnut-brown and maroon flowers. The Russian sunflower is a tall (180-240 cm) which produces edible oil and cattle feed.
	• Planting distance:60x90cm
	• propagated by seeds
	• Seed are source of oil
	• The plant is hardy, vigorous and produces magnificent flowers

Tithonia	The scientific name of Tithonia is *Tithonia rotundifolia* syn. is *T. Speciosa* and it belongs to the Asteraceae family. Tithonia is commonly called as Mexican sunflower and is considered to be a native of Mexico.The plant attains a height of nearly 120-140 cm and starts flowering after80-90 days of planting.
	Flowers are large measuring about 5-7 cm.
	Branches are brittle and break very easily
	Colour range: deep orange to scarlet colour with yellow colour
	Plant to plant distance:60-70cm.
	Suitability: Suitable for borders
Zinnia	The scientific name of zinnia is *Zinnia elegans* and it belongs to the Asteraceae family. It is considered to be a native of Mexico and named after johnan Gothifried Zinn-a professor of medicineThe plant attains a height of nearly 25-120 cm and starts flowering after 70-80 days after planting .The plant dominates garden due to wide variation in height
	It has become a very common flower in garden during summer season flowering of which continues upto September – October. Important varities of different groups are:
	Giant Dahlia: Canary Bird (yellow); Dream (Lilac); Meteor (dark red); Oriole (Orange scarlet); Polar Bear (White);
	Giant of California: Brightness (pink), Cherry Queen (rose); Orange Queen (golden orange). Lavender Gem (Lavender), Purity (white).
	Giant cactus: Empress (pink); Red Man (scarlet): Snow Man (white); Sun Gold (light yellow).
	Lilliput or Pompon: Peach Blossom, Rose Gem, Canary yellow, white Gem.
	Cupid: Flowers are like small button. Goblin (burnt orange), Pixie (yellow); Snow Drop (white); Pink Buttons (pink).
	Other groups are Fantasy, Dwarf Giant, Gaillardia flowered, Peppermint stick, Ortho Polka, Tom Thumb and Thumbelina.
	F_1 hybrids are very common and are being marketed. Flowers of big size (12-13cm) are produced on long sturdy flower stalks and are ideal for cut flower. These are available in Dahlia and Cactus group. In Dahlia group important varieties are: Blaze (orange scarlet), Eskimo (creamy white), Riverside Beauty. Latest addition in this is a Peter Pan series which is available in different colours and Fruit Bowl. In cactus group varieties are Bonanza (golden orange), Fire Cracker (red), Princess (Salmon pink), Sunny Boy (deep yellow), Cherry Time (Cherry rose). Tetraploids are also very popular due to free flowering and vigorous growth.
	Z. angustifolia (*Z. haageana* or *Z. mexicana)* is also common and important varieties are old Maxico and Gold. *Z. linearis* is ideally suitable for edging, beds and mass effect. Flowers are small and profusely produced in September-November. Deep yellow, light yellow and white colours are common.

Water Annuals	
Acroclinum	The scientific name of Acroclinum is *Acroclinum roseum* and it belongs to the family Asterace. It is considered to be a native of Australia.The plant attains a height of nearly 60-75 cm and starts flowering after 80-120 days of planting. Popularly known as paper flower and also ever lasting flower on account of its hard and paper like petals.
	Rose coloured flowers are produced profusely. Flowers are single or double and keep their form and colour on drying..
	A. album :bears pretty white coloured flowers.
	A. *grandiflorum* produces very large flowers of pink colour.
	Suitability:suitable for drying
	Remarks:flowers keep their form and colour .even they dry up ;so these can be used for interior decoration colour range: pink and white. important varieties: Double hybrid and Giant Flowered mixture
Ageratum	The scientific name of Ageratum is *Ageratum houstonianum* and it belongs to the family Asteracea. It is considered to be a native of central America.The plant attains a height of nearly 15-60 cm and starts flowering after 55-70 days of planting.It is commonly called as floss flower.
	A tetraploid form having bigger flowers is also grown in the garden.
	Colour range:Flowers are available in blue white or pink colour
	Species: The garden varieties have been evolved from two species *A..conzoides* and *A.houstonianum*
	Suitability: for rock garden.,beds,mixed borders&corners
	Remarks:grown for bedding purposes
	Transplanting:September-october
	Spacing:25x25cm
Anchusa	The scientific name of Anchusa is *A. capensis* and it belongs to the family Boraginaceae.
	It is considered to be a native of South Africa. The plant attains a height of nearly 45 cm and starts flowering after 80-120 days of planting
	It is a perennial but is grown as an annual flower in Indian gardens. The flowers are bright blue and produced in clusters.
	Important varieties :Blue Bird, blue with white centre; Bedding Bright Blue-azure. *A itailice* a perennial species that can be grown as biennial in the hills
	Suitability: highly suitable for pot.
Annual chrysanthemum	The scientific name of Annual chrysanthemum is *chrysanthemum sp* and it belongs to the family Asteracea. It is considered to be a native of mediterranean, North Africa and Europe.The plant attains a height of nearly 50-100cm and starts flowering after 120-150days of planting.
	Common annual species: There are three common annual species which are cultivated in Indian gardens
	1. **C. Coronarium** commonly called as garland chrysanthemum or crown daisy (in Europe)
	Bhambiree or Guldhak (in Punjab)

	Gendi (in UP)
	2. **C. Carinatum (Summer marguerite) varieties** : Court Jester, Polestar, torch
	3. **C. Segetum (Corn marigold) varieties** – Evening star, golden glow, morning star, Eldorado, Evening Star, Golden Glow and Morning Star
	Plant height - 50 – 200 cm
	Flowering -After 120 – 150 days
	Spacing - 50 – 100 cm
	Amongst these species only C. *coronarium* is grown in large areas of western parts of U.P., Delhi and Punjab. In gardens it is ideally suited for shrubberies, beds and as cut flower.
	C. *coronarium nanum compactum* is a dwarf and plant grows upto only 30 cm. Leaves are deeply cut of shining green colour. Numerous single, semidouble and double flowers are produced of large size measuring 5-7.5 cm across weighing about 2.917 kg per plant which are plucked in 9-10 pluckings. The flower colour varies from white, crearnish white, creamish yellow and yellow in C. *coronarium* and deep yellow in C. *segetum.*
	In C. *carinatum* flower colour is white, yellow colour having band of purple or crimson colour and thus flower looks like tricolour and is good for garden display.
	There are several varieties available in all three species.
	Important varieties of C. *carinatun* :Court Jester, Rainbow mixed, Pole Star, Torch, Spectalite and Chelsea.
	important varieties of C. *segetum:morning star,golden glow,evening star,eldorado*
Antirrhinum	The scientific name of Antirrhinum *is**Antirrhinum majus*** and it belongs to the family. Scrophulariaceae .It is considered to be a native of South America.The plant attains a height of nearly 20-80 cm and starts flowering after 65-120 days of planting **.** Due to curious shape of flowers which resemble to dog or rabbit, it is popularly called as snap dragon ,dog flower, or bunny rabbit or bunny mouth.
	Leaves are simple. Magnificent flowers are produced on long spikes of many colours and various shades like white,cream, yellow, rose, salmon, pink, mauve, red, magenta, orange, bronze. Flowers have good keeping quality and remain fresh for 6-7 days.
	There is a wide range of varieties suitable for various purposes. The important varieties of tall Giant or Grandiflora group are Tip Top Canary yellow, Tip Top Apple Blossom, Tip Top White, Tip Top Orange Rose, Triumph, Bright Orange, Triumph Scarlet, Triumph Gold whereas the varieties of intermediate or semi-dwarf are Intermediate Bright Pink, Intermediate Guardsman, Intermediate White, Intermediate Mauve, Bedding Scarlet. Dwarf or Tom Thumb varieties hardly grow about 30 cm and important variety is Orange Scarlet. The crosses between *A. majus* and *A. molle* resulted into a new series which is known as miniature or magic carpet and important varieties are Magic Carpet and Floral Carpel.

	F_1 hybrids are getting very popular and two series are very common *i.e.* Rocket type with prominent varieties like F_1 Golden Rocket, F_1 White Rocket, F_1 Rose Rocket, F_1 Bronze Rocket. Super Giants are another series in which plants grow tall and produce standard blossoms. Different coiours like red, yellow, white, gold, bronze, pink and rose are available. Other important varieties of this series are Candel Light, Sun Set, and Sky Scraper.
	Lollipop Nanum and F_2 hybrid are also popular due to their variable height and mixture flower colour. In double Azalea series of snapdragon, flowers are double like azalea and are bigger. Madame Butterfly is a good variety of double azalea series. Sweet Heart series, a tetraploid, is also gelling popular because plants grow 30 cm tall and are double. The different colours such as bronze, pink, red, white and yellow are available. Super tetraploids are resistant to rust and important varieties are High Moon, Glacier, Crimson Giant and Volcan.
	Recently there are flowers in such varieties which do not snap and are called without snap or pensternon type. The common series is Bright Butterflies in which each floret looks like a colourful butterfly. Plants grow 60-75 cm tall, produce branches freely. Flowers are available in a wide range of colours *i.e.* pink, red, bronze, rose white and yellow. There is another Pixie series available in different colours like Orange Pixie, Pink Pixie, White Pixie, Rose Pixie, Red Pixie, etc.
	There is scented antirrhunum also which have soft clove like fragrance. The scented varieties are Super Jet, Vanguard and Venus.
	Remarks :Require full sun,Prefers cool temperatures
	Suitability: It is most ideally suited for beds, pot, edging, window boxes, herbaceous border and rock garden.
Adonis	The scientific name of Adonis *is Adonis aestivalis* and it belongs to the family Ranunculaceae.
	The plant attains a height of nearly 25-40cm and starts flowering after 100-120days of planting.
	Spacing: 25 – 30 cm
	Remarks-Small flowers, like butter cup, leaves just like fern
	Suitability:rock garden
Arctotis	The scientific name of arctotis is *Arctotis stoechadifolia* and it belongs to the family Asteracea. It is considered to be a native of south africa. The plant attains a height of nearly 35-50 cm. and starts flowering after 85 days of planting .Commonly called as African daisy.
	Plant has deeply cut foliage
	Transplanting time: September-october
	Spacing: 30-45x30-45cm
	Suitability: Suitable for pot,bed, and herbaceous border
	Colour range:white

Aster	The scientific name of Aster is *Callistephus chinensis* and it belongs to the family Asteraceae.
	It is considered to be a native o china and japan and introduced in Europe in 18th century.The plant attains a height of nearly 25-45 cm and starts flowering after 75-125 days of planting.commonlly called as china aster
	Suitablity:Excellent cut flower.
	Transplanting:sep-oct.
	Spacing:20-35-x20-35cm.
	Colour range:white pink and blue
	Remarks:bedding and pot growing
Bells of ireland	The scientific name of Bells of ireland is *Molucella laevis* and it belongs to the family labiatae.
	It is considered to be a native of Mediterranean region.The plant attains a height of nearly 15-25cm and starts flowering after 80-120 days of planting..the molucella flower come out in leaf axils the calyces which appears like bellare big pale, translucent, green and veined
	Bellis perennis:Commonly called as English daisy, white, light pink
Brachycome	The scientific name of brachycome is *Brachycome iberidifolia* and it belongs to the family Asteracea
	It is considered to be a native of Australia. The plant attains a height of nearly 15-25cm and starts flowering after 85days of planting. Popularly known as swan river daisy.In greek language brachycome meaning soft short hair.
	Flowers are small 2.5cm across,producedin abundance.
	Transplanting:sep-oct
	Spacing:20x-20cm
	Suitability:for pot, bedding and rock garden
	Colour range:white, blue, light pink
Calendula	The scientific name of Calendula *is Calendula officinalis* and it belongs to the family asteraceae It is considered to be a native of south Europe. The plant attains a height of nearly 20-50cm and starts flowering after 80-120 days of planting. Also called as pot marigold. Leaves are long, hairy and some what sticky.
California poppy	The scientific name of *California poppy* is *Eschscholtzia californiaand* it belongs to the family papaveraceae
	It is considered to be a native ofcalifornia (U.S.A.).
	The plant attains a height of nearly 30-40 cm and starts flowering after 80-120 days of planting.Leaves are finally cut and smooth.
Candytuft	The scientific name of candytuft is *iberis sp* and it belongs to the family cruciferae
	It is considered to be a native of Europe
	The plant attains a height of nearly 45 cm and starts flowering after 110-150 days of planting

Carnation	The scientific name of carnation is*Dianthus caryophyllus*. and it belongs to the family caryophyllaceae. Itis considered to be a native of Europe. The plant attains a height of nearly 45-75 cm and starts flowering after 80-120 days of planting
Cineraria	The scientific name of cineraria is *Senecio cruentus* and it belongs to the family asteracea It is considered to be a native of canary islands.
	The plant attains a height of nearly 30-60cm and starts flowering after 80-120 days of planting.
	Shade loving plant.
Clarkia	The scientific name of clarkia *is Clarkia elegans*. and it belongs to the family onagraceae. It is considered to be a native of california (U.S.A.) The plant attains a height of nearly 60-90cm and starts flowering after 100-120 days of planting It is generally grown in semi shady situations, plants are stately growing. Leaves are ovol and flowers are produced in axilof leaves.The flowers are single or double.
	Colour range:white, rose pink, salmon, or purple.
	Direct sowing:sep-oct.
Clianthus	The scientific name of Clianthus is *Clianthus dampieri* and it belongs to the family Leguminosae.
	It is considered to be a native of Australia .Due to its peculiar shape of showy flowers resembling to parrots beak. It is also called as Parrot's Bill. Plant grows upto 60-75 cm in height.
	Flowers of dark scarlet colour are produced in clusters of 4-6 blooms. Flowers attract the attention of viewers in exhibition due to unusual shape and its pretty look.
	Suitability: most ideally suited for pot culture.
	Important variety : Dampieri.
Coreopsis	The scientific name of coreopsis is. *Coreopsis tinctoria* and it belongs to the family Cornpositae).
	It is considered to be a native of California (U.S.A.) The plant attains a height of nearly 25-40cm and starts flowering after 110-120days of planting commonly called as Tick Seed on account of seed colour and seed shape. It is a dwarf annual The yellow flower heads with brown spots are produced in abundance. It comes in bloom quite early
	Transplanting - September – October, May
	Spacing - 25 to 45 x 25 to 45 cm
	Suitability: suitable for bedding purpose and along with walks, paths in the garden.
	Important varieties: Golden Crown, Dwarf mixed. Double Sunburst, Mayfield Giant (Deep Golden Yellow), Baby Gold, Sunray, Grandiflora Sun Burst, Gold fink, Grandiflora Mayfield Giant.
Corn flower	The scientific name of Corn flower is Centaurea cyanus and it belongs to the family Astraceae. It is considered to be a native of Europe and britain
	The plant attains a height of nearly 90-120cm and starts flowering after 80-120 days of planting

Cosmea	The scientific name of **cosmea** is cosmos bipinnatus and it belongs to the family Asteraceae. It is considered to be a native of mexico
	The plant attains a height of nearly 30-45 cm and starts flowering after 80-120 days of planting
Dahlia	The scientific name of **dahlia** is *dahlia variabilis.* and it belongs to the family **Compositae**
	Cock' Comb is considered to be a native of Tropical Asia, Africa and America.
	The plant attains a height of nearly 20-150 cm and starts flowering after 80-120 days of planting This is one of the most important garden plants and is useful for cut flower. name to this flower has been given after a French botanish Andres Dahl. There is a wide variation in size of flowers, varying from 5-25 cm across. Plant height also shows great variation which may range from 20- 50 cm. Flower colour range is also very remarkable and almost all possible colours are available. Flowers are of white, cream, yellow, orange, scarlet, pink, mauve, purple, chocolate and deep crimson almost approaching to black and many intermediate shades. According to flower shape, dahlia has several groups. Important groups arc Single, Anemone, Collareue, Paeony, Decorative, Cactus and Pompon. It is highly suitable for bedding, and pot culture. Propagation of dahlia is done by seeds, division of tubers and terminal cuttings. The propagation through seeds is easy and the best way to achieve striking mixtures of colourful flowers which are sown in September-October. The varieties which are being marketed in India are Giant Exhibition mixed, Dwarf Double Red Skin, Coltners hybrids, and Border Jewels, Rigoleuo, and Citation.
	Tubers are stored during summer in cool place or in refrigerator. After careful separation, tubers are planted directly in field in August. The care should be taken while separation that each tuber contains the portion of stem with a vegetative bud. The terminal cuuing should be solid and made in September-October from plants and after treatment with seradix-I are planted in sand. It takes about 2-3 weeks for rooting and after that they are transplanted in pots (25-30 cm) or in beds.
	Dahlia is very rich in its varietal wealth and specific variety can be selected for a particular effect. The important varieties are: Decorative-Large-Amaranth, Amrita Dignity, Masterpiece, Croydon White, Croydon Masterpiece, Nasturtium, Liberator; Medium-House of orange, peace; Small-Edinburg. Mary Richards. Trendy; Miniature-Arabian Night. Doris Duke.
	Cactus Large-Arab Queen. Albert. The colonel. Radio; Medium-Eclipse, Beaudelaire, Polar Beauty, Carnival; Small-Preference, Pinnacle, Grace; Miniature-Lovely Looker. Little mermaid; Pompon-Large-Jean Lister, Ascot, Kinky. Medium-Chamirs, Bonny. Liule David; Small-Glow, Yellow Gem. Doria.
	To get a large size bloom extra care in feeding. watering. staking and disbudding should be taken.
	• Dahlia -30 – 180 cm

	• Planting - September – October, Planting of rhizome and suckers
	• Spacing - 30 to 45 x 30 to 45 cm
	• Start flowering - After 80-110 days
	Staking is required for tall variations
Daisy	The scientific name of **Daisy** is. *Bellis perennis* and it belongs to the family Compositae.
	It is considered to be a native of Europe.The plant attains a height of nearly 20-30cm and starts flowering after 60-70days of planting It is also called as 'English daisy'.
	Plants are dwarf. Stem is thick and leaves are strap shaped. The flowers are single or double which are produced in while and pink colours. Flowers are small measuring about 2.0-5.0 cm. The showy varieties producing double flowers are Dwarf White, Snow Ball, Long Fellow, Ruby, Gigantea mixed.
	• Single stem plant
	• Transplanting - September – October
	• Spacing - 20 x 20 cm
	Suitability: It is mostly planted in pots, beds and rock gardens.
Dimorphotheca	The scientific name of Dimorphotheca is. *Dimorphotheca aurantiaca* and it belongs to the family Compositae. Itis considered to be a native of. south AfricaThe plant attains a height of nearly 30-60 cm and starts flowering after days of planting It is popularly known as African Daisy.
	It is very sensitive to weather conditions and flower shuts in dark or cloudy weather. *D. auriantiaca* and *D. sinuata* have been crossed with *D. pluvialis* to produce an attractive race of variously coloured hybrids. It is a bushy and medium plant. Leaves are narrow either toothed or entire. Flowers are white. yellow. orange and salmon in colour with dark brown disc in center measuring about 5-6 cm. Important varieties are Glistening White. Giant Orange. Salmon Beauty. White Sparkle and Buff Beauty. Tetra Goliath is a tetraploid variety with large orange flowers with dark green disc
	Suitability: It is a very good for bedding and for pots
Gamolepis	The scientific name of Gamolepis is *Gamolepis tagetes* and it belongs to the family Compositae)
	The plant attains a height of nearly 20-25cm and starts flowering after 80-120 days of planting
	It is highly suitable for bed. Edging pots and rock garden. Plants are dwarf. Leaves are fine and deeply cut. Flowers are small measuring 1-1.5 cm, yellow in colour and are produced profusely.
Gazania	*Gazania splendens* (Compositae). It is native of South Africa. The plants are dwarf and grows about 25 cm. Leaves are long, narrow and silvery on underside. The flowers are very showy, large and are available in different colours varying from white, pink, orange, yellow, red or brown. Flowering continues for a long period, but flowers close in the afternoon. Sunshine hybrids are very common

Gypsophila	***Gypsophila elegans*** (Caryophyllaceae). It is native of Caucasus region and Popularly known as Baby breath. Plan grow 60-75 cm_tall and produce numerous flowers of white, pink, and crimson colour. Flowers are borne in mist like sprays and look very graceful. Flowers are highly suitable for bouquet arrangement and are being, sold in the market along with other cut flowers. Important varieties are King of Market, London Market, Rosea, Convent Garden.
Helichrysum	Common Names: Golden Eternal Flower, Everlasting, Strawflower, Curry Plant, Immortelle, Licorice Plant
	Latin Name: Helichrysum italicum bracteatum
	History: A plant much admired for the beauty of its blooms, Helichrysum comes from the Greek word helisso (meaning "to turn around") and chrysos (meaning "gold"). Europeans historically used Helichrysum as an anti-inflammatory. Native to Africa, it has also been used by East and West African cultures, and is particularly wide-spread in its use in traditional Southern African tribal medicine. The Xhosa tribe used it to treat wounds topically, and the Zulu and Xhosa burned the leaves of the plant as an incense for ceremonial rituals. Historically, it was also revered as a powerful aphrodisiac for attracting a lover. Medically, it has been used as a traditional herb for chest complaints, colic, fever, internal sores, coughs, colds, headaches and topical uses.
	Herbal Properties And Uses: Helichrysum offers powerful tissue regeneration properties, and aids in the formation of scar tissue. European researchers have found that the helichrysum oil can reduce tissue pain, improve overall skin conditions, increase circulatory function, reduce cholesterol, stimulate liver cell activity, and reduce skin discoloration and scarring. It is a known mucolytic, antifungal, expectorant, anticoagulant, antispasmodic and anticatarrhal.
	Helichrysum Cultivation and Growing Methods
	Annual/Perrenial Plant: May be annuals, herbaceous perennials or shrubs.
	Parts Used: Flowers, stems, leaves, roots
	Soil Requirements: Does best in clay, loam and sandy soil, with a 6 to 7 pH level. This plant is tolerant of poor soil.
	Sun Requirements: Thrives best in partial to full sun.
	Height: 60-90 cm in height
	Spacing: Space seedlings around 20cm apart for smaller varieties, and 40cm apart for larger ones.
	Growing Zones: Grows well in U.S. Zones 8-11
	Planting Time: Plant seedlings indoors in early spring, or sow seeds on the surface of soil after the last frost of spring.
	Pollination: Propagation by seed and cuttings.
	Flowering/Seeding Time: Seed germination occurs from one to three weeks after planting. Seeds germinate best at a temperature of 18 to 23 degrees Centigrade.

	Harvesting: Flowers can be as harvested as they open in summer and autumn.
	Drying Methods / Yield: Flowers and leaves can be dried in the sun directly.
	Plant Yield: The life-span of this plant is from 4-6 years, making for a good yearly harvest from one plant.
	Preservation / Packaging Methods: Flower buds and leaves may also be stored in an airtight glass container for up to one year.
	Essential Oil Use: Extensive use as an essential for cosmetic and medicinal purposes. Particularly used for the treatment of skin conditions and liver ailments. The essential oil has known antiallergenic, anti-inflammatory, antimicrobial, antioxidant, antibacterial, antispasmodic, cholagogue, cicatrizant, astringent, diuretic, hepatic, nervine and stimulant properties.
	Plant Chemicals: The main constituents responsible for the actions of this plant include a-pinene, b-pinene, myrcene, camphene, limonene, eugenol, 1,8-cineole, terpinen-4-ol, linalool, neryl acetate, italidone, geraniol, nerol and several other b-diketones.
	Is This An Edible Plant: Yes
	Cautions / Contraindications: Helichrysum is considered to be a non-toxic, non-irritant safe oil. There are no known contraindications for use, and it is even considered safe for babies and children. That said, pregnant and breast-feeding women should consult a health professional before taking.
	Drug Interactions: None to date, but care should be taken with all herbal medicines.
Holly hock	The scientific name of Holly hock is *Althea rosea* and it belongs to the family Malvace**a**
	It is considered to be a native of China.
	The plant attains a height of nearly100-130cm and starts flowering after 100-130 days of planting
	Plants are tall, stately growing. Leaves are deep green, coarse and round in shape. Flowers are single, semi-double and double which are produced in the axil of leaves in various colours varying from white, cream, yellow pink, mauve, lilac, rose, salmon, red, scarlet cn,mson and many intermediate shades. Transplanting:September – October
	Suitability:Back row of herbaceous border or for screening purpose
	Flowers – In axils of leaves, large in size about 7-10 cm
	Spacing: 45-75 x 45-75 cm
	Remarks: Require full sun ,frost free,biennia loften treated like as annual tolerate poor soils ,reseeds itself readily
	Highly ornamental varieties suitable for growing in the garden : Giant Double, Chater's Double, Powderpuff, Summer Carnival and Tnumph Double mixed.

Ice plant	Mesembreyanthemum criniflorum (Aizoaceae) It is native south Africa and is commonly called as Living stone Daisy or Fig Marigold. It is very dwarf plant and grows about 20 cm. It is best suited for sunny situation, rockeris, shallow baskets, pots etc. It can also be planted to cover the space under standard roses. The branches and leaves are succulent. Leaves are elongated thick and fleshy and dew depoists on them into small droplets which look like snow crystals. The flowers open in sun which are very shining and attractive and close at night. Flowers are sinle measuring about 2.5 cm across in many colours like pink, white, salmon, orange, red, crimson, rose, apricot colours. Flowers are available in self coloured or white edged with countrasting colours.
Lady's lace.	**Lady lace:** *Pimpnella monoica* (Umbelliferae). It is a tall annual with finely cut foliage and is natie of India. Flowers are small, white, delicate and are produced in umbels. Dry flowers maintain their shape and dried flowers are commonly used for dry arrangement. Queen Anne is the important variety.
Larkspur	Deliphinium hybridum (Ranunculaceae) it is a native Europe and other temperate regions. Other important species are *D. elatum, D. formosum, D. cardinale, D. belladonna, D. nudicale*. It is a good cut flower and also suitable for mixed annual borders. Plants are much branched with finely cut deep green foliage. Flowers are spurred and are produced on long column. The common colours are blue, white, pink, lilace, and mauve. Flowering occurs late in season *i.e.* end of February-March. The double flowered strain known as 'Hyacinth flowered' has been produced. Another strain, stock flowered Larkspur has been produced in several fine colour forms in dark blue, rose pink, lilac rose, rosy scarlet, white and soft salmon-rose. The plants of these varieties grow about 75 cm tall of compact erect habit. Recently selection fand development of upright growing type known as 'Gaint Imperial' have been done. It is characterized by plants of erect branching habit growing upto 120-130 cm tall with graceful spikes of double flowers in a wide range of delicate shades. The important varieties of this class are Blue Bell, Blue Spire, Brilliant Rose, Carmine King, Daintiness, Miss California Rosalie and White King Planting : 20x30 cm Flower : 90 to 100 days
Linaria	***Linaria bipartita* (Scrophulariaceae).** It is also known as Toad Flax. It is native of Spain, Portugal and Morocco. The shape of flower is similar of snap dragon but flowers are smaller in size. Plants are dwarf and attain a height of 30-40 cm. Branches are erect and are thin. The flowers are borne on these erect branches which are tiny and look peculiar due to their shape. Flowers are of self colour or bicolour and important colours are purple, blue, deep pink, yellow and white and combinations of these. The important varieties are Fairy Bouquet, Fairy, Brides Maid, Ruby King, White Pearl and Yellow Prince.

Linum	***Linum grandiflorum* var. *rubrum* Linaceae)**. It is a native of North Africa and Europe and is commonly called as flax. It is ideal for bedding purposes. Plants are medium and grow upto 45-60 cm height. Stems are slender and leaves are narrow and pointed. Flowers have five petals which arc united and have double centre. Flowers measure about 2.5 cm. The common colour of flowers is red and white. Blue colour flax is also grown in the garden.
Lupin	The scientific name of Lupin is *Lapinus hartwegii* and it belongs to the family Leguminosae
	It is considered to be a native of. N. America specially of California and Virginia states
	The plant attains a height of nearly 50-75cm and starts flowering after 80-120 days of planting.The name lupins has been originally derived from Greek word i.e. lupe which means grief. There are many species like a *L. perenne, L. luteus, L. varius, L. hirustus.* Romans used to grow *L. albus* as food for man and beast. Modem lupins i.e. *L. hartwegii* have been derived from *L. polyphyllia* and *L. arboreum.* Lupins are most ideally suited as cut flower, and as bedding, border and pot plants. The plants have palm shaped foliage. Flowers are borne on a long spike and resemble pea !lowers. The colour range varies from white. blue, pink and disco loured. The important varieties are Azure Blue, Roscus, Colestinus, Albus, Pixie Delight, Russel Hybrids, dwarf Russel hybrids, Blue Jacket, Radiant, Day dream, Heather Glow, Freedom *etc.*
Mignonette	*Reseda ordorata* (Resedaceae) is native of North Africa. Although plants do not produce attractive flowers but they are valued for fragrance. Flowers produced nectar and lot of honey bee activity is observed around this flowers. Plants are dwarf growing about 35-40 cm and have crawling habit. The flowers of white light yellow, red or crimson are small in size and produced in loose cluster. It is suitable for pots, beds and window gradens. Machet is the variety which is being marketed in India.
Mimulus	The scientific name of Mimulus is *Mimulus tigrinus* and it belongs to the family Scrophulariaceae.
	It is considered to be a native of. Western parts of North and South America and also commonly called as Monkey flower due to its sported flowers.
	The plant attains a height of nearly 45-90cm and starts flowering after 80-120 days of planting
	In Latin language it means mimick. and angular branches are produced. Leaves are toothed and heart shaped. The flowers are large, tubular and yellow, pink, red, generally biocoloured with burnt and maroon spots. The plants are free flowering and numerous flowers are produced. It is most ideal for pot and for bedding purposes. The modern varieties are hybrids of *M. luteus, M. cupreus* and *M. guttata.* The common varieties are *A.T.* Johnson, Bee's Dazzler, Bonfire, Canary Bird and Queen's Prize.

Nasturtium	*Tropaeolum majus* (Tropaeolaceae) it is of Mexico and South America and is very common is Indian gradens. Plants have wiry stems and green round leaves. There are dwarf and trailing type nasturtium and in both groups flowers are single or double. Dwarf type hardly grows about 25-30 cm and most ideally suitable for pot, and dbedding purposes whereas trailing types can reach the height of about 2 m and need support for climbing. This type is most suitable for temporary screening, training in different forms and against wall. Flowers are large and have long spur. Flower are of yellow, orange, scarlet and mahagony colour and in some cases have spots and markings of contrasting colours. Flowers are generally hidden by foliage so production of leaves may be checked by restricting supply of nutrients and water. The common varieties in dwarf single are Empress of India King ot Tombs (scarlet), Gold Kind (yellow). The dwarf double varieties are Orage gem, Salmon Gem, Golden Globe, Scarlet Globe Cherry Rose and Jewel mixed. The important trailig single varieties are Lucifers and Spot Fire (scarlet). Recently gleam hybrids have been introduced which are very attractive. The common varieties are Golden's Orange, Scarlet, Salmons Gleams and Gleam mixed. Now-a-days varieties like Cherry Rose and Golden Jewel. Golden Yellow, Scarlet Jewel are preferred because they produce flowers above foliage. Other important varieties are peach Melba, salmon Baby. Scarlet Express and Canariense.
Nemasia	The scientific name of Nemasia is *Namesia strumosa* and it belongs to the family Scrophuliaraceae.
	It is considered to be a native of South Africa .The plant attains a height of nearly 30-45 cm and starts flowering after 80-120 days of planting.
	It is semi hardy and growing about 20-45 cm in height.. Plants are bushy and compact with erect branches on which flowers are produced freely. These flowers are very pretty and attractive on account of their orchid like appearance. Wide range of flower colours and throat markings are available in nemasia. The flowers are of yellow, white. pink, purple, scarlet, crimson. Popular tall growing varieties are suttoni of separate colours as well as of mixed colour and Carnival mixture whereas amongst dwarf group. varieties are Triumph (mixture), Orange Prince (Orange), Fire Ball (Scarlet), Fire King and Blue Gem.
	Suitability: It is ideally suited for pot, bedding purpose and dwarf varieties are suitable for window boxes and rock gardens
Nigella	The scientific name of Nigella is ***Nigella damascena*** and it belongs to the family Ranunculaceae
	It is considered to be a native of of North Africa, and Europe
	The plant attains a height of nearly 45-60 cm and starts flowering after 80-120 days of planting

	It is popularly called as Love in a-mist or Devil-in-the bush. It is mostly liked in its dried stage when seed capsules become egg shape and can be arranged for dry decoration. It is also mostly suitable for pot' as well as cut flowers. Plants attain the height of 45-60 cm and have finally cut thread like leaves which cover bloom. Flowers are semi double measuring about 3-4 cm of white light blue or rose in colour. The popular varieties are Persian Jewel and Miss Jekyll which produces sky blue flowers. Oxford Blue is also another good variety.
Pansy	The scientific name of Pansy is *Viola tricolor var. hortens* and it belongs to the family **Violaceae**
	It is considered to be a native of Europe. The plant attains a height of nearly 20-30 cm and starts flowering after 40-80 days of planting
	Pansy is one of magnificent flowers which is mostly sought in the garden due to its pretty shape and contrast colour markings or blotches of the flower. These markings or blotches resemble the face of cat. Leaves are heart shaped. Flowers are produced in great profusion and size varies from 5 to 10-13 cm across. Flowers are of white, red, deep violet. blue, yellow, self coloured or have blotches or markings of' contrast colours. Flowers are mildly sweet scented, particularly early in the morning.
	The pansy varieties are grouped into two groups depending upon the size of flowers *i.e.* small flowered or large flowered pansy. Small flower varieties produce flowers into a great profusion which are most suitable for bedding and mass effects. The important varieties are Lord Beacot Field, Tormordeau mixed, Hiemalis mixed. For getting a colourful mixed population, seeds of separate colours are produced and different colour are mixed in a certain proportion. Under North Indian conditions, there is: no problem of seed set in small flowering pansy.
	The large flowered pansies are also known as Show pansies or Giant size These varieties produce less number of flowers but of good size around 10-13 cm. The important varieties are Sakata's Giants, Roggolis Swist Giants, Aalsmeer Giants, Floridaie Giants, Her Majesty, World's Seventh Wonder, Triumph of Giants, Fancy Queen, Fancy Giant etc. F1, hybrid of Super Giants are also available. F_2 and F_3 hybrids are also available for mixed colourful planting though the size of flower is little less. Under North Indian conditions, seed set in these giant types is poor unless flowers are hand pollinated.
	Transplanting :September – October
	Spacing:15 to 30 x 15 to 30 cm
	Suitability: It is most ideally suitable for pot, edging, border, rockery, bedding, window boxes and makes good combination with roses when planted in rosery The large flowered pansies are specially preferred for pot culture and window boxes.

Petunia	The scientific name of Petunia is *Petunia hybrida* and it belongs to the family Solanaceae. It is considered to be a native of South America The plant attains a height of nearly 30-40cm and starts flowering after 80-120 days of planting. Very popular in Indian gardens due to its floriferous and hardy nature. commonly grown as bedding, pots, hanging basket, window boxes, rockery and for most planting. and have spreading habit with trailing branches. Leaves are small, round and thick. The flowers have five petals which are joined and are trumpet shaped. The colour and form of petals differ widely. The flowers are self coloured of white, cream, yellow, pink blue, purple mauve, salmon and bicoloured with star like patterns. The petals may be entire or frilled. The seeds of double petunia and fringe. varieties do not produce the plants of true-to-type. For F_1 hybrid seed production, the single petunia is used as female parent which is fertilized with pollen of a double variety.
	There are different types of petunia and large number of varieties available in different groups. The common varieties of dwarf and compact bedding are: Blue Bird (blue-violet), Cream Star, Peach Red, Rose of Heaven, Snow Ball, Butter Scotch, Fire Chief, Lady Bird. Smooth edged grandiflora varieties are Bingo, Dazzler, Pop Com and Purple Prince. The important varieties of frilled type are Giants of California, Superbissima, Ramona, Snow Storm, Theodosia, Defiance, Super Frills, etc. Balcony and Pendula's petunia's are trailing type and produce small flowers and common varieties are Blue wonder, Rose Wonder and Rose. The varieties of all double petunia are Son nata, Prestos, and Alegro. Multiflora F_j hybrids poduce small flowers of smooth edge of petals and common varieties are Sugar Plum, Montana, Polaris, Coral Satin, Glitters, etc. whereas F_j grandiflora petunia produce large flowers with ruffled petals. The important varieties are White Magic, Pink Magic, Lapalona, May Time, Spring Time etc. The varieties of F2 hybrids of grandiflora are carnival and of multiflora are Colorona and Canfetti. There is a recent introduction of Single Joy Fest series of F, hybrids multiflora and important are Blue, Rose Red, Rosy Star, Blue Star, Fiery Star, and White.
	Planting: September – November
	Spacing: 20 to 30 x 20 - 30 cm
	Flowering: Start after 80 – 120 days
	Require full sun
	Easily grown
	Available in grandiflora,multiflora and doubled types in wide array of colour
	Cultivars from cuttings especially floriferous
Phlox	The scientific name of Phlox is *Phlox drummondii* and it belongs to the family Polemoniaceae. It is considered to be a native of U.S.A., specially the region of Texas
	The plant attains a height of nearly 30-45 cm and starts flowering after 70-100 days of planting

	It is also known as Star flower. It is very popular in all gardens due to its easy culture, free flowering and wide range of colours with long blooming period. It is highly suitable for pot culture, beddings, border, window boxes and is a good cut flower. Phlox is a dwarf annual and grows about 15-40 cm tall. Plants are bushy with medium sized, narrow and pointed leaves. The flowers are produced in clusters at the end of branches well above foliage and covers the whole plant. The individual flowers are small, about 2 cm across with round or pointed petals. The flower colour is wide which varies from white, cream, pale yellow, rose, pink, salmon, mauve, blue, scarlet, red, crimson etc.
	There are numerous varieties in mixed or separate colours in both groups of phlox *i.e.* Grandiflora with large flowers and Nana Compacta which produces dwarf and compact plants. The important varieties of Grandiflora are Snowball, Vermilion, Coccinea, Ford hook, Art.Shades Brilliant, Yellow Beauty, Blue Beauty etc. Common varieties of Nana Compacta are Globe, Cecily, and Beauty. Cuspidata and Twinkle are good varieties of star phlox. Tetraploid varieties like Tetra Road and Giant Tetra with stronger stems and larger blooms are also available and are Quite popular.
	Transplanting: August – November
	Spacing: 20 to 30 x 20 x 30 cm
Rudbeckia	The scientific name of Rudbeckia is *Rudbeckia biocolour* and it belongs to the family *Compositae*
	It is considered to be a native of North America .Also, called as Cone flower . The plant attains a height of nearly 40-60 cm and starts flowering after 120-150 days of planting.
	Flowers are like daisy flower i.e. yellow with a mahagony crimson central zone.
	The important varieties are Hirta, Gloriosa, Daisies Mixed Golden Flame, Kelvendon Star and Summer Festival.
	suitable for bedding purpose and border.
Saliva	The scientific name of Saliva is *Saliva splendens* and it belongs to the familyLabiatae. It is considered to be a native of South America, specially the region of Mexico and Brazil. The plant attains a height of nearly 30-90 cm and starts flowering after 110-120 days of planting.
	It is also called as sage flower. Saliva is ideally suited for shady, situation and comers of the garden. It is an ideal plant for pots. bed and under the trees. Plant has many square, smooth branches of erect growth. Leaves arc broad, pointed and their edge is slightly cut. The flowers are produced on long spikes which are 15-30 cm in length which are long, tubular with a long tip. The common colours are red, white, cream and purple. There are also pink, violet and salmon." There are several varieties and common

	dwarf varieties are Hussara (Red), St. John's Fire, Blaze of Fire, Scarlet Pygmy, Hot Shot whereas tall varieties are Scarlet Cream and Crimson King. S. *coccinea* is commonly grown in, South India and important varieties are Red Indian, White Dove and Pink Pearl
Saponaria	The scientific name of Saponaria is *Saponaria vaccaria* and it belongs to the family Caryophyllaccae It is considered to be a native of Europe.The plant attains a height of nearly 75-90 cm and starts flowering after 90 days of planting and is also popularly called as soap wart. Plants make bushy growth and have straggling branches. Leaves are long. Numerous flowers of star shape are produced in loose clusters which look very attractive. Pink and white colours are common. Flower is suitable as cut flower.
	Another species- S. *calabrica* which is dwarf (20-30 em) is suitable for edging or rock garden
Schizanthus	The scientific name of Schizanthus is *Schizanthus wisetonensis* and it belongs to the family Solanaceae. It is considered to be a native of Chile and Peru. The plant attains a height of nearly 90 cm and starts flowering after 80-120 days of planting
	It is commonly called as Butterfly flower or Poor man's Orchid This is excellent for growing in pots and cut flowers. The modem varieties have been developed by crossing two species *i.e.* S. *grahimi* and S. *pinnatus.* foliage is deeply cut like ferns. Numerous small flowers about 2 crn across are produced which are attractively colourcd and cover almost the entire plant, The common colours are white, apricot, yellow, rose purple, mauve, lilac, pink, salmon or cardinal red and marked beautifully and blotched in contrasting colours. The common tall varieties are Butter Giant, Monarch; Brilliant, Bcnery's Giant, Dr. Badger's Hybrids, Angelwings, Cauleya orchid. Excelsior while Dwarf Pansy and Dwarf Bouquet arc dwarf varieties.
Shirley Poppy	The scientific name of Shirley Poppy is *Papaver rhoeas* and it belongs to the family Papaveraceae.
	It is considered to be a native of Europe.The plant attains a height of nearly 50-80 cm and starts flowering after 100-120 days of planting.and is also commonly called as corn poppy.
	Stems are long slender. Leaves are bluish green. The flowers are cup shaped, single or double with crinkled petals. There is a wide range of colours available varying from dark crimson, salmon, scarlet, pink, mauve, yellow to blue. The common varieties are Shirley Single, Double Paeony flowered, Oriental Mixed, Iceland Mixed, American Legion, Sweet Briar, and Mixed. Other species of poppy are *P. glaucum, P. nudicaule, P. somniferum, P. orientale*
Statice	The scientific name of Statice is *Limonium sinuatum* and it belongs to the family Plumbaginaceae . It is considered to be a native of Mediterranean region.The plant attains a height of nearly 60-70 cm and starts flowering after 100-120 days of planting .It is also popularly known as Sea Lavendar or Pink because some species were found growing in salt marshes.

	Statice is suitable for planting in beds, borders and for flowers which keep colour after drying. Branches are angular, leaves are leathery and deeply lobed. These branches carry dense cluster of numerous small flowers. These flowers have papery texture and are about 1.25 cm across, usually blue, lavender or rose and a tiny yellowish corolla hidden inside. There are several varieties available for commercial growing and important varieties are Mid-Night Blue, Twilight Lavender, Blue Rennet, Iceberg, Gold Coast, Blue Perfection, Charmois Rose, Lavender Queen, Market Growers Blue, Market Rose, Purple Monarch and White.
	Other Species:*L. suworowii* is very ornamental. ,*L. latifoliun* is also highly suitable as cut flower and can be used as dry flowers which can be kept for several years. Blue Cloud and Violetta are good varieties.
	Remarks:Requires full sun ,Needs good drainage and Excellent for drying
Stock	The scientific name of stock is *Matthiola indica* and it belongs to the family cruciferae. It is considered to be a native of Mediterranean region. The plant attains a height of nearly 45-90cm and starts flowering after 60-90days of planting.
	Leaves are single and dark green. Flowers are fragrant and single or double.single flowers have 4 petals,4 stamens and a pistal having 30-60-ovules whereas double flowers have 40-70petals:
Sweet alyssum	The scientific name of Sweet Alyssum is *Alyssum maritimum* and it belongs to the family Cruciferae. It is considered to be a native of Western Asia and Europe and is very common in Indian gardens.The plant, having spreading habit, attains a height of nearly 15-30cm and starts flowering after 45 -60days of planting
	Leaves are narrow of light green colour and produce spike of tiny sweet scented flowers which cover whole plant and look a white carpet of flowers.
	Important varieties:Snow Carpet (white), Royal Carpet (violet), Pink Heather (rose), Violet Queen and Snow drift.
	Suitability: Sweet Alyssum is an excellent flower for edging, pot growing, hanging baskets, beds and window boxes.
	Colour range:white, lilac
	Transplanting: Sep-Oct
	Spacing:10-15x10-15cm
Sweet Pea	The scientific name of Sweet Pea is *Lathyrus odoratus* and it belongs to the family Leguminosae .It is considered to be a native of Sicily and Greece .The plant attains a height of nearly 90-150 cm and starts flowering after 75-90 days of planting

	It has climbing habit and needs support to climb up. Therefore, it is planted for artifical screening or as temporary tall hedge. or trained on stumps. Seeds are sown directly at 6- 9 cm apart, 3-5 cm deep and in double rows spaced 30-40 cm apart in deeply dug (5-7 cm deep) and well prepared land by adding organic manure. When the plants are about 5-7 cm tall it need support which can be of various materials like sarkanda, chicken wire netting, bamboo poles or galvanized pipes or strings. There is a wide range of flower colours varying from white, light blue. lilac, mauve. pink, rose, salmon. cherry red, red, and maroon to crimson. There are numerous varieties which are being grown. The original hooded types and plain grandiflora varieties have been replaced by spencer type having frilled waved edges. There are six different strains of sweet pea. They are: Giant Frilled, Late Flowering Spencers: Early-Flowering Frilled: The Cuthberston, Frilled: Multiflora or Zvolanik's rnultiflora (5-7 blooms to a stem); the Dwarf cupid (without tendril-non trailing) and the Dwarf Cupid Frilled or the Little Sweet Heart. Important varieties are Early Multitlora Galaxy, Late Spring Galaxy, Giant Ruffle Mixed, Royal Family mixed, Knee Hi Mixed, Vulcan, Monarch, Blue W onder and B lack Prince.
	Remarks: Mainly grown as background of herbaceous border and screening purpose.sown directly in the permanent places in September at15-75cm spacing.
Sweet Sultan	The scientific name of *Sweet Sultan is Centaurea moschata* and it belongs to the family *Compositae.* It is considered to be a native of Caucusus region, Middle East Asia and Eastern Parts of Mediterranean region.
	The plant attains a height of nearly 90-120 cm and starts flowering after 90-120 days of planting
	It is another important seasonal flower belonging to genera Centaurea. It's common name Sweet Sultan is due to the fact that it was brought from East which was under the rule of Ottoman Sultan in the 17th Century. Like other seasonal flowers, it is also mostly planted in the Indian gardens and home landscapes due to its delicate and sweet scented flowers. It is most suitable for herbaceous border and for mass effect. . Flowers are soft and fully which are borne at the tip of them. Flowers are available in white, mauve, rose and sulphur yellow colours. Important varieties are the Bride-white, Flavo-yellow and Rosea-pink.
Sweet William	The scientific name of Sweet William is *Dianthus barbatus* and it belongs to the family Caryophyllaceae.
	It is considered to be a native of Northern France and is closely related with carnation and pink The plant attains a height of nearly 30-45 cm and starts flowering after 80-120 days of planting

	Sweet William is biennial but is grown as an annual in North Indian plains. It is ideally suited for bedding, borders, cut flowers and pots. The dwarf varieties are mostly planted for edging, rock garden, window boxes and pots. Leaves are flat and tips are pointed and green. Flowers are produced in clusters. There is large variation in colour of flowers and flowers of pleasing colour such as crimson, dark red, dark maroon, purple, salmon and while are produced. The flowers may be of self, mottled, or have markings of different colours. Diadem, Indian Carpet, Messenger Mixed, Pink Beauty and Scarlet Beautyare common varieties.
Venidium	The scientific name of Venidium is *Venidium fastuosum* and it belongs to the family Compositae. It is considered to be a native of South Africa and is a popular flower for bedding purpose.The plant attains a height of nearly 60 cm and starts flowering after 90-100 days of planting.
	Plant makes a bushy appearance. Leaves are irregular and lobed. Leaves and flowering stalk have silvery white hairs which give a wooly or fuzzy appearance. Flowers are large measuring about 10 cm across of brilliant orange,ivory,cream, yellow colour with a purple black centre. These are produced on long stem. The important variety is Monarch. Dwarf hybrids which grows about 35-50 cm high are also available.
Verbena	The scientific name of Verbena is *Verbena hybrida* and it belongs to the family Verbenaceae. It is considered to be a native of south America.The plant attains a height of nearly 25-30cm and starts flowering after 80-90 days of planting.
	Leaves are dark green,wrinkled, small and deeply cut. Flowers produced in loose clusters are above the foliage. These clusters consist of several star like small flowers that give an appearance of mass of flowers.
	Remarks: Good for bedding, pots, hanging baskets, window boxes and rockery
	Spacing:15x25cm
	Propagation: Seed
	Sowing season: July-Agust in plains and October-November in hills
	Requires full sun
	Prefers cool temperatures. Available from seed or cutting. Cutting types more heat tolerant.
Wall flower	The scientific name of Wall flower is *cheiranthes cheiri* and it belongs to the family Cruciferae. It is considered to be a native of Europe. The plant attains a height of nearly 30-45cm and starts flowering after 90-100 days of planting. The leaves are long having green colour.
	The flowers are produced on a long spike. These are single and common colour is golden orange.
	Remarks:Bedding and pot growing

7.2 Flower Arrangements

Introduction

Flower arrangement is a very old art. In India, flowers were earlier arranged in temples and during festivities. The first rules of *ikebana* were laid down in Japan more than a thousand years ago. Flowers were widely used for interior decoration, but they were cut from the garden and simply massed into water-filled containers to brighten the home. The beauty of the display relied upon the blooms themselves rather than the aesthetic appeal of the design. Even at homes and venues of festivals/functions/on auspicious occasions, flowers are used in a big way in the form of garlands, wall hangings, and floor decorations. Flower arrangements grace table tops, window sills, corners, fire places, and so on to suit the occasion.

Flower arrangement may be defined as the art of organizing and grouping together plant materials (flowers, foliage, fruits, twigs etc) to achieve harmony of form, colour and texture, thereby adding cheer, life and beauty to the surroundings.

Flower Arrangements

Various types of arrangements are chosen, as appropriate to the area and occasion. Medium sized 'round' arrangements are often provided at the guest relations executives' desk in the lobby and on coffee tables in the lounges. In most five-star hotels, one can see huge, spectacular arrangements in the loggies. Table arrangements for conferences must be low so that guests may see over them. At informal banquets, large arrangements may be seen. At wedding banquets, wall arrangements using gerberas are very popular nowadays. On special occasions and festivals, a large amount of flowers is required for making up various types of arrangements. The extent to which flowers are used in hotel interiors depends on the degree of luxury provided, the number of special functions held.

The housekeeper is responsible for all flower arrangements and their placement. Simple arrangements such as a bud in a vase can be done. Alternatively, flower arrangements may be provided on contract, in which case the arrangements are brought in and taken away at agreed times and little or no floral work is carried out on the premises. Arrangements like running water, containers, buckets, vases, scissors and flower pots are important.

Flower Arrangement Basics

Making up a good flower arrangement requires a lot of creativity on the part of the arranger and beginners can develop this art through study and experimentation with different plant materials. Studying pictures of interesting arrangements in books and magazines for ideas is one way of learning this art, but actual practice is essential for developing skill in flower arrangement. The materials used for making flower arrangements are not necessarily expensive or elaborate (compared to other crafts); but as with all other crafts, they are a necessity. The following groups of ingredients and aids are essential to flower arrangement:

Mechanics: These are items used to keep the flowers, foliage and stems in place within the container. Mechanics must be fixed securely and should be hidden from view. The most popular and basic mechanics are florists' foam, pin holders, and chicken wire.

1. **Floral foam:** This is also called 'oasis'. It is cellular plastic material. A few plants, such as tulips, find water intake difficult when set in foam. There are two types available like green foam and brown/grey foam.

2. **Green foam:** This need to be soaked in water for at least half an hour and then fresh plant material may be inserted into it. The popular shapes for green foam are 'rounds' and 'blocks'. This type of foam is extremely light when dry, but its weight increases by over 30 times when saturated with water. The green foam should be stored wrapped in plastic and foil after use to prevent degradation from atmospheric moisture.

3. **Brown/grey foam:** This is used only for dry plant material or artificial display materials. Stems can be held at any angle in both shallow and deep containers. This problem of smelly water is also eliminated for long lasting arrangements. In case of large arrangements, however extra support with chicken wire is required.

4. **Chicken wire:** This is also called 'wire mesh' or 'wire netting'. A fine-gauge wire should be selected. To begin with, a 2-inch mesh may be bought. This 1-inch mesh grade is used to cover floral/foam blocks in large displays. Florists' wires may be of two kinds; galvanized wire and plastic coated wire.

5. **Pin-holders:** These are also called *kenzan* or needle-point holders. A series of sharply pointed pins are firmly held in a solid lead base, which may be circular or rectangular. It holds thick and heavy stems securely by impaling them on the pins. The holder may be used on its own in a shallow dish or with other mechanics for a large display in a deep

container. Choose one with a heavy base and a large number of sharp brass pins placed close together. Avoid iron ones, as they rust in water. It is best to start with one basic pin holder, as they are expensive - most useful is a round shape of 3 inches diameter. It may be stuck to the base of the container with adhesive clay. Well type pin holders are also available, which do not call for a container as the dish around the pin holder holds water.

6. **Prong:** This is simplest type of floral foam anchor. It is a small plastic disc with four vertical prongs. The base of the prong is attached to the container with adhesive clay and the block or round floral foam is pressed down onto the prongs. More than one prong may be required if a large block of floral foam is used.

7. **Florist's cone:** This is also called a 'flower tube' or 'flower funnel'. It acts like a miniature vase. It is used in large arrangements, where foliage or flowers need to be placed above their stem height. Fill the cone with water before inserting the stem.

8. **Adhesive clay:** This is also referred to as 'oasis fix'. It is non-setting sticky clay in strip form which holds dry surfaces together. It is used for securing a prong, pin holder or candle cup to the container. Adhesive clay is sold in brown or green colours.

9. **Setting clay:** This is sometimes available under the name of 'dri-hard' and is used in permanent dry and artificial flower arrangements. This material sets solid after a few hours, which means that neither the clay nor the plant is reusable. Plaster of Paris is a popular alternative for securing the stems of topiary trees in pots.

10. **Non-setting clay:** This is also available under the name 'stay-soft'. It is used for dry and artificial flower arrangements, where the plant material is to be removed and reused at a later date or where non-permanent accessories such as candles are to be inserted. Plasticine can be used as an alternative.

11. **Glue:** Quick-drying glue is used in dried flower arrangements to attach flowers or leaves to the container or to other plant materials. The most convenient way to apply the glue is using a glue gun.

12. **Pebbles and marbles:** Small pebbles have long been used to hold the stems of cut flowers. Round marbles or flattened glass nuggets in a glass vase can also add to the attractiveness of the display.

Equipment: This includes tools or other aids used to ensure that a satisfactory arrangement of plant material is created within the container. Only a few pieces of equipment out of all those listed below are essential for a beginner like bucket, scissors, knife and watering can.

Bucket: A water-filled bucket is a vital piece of equipment for collecting flowers from the garden and for conditioning the blooms before making an arrangement.

Florist's scissors: Ordinary scissors are not suitable for cutting plant stems, they tend to crush the tissues. Choose a pair of florist's scissors which contains short blades and one is serrated. At the base, there may be a notch to be used for cutting thin wires.

Mister: A hand-held spray bottle to produce a fine mist of water droplets is an aid to keeping an arrangement looking fresh in warm weather. Spray the mist slightly above the top of the display as soon as the arrangement is done.

Secateurs: These are used to cut through thick and woody stems. The garden type is commonly available, but there are narrower ones made especially for the florist.

Watering can: This is used for topping up the water supply in the container or re-wetting the florists' foam for holding a fresh flower arrangement. Buy a plastic one and look for two important features - the spout should be long and narrow and it should arise from the base of the can.

Wire: This is used to support drooping stems and for making posies, corsages, and so on. It is also used to make false stems for dried and artificial flowers and to bind clumps of blooms together. Three types of wires are used as ***Stub wire*** (strongest), ***Rose wire*** (Thinner silver wire), ***Reel wire*** (extensively used for binding plant material).

Knife: A craft knife with a sharp blade for scrapping stems, removing leaves, and stripping away thorns. It is also employed for preparing stem ends by making a sloping cut and occasionally a vertical slit. It may also be used to cut floral foam and to remove excess clay.

Wire cutters: These are useful for heavy cutting work such as cutting chicken wire, plastic stems of artificial flowers, and thick stub wires.

Paints and finishes: Paints can be used on containers, mechanics, and bases as well as, plant material.

Cut-flower preservative: This is available in powder or liquid form under different brand names. It is basically a bactericide to prevent slime and smell from developing in the vase water, plus sugar to prolong the life of fresh flowers. A preservative can be made in-house by adding three teaspoons of sugar and one drop of bleach of half a litre of water.

Containers: The container must be waterproof if fresh flowers are used. The base material from which the container is made determines its texture. Neutral colours such as soft grey, dull brown, off-white, or earth colours are most suitable because they are inconspicuous and do not detract attention from the flowers displayed. A vase is a container that is at least as tall as it is wide and is often quite narrow, with a restricted mouth. It is a favourite container for cut flowers. Metal vases were once very popular, but now pottery and plastic ones are common. A jug is a lipped container with a single handle and is useful for old world and 'natural' arrangements.

Basket is a popular container for dried flower arrangements. Willow and bamboo baskets are easily available. For fresh flower arrangements, it is necessary to have a waterproof container within perhaps a hamper, a square or rectangular lidded basket.

Plant materials: These can be divided into three basic types. Most arrangements use all the three types of plant materials.

Line material: This consists of tall stems, flowering spikes or bold leaves that are used to create the basic framework or skeleton. This line material may be straight or curved and it sets the height and width of the finished arrangement. Examples are Gladiolus, bird of paradise, golden rods, larkspur, asparagus ferns, palms, and tuberoses.

Dominant/focal point material: This consists of smaller flowers or all sorts of leaves and foliage that are used to cover the mechanics and edges of the container and also provide added interest colour to the display. Unwanted bare spots are filled by these. Examples are Asters, ivy, marguerites, button chrysanthemums, carnations, *Gypsophila*, and *Limonium*.

Some versatile accessories are baskets, bronze lamps, miniature dolls, grain scoops, wooden shapes, ribbons, pottery items, artificial glitter and beads, wooden fruit shapes, silk flowers and foliage, driftwood, carved objects, tree barks and interesting pebbles.

Cut Flowers: Flowers are a highly perishable commodity and if the vendors themselves have not kept them in good condition, they will not last long. Exotic flowers are expensive and it is best to buy them from a wholesale market, where one can get a lot of variety at a reasonable price. The following points should be kept in mind while selecting cut flowers:

1. The flower buckets should be placed out of direct sunlight and the water should be clean and not smelly.
2. Foliage should be firm and the cut ends properly immersed in water.
3. Choose blooms at the just-open stage and not the full-blown stage for a long-lasting display. The bud stage is too early closed; green buds do not often open indoors. The problem with the full-blown stage, though it seems ripe for display is that all the flowers are fully open and so the display will be soft-lived.

Care and conditioning of Flowers: A flower or leaf cut from a plant has a short, though beautiful life. It is possible to prolong this for a little while by a few methods. This is well worth doing, as having spent time and money on a flower arrangement, it is gratifying to have it last as long as possible. Flower arrangers use the term 'conditioning' to refer to the preparation of cut plant materials for a long life, the filling of stems with water and prevention of wilting. Cut flowers can be cared for and kept fresh for longer if the point discussed below is kept in mind.

Guidelines for flower arrangement: While preparing flower arrangements, adhere to the following guidelines:

1. Plant materials should be cut at a slant, using sharp scissors or knife, either early in the morning or after sunset.
2. It is best to cut flowers before they reach maturity as they contain proper moisture at this level.
3. Carry the cut flowers in a heads-down position so that heavy-headed flowers will not snap off.
4. Wrap the flowers in newspaper upto the neck of the flowers. Plunge this bunch into a bucket of water for 3-4 hours or overnight for conditioning. In case of foliage, submerge them in water for about two hours.
5. Use a good pruning knife or scissors to make clean, slanting cuts, causing minimal damage or bruising to the little ducts in the stem.
6. Make slanting cuts in stems rather than straight ones preferably underwater, to avoid the introduction of air bubbles immediately before putting the stems in water.
7. Remove all leaves from the stems of flowers that have shorter lives than most.

8. Re-cut any stem that has been left out of water and removing about 2 inches of the stem.
9. Preserve or revive woody stems by pounding the bottom 2 inches of the stems before plunging in water and ensure enough water.
10. To reduce underwater decay, strip the stems of all foliage and thorns that fall below the waterline. However, de-thorning roses may shorten their life.
11. Flowers with hollow stems, such as dahlias and marigolds, should have the stem ends seared over a candle flame to coagulate the sap at the ends, thus preventing the sap from bleeding out.
12. Some plant materials are long lasting when mature, such as stems of pomegranate, sweet lime and sapota. These could be used as basic lime material.

Aftercare for flower arrangement: The following guidelines should be kept in mind for aftercare:

1. Never place a fresh flower arrangement where it will be exposed to direct draughts from a fan or window. To prevent dehydration, keep cut flowers away from direct sunlight and large appliances as well.
2. Do not put flowers near a bowl of fruit, especially apples, pears, and plums. They emit ethylene gas when ripening, which causes wilting of flowers.
3. Prolong the freshness of the arrangement by spraying with lukewarm water from a mister morning and night.
4. Change the water every day if the arrangement is meant to last a while. Never use chilled water, as cut stems fare best in warm water of about 45°C.
5. Use commercial cut-flower preservatives available in the market.
6. Use clean containers to prevent premature fouling and bacterial growth. Use coloured glass containers if possible the darker the glass, the harder it is for nasty green algae to grow. Do not use aluminium containers for flowers.
7. Re-cut the stems every three days, clean the vase, completely replace the water, and add more preservative.

Designing Flower Arrangements

Decorating with flowers is a creative and stimulating art, which often carries a message or theme and expresses the mood or emotions. Blending together the eight features of good design helps in creating beautiful flower arrangements. An arrangement made keeping these features in mind will turn out to be a beautiful piece of floral art.

Style: Following styles already established by experts ensures a beautiful flower arrangement. There are many styles in flower arrangement and new one are constantly being added, as this is now a professional art Styles can be of various kinds. Based on the angle from which they are seen, the style could be an all-round arrangement or a facing arrangement. Style can be based on amount of space present, type of plant material used, effect of the arrangement; it could be formal; semi-formal, informal or modern or free style. The various styles of flower arrangement are:

Based on the angle: On the basis of the angle from which a flower arrangement is viewed, it can be classified as **all-round arrangement, and facing arrangement (**flat-back arrangement).

Based on the space present: On the basis of the space present in the arrangement, flower arrangements can be classified as mass style which are as follows :

Bunch in a vase: This is the simplest arrangement. The stem bases of the bunch are cut and then the flowers are put in a vase half-filled with water.

Biedermeier: This is a flat or domed mass in a round and shallow container. These flowers may be fresh, dried or artificial. The blooms are arranged to give concentric circles of different colours and there is an outer collar of foliage.

Traditional mass: This is the term for the classic massed arrangement that is held in place by florists' foam or crumpled chicken wire. The first step should be to create a central upright axis with line material and then the dominant flowers should be inserted. The final step is to use filler material to cover nearly all of the line material.

Line style: In this style, open spaces within the boundary of the arrangement are the main feature. Most of the display is line material. The line concept originated in the East and the rules were laid down in China and Japan more than thousands of years ago. The basic feature of a line design is limited use of plant material with support often provided by a pin-holder.

***Ikebana*:** means 'making flower life' in Japanese. This Japanese style has been practised for thousands of years. These arrangements are more than an aesthetic grouping of plant materials. They are symbolic representations of an ideal harmony that exists between earthy and eternal life. It is a 'Japanese flower arrangement' type.

Vertical line: This type of line style is formal, geometric and defined by clear-cut rules. The important feature is the bold line material set vertically to form a central axis.

Triangular shape: This triangle is a popular shape for symmetrical arrangements. The first step is to establish lines of height and width, usually with flowers or foliage of finer form or paler colour. The next step is to establish a focal point of interest with large or darker-coloured flowers. ***Circular shape***: The circular or round shape is loved by mature since a majority of flowers fall into that shape. Arranging flowers in circular designs adds a pleasing element of repetition.

Crescent shape: The crescent is asymmetrical and formal in character. It requires more skill and experience on the part of the arranger than other basic styles. For this arrangement, choose plant materials with pliable stems.

Parallel style: Also called the European style, it spread from Holland. The mechanic here is a rectangular block of florists' foam in a shallow dish. A group of stems arising from it stand vertically. The foam is hidden by a horizontal groundwork of flowers, foliage, fruits and stems.

Based on the type of plant material used: On the basis of the type of plant material used in the arrangement, it can be classified in the following ways.

Foliage arrangement: Nothing does more than cut green foliage to freshen up a room at a minimum time and money. Foliage arrangements have a natural affinity for modern furnishings and contemporary architecture. They do take to a traditional setting also if styled properly and placed in a suitable container.

Dried flower arrangement: Preserved or dried plant material can be arranged in containers either on its own or combined with fresh plant materials. These can be used for permanent or semi-permanent decor. During those months when little is available from the garden and flower prices shoot up in the markets, an arrangement of dried flowers and foliage is extremely useful. Fresh flowers could be added and held in place by the use of wires, test tubes, florist's cones, cello tape, plasticine etc. For drying flowers and foliage, first place the stems in a solution of two parts of water to one part glycerine for two weeks. Dried materials may be painted silver, white, black, or gold.

Based on the effect: The flower arrangement styles discussed so far could be formal, semi-formal, or informal based on the effect they create.

Formal arrangement: This is symmetrical and precise.

Semi-formal arrangement: This is more or less symmetrical in outline, but not in the details of arrangement.

Informal arrangement: This is asymmetrical and 'free' style of flower arrangement.

General Guidelines for Flower Arrangements: The following are some general guidelines for flower arrangement:

1. Make a definite plan for any flower arrangement based on the purpose, area available and location of the arrangement.
2. Select containers, flowers and foliage that express the mood of the room, the occasion, and the colour scheme of the interiors.
3. Use flowers with stems of different sizes and select flowers according to the size of the vase. Arrange the tallest stems first and then others according to the type of arrangement.
4. Large flowers with bright, bold colours can be used in small numbers and at the centre in tall vases, small, short-stemmed flowers may be easily arranged in groups in low vases.
5. Avoid mixing up fresh flowers and artificial flowers.
6. Low containers are suitable for all types of arrangements.
7. Small arrangements look good grouped with other objects and accessories.
8. Pour enough water into the vases.
9. Follow the points given for the care and conditioning of flowers.

Japanese/ Oriental Flower Arrangement

The Japanese lay great emphasis on the art of flower arrangement. People in Japan use flowers to symbolize seasons or particular occasions. In all their arrangements, a single principle is followed, and the most striking characteristic is that they give the impression of naturally growing plants. ***Ikebana*** literally means 'making flowers live' in Japanese. In all such arrangements, Heaven, Man and Earth are represented by means of three main branches. The Japanese use tall vases as well as low bowls. Tall vases are usually made of bamboo, bronze, or pottery. Sometimes the bamboo ones are painted with black lacquer. Low bowls are made of bronze and pottery. For holding flowers, metal holders are used in vases and bowls. A naturally forked branchy is also used to hold the stems in place.

A formal arrangement called the *seika* style has strict rules governing the lengths and angles of the stems. It is basically a triangular arrangement and usually stiff so that all stems arise from a single point. A floating arrangement is called *ukibana* and a basket arrangement is *morimano*. Another classical arrangement in a tall cylindrical vase with a flowing and natural effect is called *nagerie*.

Common Flowers and Foliage

Flowers: Some common flowers used in arrangements are Roses, Lilies, Gladioli, Dahlias, Chrysanthemums, Gerberas, Tulips, Asters, Carnations, Freesia, Tuberoses, Lotus, *Anthurium*, Birds of Paradise, Marigold, Orchids, Irises, Petunia, *Hibiscus*, Poppies, Camellia, Peonies, Hydrangea, *Gypsophila* (baby's breath), Bottle brush, Hollyhocks, Geraniums, Daisies, Larkspurs, Spider Lilies, Water Lilies, Zinnias, Lady's lace.

Foliage: Commonly used foliages are: True ferns, Asparagus ferns, Palm leaves, Umbrella palms, Bamboos, Pine, Cyprus, Goldenrods, Citrus branches, Crotons, Boxwood, Oleander, Ivy, and *Caladium*.

Floral/dry flower arrangements

Dehydrated flowers and plant parts have been used for designing distinctive and artistic greeting cards, landscapes, interior decorative items with dry flowers sealed in glass containers, etc. It can also be used in the preparation of pot pourri, flower baskets, twig baskets front facing arrangements, mirror frames, tables centres etc. Dry flowers and floral crafts have an everlasting value that can be cherished for long periods if they are protected from moisture and dust. Now days the dry flower products are a replacement of various artificial and unnatural ways of decoration. The floral crafts can be made cost effective by using the locally available materials as fillers. The dry flower production is labour intensive provides employment opportunities for a large number of workers and aids in the development of subsidiary industries at developed as well as developing countries.

Tips for Dry Flower Arrangements

- Dry flowers are light in weight, so the container holding the dry flowers should always be weighted with sand, pebbles or gravel to give stability.
- Use wire cutters to shorten stems. Stems can be lengthen by using wooden floral picks
- Never use a bare stub wire in an arrangement

- Arrange the flower in a manner to give them a natural look
- When using clean containers, add marbles, layers of interesting pebbles, shells, or moss to hide the foam
- Think about the size of the space in which the arrangement has to be placed and choose the size and shape of the container accordingly.
- Use dry flowers and foliage with different shapes, colors and textures for a more interesting design
- Always allow some space between dry flowers to prevent a crowded effect
- Make sure that the colors of the flowers are evenly balanced
- If the arrangement is permanent, then dip stems in pan glue, white glue or hot glue before inserting them into foam for greater stability and permanence.

Pot pourri

Pot pourri (pronounced as popu-re) literally means miscellaneous mixture in French. Traditionally used to describe a pretty ceramic container filled with a collection of aromatic fruits, spices as well as petals of flowers that gave a pleasant fragrance as the mixture smoldered through the perforated cover.
Pot pourri is available in big bags or filled into dainty containers. These are placed in containers around the house where their fragrance can gently waft around perfuming the air where Simmering pot pourri container is another popular choice.

Pommanders are essentially ball-shaped containers with perforations around them filled with pot pouri that are hung up in cup boards or placed in the closet to keep the clothes fragrant. Apart from single fragrances like strawberry, lemon and vanilla, pot pourri is available in mixed fragrances that use a variety of different fruit and flower perfumes in unique mixtures. "Pot pourri" a special dry floral arrangement, is very popular in European countries as a decorative pieces and natural room fresheners. Large number of products like rose buds, ferns, pine cones, lily pods, marigold, driftwood and many other items are collected by enthusiastic suppliers as the primary raw material for the floral arrangements. The materials are stored and graded by experts before sending. The materials used for this purpose should be resistant to mould, nontoxic, free from noxious odours and sufficiently robust to withstand mechanical blending. Pot pourri is normally designed in a glass bowl or a ceramic jar or stored in a colourful satin or muslin sachet, while the other arrangements are designed in beautifully coloured or shaped pots. A huge amount of raw materials are exported from India. Market watchers are of the opinion that in view of expanding clientele, lucrative returns and limited competition, more and more entrepreneur are expected to enter this booming business in near future.

Pot pourri fragrances tend to evaporate after a certain time of being kept in open containers. These can be replenished with a couple of drops of pot pouri oils every couple of months which are also available. For pomanders as well as other closed containers fragrances replenishing pallets are also available.

Types of pot pourri

Pot pourri is a mixture of dried, sweet scented plant parts including flowers, leaves, seeds, stems and roots. Two kinds of pot pourri can be made, dry and moist. The dry method is quicker and easier, but the pot pourri does not last as long. The herbs and fruits are to be thoroughly dried to prevent mildew. Both methods require a fixative which is responsible for absorbing aromatic oils and slowly relasing them. Common fixatives include finely ground non iodised salt, iris root (dried rhizomes of iris plant), sweet flag (calamus root), gum benzoine, storax (styax) and amber gris. The fixatives are to be ground finely so that they can better absorb the aromatic oil.

Material used

The materials used for this purpose should be resistant to mould, non toxic and able to withstand mechanical damage. The basis of a pot pourri is the aromatic oils found within the plant. Herbs such as Artemesia, thyme, sage, rosemary, rose, basil, achillea (yarrow), lavender, scented geranium, mint, verbena, anise and fennel can be used for scent. The flowers should be collected at their best when they are most fragrant. In rose, the essential oil is present in glands in the petals where it is stored in an inert form, as a mixture of oil and sugar known as glucoside. This is not released in the bud form, but only when the flower opens and continues till the flower is alive with their thick and leathery petals roses retain their scent for several years after drying and are one of the most important ingredients of any pot pourri.

How to make pot pourri?

Pot pourri can be made by blending together 2 to 3 cups of dried flowers, roots and leaves (herbs and flowers), 2 to 3 table spoons crushed cinnamon, star anise and cloves, ¼ cup dried orange or lemon peel, 2 tablespoons of a fixative and 5 or 6 drops of an essential oil. Mix this into flowers, cones etc. By doing this the fixative has time to really absorb the aroma of the oil. Add the essential oil to the fixative and allow that to blend and age for about 4 weeks. Mix this into the flowers, leaves, cones etc. Those who prefer less sweet pot pourri could replace the orange peel with that of a lemon and use lemon thyme with rosemary. Add some dry leaves of lemon scented geranium and of southernwood, together with a pinch of powdered nutmeg and mix well together. The pot pourri will release the crisp, refreshing scent of lemon. It can be designed in a glass bowl or a ceramic jar or in muslin or in sachets. If an open bowl is used, to retain the perfume in the mixture a polythene is stretched over the top and fastened around with a piece of ribbon, when the room is not in use.

Tips for making a Pot pourri

- To create a unique fragrance, add a few drops of favorite essential oil to the fixative. Because essential oils are so concentrated, be sure to use oils sparingly.
- Fixatives are either ground or powdered. The ground fixative is more suitable and powders leave a film on the glass.

Flower arrangements in glass or plastic containers

Flowers and leaves, after dehydration may be arranged aesthetically and can be used for interior decoration. They are covered air tight with transparent glass/ plastic containers to protect them from atmospheric humidity, wind and dust. A well cleaned and dried transparent container is taken. A slightly over sized glass or plastic disc or plate is taken on which the cut thermocole piece is pasted with little of synthetic resin adhesive (fevicol). Velvet sheet is also cut to the same size and pasted on the thermocole. The flower arrangement with dried flowers and leaves is then made by fixing stems on the thermocole and according to the size of the container. Adhesive is applied on the brims of the container which is inverted over the disc thus accommodating the arrangement. It is then kept in the oven at about 45°C for about half an hour. The bottom 2.5 cm of the container is painted with enamel paint.

Floral crafts with press-dried flowers and foliages

Greeting cards, wall hangings, landscape calendars and such other creative displays can be made by embossing the press dried flowers and foliage on various backgrounds such as velvet paper, handmade paper, linen, velvet cloth and silk. Pre-cut velvet paper or cloth on the trimmed card is pasted leaving a margin all round the card and placed under the table glass for a few minutes to dry. Arrange the flowers and foliage on the velvet of the card one by one with forceps after applying adhesive as sparingly as possible so that when pressed, it does not come out of flowers and leaves. Floral material is gently pressed with finger tips. This card/floral item may again be placed under the glass table top for about an hour. After this it should be kept away from moisture and dust. Using this technique several other items, like floral designs or pictures, landscapes, calendars, etc. may be prepared. Some of the floral items can be framed or laminated.

Basket arrangements

Material required: basket, florist's foam, stub wire, moss, glue gum or adhesives, knife, scissors, etc.

Procedure: Fill the basket with florists foam and cut to size. Glue the foam to the bottom of the basket, if necessary. Secure the foam in place. Choose the moss to coordinate with the arrangement and sprinkle it over the foam. Bend stub wires into hair pin shapes and push them into the foam to hold the moss in position. Allow the moss to dry. It is an integral part of the basket.

Select first wheel of sea lavender/ foliage (uneven number) and arrange them at right angles to the foam, so that they come out of basket horizontally. Fill with more of this. Select flowers which blend well with the colour and texture of the sea lavender/ foliage. Use odd number to create the second wheel of flowers, thus providing the outline for the arrangement. Flower stems with foliage can be used as foliage tiller. Select another flower and fill the same way as did for second wheel, if necessary.

Centre table arrangement

Arrangements of all types of centre table should be low so that they do not obstruct from opposite sides and it should look attractive from all sides. A clear simple design is far better than clumpy decoration with too many flowers. Before inserting stems inside the vase, first the design is to be divided mentally into two or four sections and then the floral material could be divided accordingly. It will help to create uniformity on overall design when observed from top or any side. Inserting flower or foliage with stem from both side and from vase rim is to be carried out. Proper colour combination makes an arrangement pleasing and attractive.

Front facing arrangements

Front facing arrangement is usually kept on side table. Here, emphasis is given on its front appearance. The colour scheme, size of display table, vase size, etc.

are to be taken into consideration. Size of decoration should be proportionate with the display table.

Take a prepared basket (florist's foam covered with moss) which should be heavy enough to provide secure base for the flower arrangement. This is essential in a front facing design because you will be grouping all the flowers along only one face of the basket. Start positioning the dried foliage. Form a fan shape. Let side branches come out horizontally to the basket. Fill up the vase design from outer boundary towards the centre with flowers and foliage. Continue to fill out the shape. When viewed from the side, the foliage and flower should be arranged so that they create a slight curve with the tips of their stems, coming down from the tops of the centre stem to the end of the foliage. Attractive flowers can be used to give a bright and beautiful focal point from which the design will radiate outwards.

Wall mounted arrangements

Free style: A florist's foam wrapped in chicken wire forms the basic structure for the arrangement. A wire loop made out of reel wire attached to the chicken wire act as a hanger. Arrange flowers and foliage in blocks in a free style fashion. The stems should look as though they are radiating out from a central point splaying out to give an uneven edge to the arrangement. Make sure that its shape is evolving correctly when it is viewed from all angles.

Wall vase: Arrangements can also be made in wall vases, made of natural material like terracotta. Take a block of florist's foam and cut it to a size and shape that will fit inside the vase. Spread glue on the edge of the foam and slide it firmly into the vase. Cover the foam with moss. Leave it for at least for a week to allow the moss to dry thoroughly. Otherwise the materials used for arrangement will trap moisture and rot. The vase size, size of flower material and display place has to be proportionate with each other.

Wreaths

The foundation of this arrangement can be a mossed wire, wreath frame or a wire wreath frame. Mossed wire wreath frame can be made using chicken wire. Join with of chicken wire together and stitch the piece with real wire. Fill up sphagnum moss. Fill the desired area and then roll or bend the chicken wire to get the desired shape. Fix the wreath to a wall with a wire loop attached to the chicken wire. Wire wreath frames are readily available. Take sphagnum moss and bind them securely on the wreath frame using reel wire. Attach a wire loop to the frame to act as a hanger. When the moss has dried out, decorate the wreath with flowers of your choice.

Tips for making a Wreath

- Once the foliage dries, spray the finished wreath with extra firm hold hair spray
- Tie a colorful bow over the area where you started and ended the wreath
- Tips for making a Sachet
- The glue used should be preferably hot
- The lace and the felt should be glued nicely edge to edge
- The opening should be sufficient enough to stuff in dry flowers

Mirror frame

Take a piece of rigid backing board and mirrored glass. The mirrored glass should be slightly smaller to the board. Make a hanger, using at the back of the board. Cut strips of florist's form to fit right around the outside of the glass. Glue the foam to the backing board. The foam surface should be slightly higher than the surface of the mirror and thick enough to accommodate flower stems. Arrange the flowers in a massed formation around the mirror to create the frame. Cover all the foam and ensure that the edges of the frame are so well covered so that no backing board is visible. Flower suitable for making mirror frame are hydrangeas, bougainvilleas, etc.

Other arrangements

Dry flowers and plant products are novel in aesthetic properties and are long lasting. Other uses are life-like plants, bouquets, gift boxes, wall hangings, landscapes, refrigerator magnets, embedded in gold or resin to use as jewellery, free standing arrangements like mossed tree and topiary tree, etc.

Tips for making a Bouquet

- Lengthen stems by attaching wires to the ends
- When selecting colors, keep in mind that dried flower colors tend to fade
- Make simple color schemes
- Keep vase colors simple and try not to use vases with small openings.
- Try not to use too many dominant flowers. Instead use more filling material that is less conspicuous in shape and color than the center flower
- Place smaller, lighter flowers higher on the arrangement
- Tips for making a Swag

- Cover the finished end with a ribbon or bow
- To have a longer swag, wire two completed swags together
- A light spray of extra-firm-hold hair spray will keep the swag looking swag fresh for a longer time.

Guidelines for Suitable Flowers and Plant Species Used for Drying and Arrangements

Plant	Specific guidelines and remarks
Acacia	The dried flower cluster is required to be steamed over a kettle for preserving the natural appearance of the flowers.
Acroclinum	Flowers immediately after picking are dried either by embedding or Hang and dry method.
African violet	Embedding of flowers for two weeks in face up position in sand.
Ageratum	Method- Borax (4 days) (Commercial preparation), Sand (2 weeks) Remarks- Embedding of flowers in face down position
Althaea	Plan part- Seed pods (pick when green) Method- hang to dry
Apple	Plant part- Foliage Method: glycerine (4-7 days)
Anemone	Sand is suitable drying material. Careful handling is required due to Fragile nature
Asters	Drying material: Borax Single varieties– 5 days time, Double varieties– 10 days.
Astilbe	Drying material: Borax Method: Hang to dry (4 days)
Baby's Breath	Method: Hang to dry (1-2wks)
Baptisia	Plant part: Foliage Drying method : glycerin (6 days) Plant part: Flowers Method: hand to dry Plant part: Pods Method: shellac
Bells of Ireland	Harvesting time: Cut when lower bells begin to turn Drying material: Borax(4 days) Method: Hang to dry (1 week) Method: Glycerin (2-3 days) Remarks: remove immature tips as they may shrivel; Green cake coloring added to glycerin will keep greenness.
Beech	Plant part- Foliage Method- glycerine (3-10 days) Remarks: Length of treatment will depend on color preferred – they change from green to brown; treat after leaves start to turn for lighter shade; cut green and remove from glycerin in 24 to 36 hours and foliage will remain green

Plant	Specific guidelines and remarks
Bittersweet	Plant part-Berries Methods- shellac Remarks: Should be dried in water to prevent excessive shrinkage and to keep longer Shellac improves their appearance
Bleeding Heart	Plant part- Foliage Method- press drying
Blackberry Lily	Plant part- Fruit Method- shellac and Hang to dry Plant part- Flowers Method- Borax and sand
Boxwood	Plant part- Flowers Method: Glycerin (4 days) upright in water
Butterfly Weed	Plant part- seed pods Drying material: Sand Remarks: difficult to dry
Calendula	Embedding of flowers for two weeks in face up position in sand. This may need diluted glue from top when dry.
Candytuft	Flowers are dehydrated in vertical position in deep containers or in horizontal position in shallow containers
Castor Beans	Plant part- Stalks & seed pod Method- hand to dry Remarks- A light coat of shellac will aid in securing the pods to the stems. Foliage may be sheared to give an oriental appearance
Cattails	Method- Hand to dry (1 to 3 weeks) Remarks- Spray with shellac or hair lacquer; let dry on stems and cut later
Chinese Lantern	Method: Hand to dry Remarks- If picked green, they will remain green
Chrysanthemum	Plant part- flowers Method- Sand and Borax (7 to 10 days) Method- Silica gel method (5days) Remarks- Yellow flowered varieties retain their colour, while red and mauve coloured flowers turn dull and dark. Not all chrysanthemums are satisfactory for drying
Christmas Rose	Method- Borax (5 days) Remarks- Wire stems before drying
Clematis	Plant parts- Flowers Method- borax (5 days) Plant parts- Seed pods Method- glycerin (24 hours) Remarks- Large flowers are difficult to treat, glue petals to stem before drying. Seed pods are most interesting to dry.
Clover (red)	Plant part- flowers Method-Hang to dry
Cockscomb	Plant part- flowers with stem (Cut when green) Method- Hang to dry (1-3 weeks)

Plant	Specific guidelines and remarks
Coral Bells	Plant part-Flowers Method-borax or press drying Remarks-Wild varieties are most desirable
Cornflower	Plant part-Flowers Method-borax (5 days) or Hang ear to dry Remarks- Pick when mature and pull back husks
Daffodils	Plant part-Flowers Method-Borax (3 days) Remarks- Remove stems, treat and store in de-moist crystals
Daisies	Plant part- flower Method- Upside down in borax Field daisy (3 days), Shasta (6 days), Gloriosa (5 days) Remarks- Cone-like center of flower may be used after drying
Dahlia	Plant parts- small flowers (5 days); large flowers (10 days) Method- Borax Remarks- Small flowered types are more suited for drying. Red colour becomes darker, white, yellow and orange flowers retain their colour after drying. Place shredded waxed paper between some of the petals,
Delphinium	Plant part- spikes (5 day), florets (3 days) Method- Sand and borax
Dogwood	Plant part- Bracts Method- borax (4 days) Plant part- Foliage Method- glycerin (7-10 days)
Dock	Method- Hang to dry or pick dry Remarks- Changes color in different stages of growth
Dusty Miller	Method- Hang to dry
Euonymus	Plant part- Foliage Method- glycerin (5 days) Plant part- Berries Method- shellac
False Dragon Head	Plant part- Foliage Method- Borax (3-5 days); Hang to dry
Ferns	Plant part- Foliage Method- Press drying
Fennel	Method- Hang to dry Bright green and feathery
Feverfew	Method- Borax (3 days) Dry upside-down
Firethorn	Plant part- Berries Method- shellac Remarks- Remove foliage when treating; dry in water

Plant	Specific guidelines and remarks
Forsythia	Plant part- Foliage Method- glycerin Plant part- Flowers Method- borax Remarks-Turns light to dark brown or purple-red
Gardenia	Plant part- Foliage Method- glycerin
Gerbera	To be kept in face up position while embedding in sand. Petals are to be reinforced when dry. Yellow, orange and pink flowers retain their colour after drying.
Gladiolus	Sand: Commercial preparation Individual flowers are cut and processed. Flowers are to be kept face up while embedding in sand.
Globe thistle	Method- Hang to dry Remarks- Cut before bracts have fully opened; allow some foliage to remain on the stem
Goldenrod	Plant part- flower Method- Hand to dry (1-3 weeks) Remarks- Pick before upper florets open
Grains – (wheat, oats, rye etc)	Method- Hang to dry (1-3 weeks)
Hedge apple	Plant part- Fruit Method- oven dry and Air dry Remarks- Pick when green, it will turn brown when dried in an oven, if hung in a warm location it will remain green.
Helichrysum	Plant part- flower Method- Hand and dry method. Remarks- These flowers can be easily air dried or oven dried. If embedded in sand, the flowers, along with stems, may be kept in shallow containers horizontally or in deep containers in vertical position
Hibiscus	To be kept in face up position while embedding in sand for three weeks. Only medium sized flowers are to be selected
Hollyhocks	Method- Borax (6 days) Remarks- Becomes transparent on drying
Huckleberry	Plant part- Foliage Method- glycerin (7-10 days)
Hydrangea	Plant part- flower Method- Hang to dry (1-3 weeks); Borax (4 days) Remarks: Peegee (flower) picked in September, Pink and blue florets type (August) or when blooms are cured on bush
Iris	Plant part- Seed pods Method- shellac
Ixora	Plant part- flowers Method- Press drying is better for these flowers

Plant	Specific guidelines and remarks
Juniper	Method- Glycerin (7-10 days)
Lentana	Method- Borax (3-5 days) Remarks- Colors may change
Larkspur	Method- Hang to dry; Borax (4 days)
Laurel	Method- Glycerin (10 days)
Leucothoe	Method- Glycerin (10 days)
Ligustrum	Method- Glycerin (7-10 days)
Lilac	Method- Hang to dry; Borax (3 weeks)
Lily	Plant part- Seed pods Method- shellac
Lily of the Valley	Plant part- Flower Method- borax (3 days) Plant part- Foliage Method- oven dry Remarks- Clean the foliage and bake in an oven at 250°C for 15 minutes
Magnolia	Plant part- Leaves Method- glycerin (10 days- 3weeks) Plant part- Flower Method- borax in upside down position Plant part- Seed pods Method- shellac
Mountain Ash	Plant part- Fruit Method- Hang to dry
Marigold	Plant part- Flower Method- Borax (7-10 days) and Hang to dry Remarks- To be kept in face up position while embedding for two weeks in sand. The petals may require gluing from underneath at the base of the petals
Milkweed	Method- Hang to dry Remarks- Cut when pale green
Mussandra	Method- press drying Remarks- Yellow colour is retained well
Narcissus	To be kept in face up position while embedding for two weeks in sand in shallow containers.
Nymphaea	To be kept in face up position while embedding for two weeks in sand. Both insie and outside surfaces of all petals should be completely dry.
Okra	Method- Hang to dry
Pansy	Plant part- flower Method- Press (10 days), Sand and Borax (4 days) Remarks-To be kept in face up position while embedding for three weeks in sand for short stemmed type. To be kept in horizontal position if long stemmed. This is also a good material for press drying.
Passion flower	Plant part- seed pods & flower Method- Borax (8 days)

Plant	Specific guidelines and remarks
Peony	Plant part- flower Method- Borax (5 days) Plant part- foliage Method- glycerin (7 days)
Pine	Plant part- foliage Method- Glycerin (10 days) Remarks-Cut from tree when green
Polygonium	Method- Hang to dry Remarks- Cut before maturing; remove foliage
Poppies	Plant part- Seed pods Method- hang to dry
Poplar (white)	Plant part- Foliage Method- Press drying Remarks- stand in a jar to dry
Queen Anne's Lace	Method- Borax (5 days)
Roses	Plant part- flower Method- Hang to dry; Borax (5 days) Sand (Commercial preparation), Silica gel drying (4 days). Remarks- If embedded in sand, to be kept in face up position for two weeks. Best when buds are half-open; lay buds horizontally. Plant part- fruit (hips) Method- Shellac
Russian Olive	Method- Glycerin (6 weeks)
Salvia	Method- Borax (4 days); Hang to dry (1-2 weeks) Remarks- Blue (deeper in color); Red (turns pink or orange)
Santolina	Method- Hang to dry
Smoke tree	Plant part- Flowers Method- hang to dry
Snapdragons	Plant part- Florets Method- borax (4 days) Remarks- Dry each separately, wire florets before drying, difficult to dry
Statice	Plant part- flower Method- Hang to dry, embedded in sand or are press dried
Stock	Method- Borax (4 days)
Strawflower	Method- Hang to dry Remarks- Cut when flowers are half open
Sugar Cane	Plant part- Pods Method- hang to dry
Sumac	Plant part- Seed pods Method- hang to dry
Sweet Gum	Method- Hang to dry
Sweet pea	Method- embedding Remarks- To be kept in face up position for two weeks in sand.

Plant	Specific guidelines and remarks
Sweet William	Entire flower cluster can be processed. To be kept in face up position while embedding for two weeks in sand.
Sycamore	Plant part- Foliage Method-; glycerin (8-10 days)
Thistle	Dry upright in jars
Tulip	Plant part- Pod Method- Borax (6 days) Remarks- Cut before fully open; use Elmer's Glue to secure petals before drying
Verbena	To be kept in face down position, while embedding for three weeks in sand
Viburnums	Plant part- Foliage Method- glycerin (3-5 days) Plant part- Berries Method- shellac
Water Lily	Method- Borax (10 days)
Yucca	Plant part- Leaves Method-: glycerin (5 to 7 days) Plant part- Seed pods Method- Hang to dry
Yarrow	Method- Borax (5 days), Hang to dry Remarks- These may be liquid dyed. To prevent shuttering spraying with clear plastic spray is suggested
Zinnias	Plant part- flowers Method- Borax (6 days); Dry upside down in mixture Remarks- To be kept in face up position while embedding in sand for two weeks. Petals are to be brushed before or after drying with coloured powdered chalk to restore velvety smoothness

Waste utilization in Dry Flower Industry

Dry flower industry facilitates the usage of several items, which are considered as waste in normal course. Such materials include:

1. Dried fruits of guava and custard apple which continue to hand on plants
2. Dried grasses as a whole e.g. Eragrostis uniloides. Themeda triandra
3. Citrus fruit rind
4. Dried cotton husks
5. Bamboo leaf sheaths
6. Wild oak leaved fem (Drynaria quercifolia) found on avenue/ forest trees

7. Wild non edible fungi which grow and dry on fallen forest plants and trees
8. Dropped petals of scented flowers such as citrus
9. Seed coats of pistachio nuts
10. Leaves from weeds, which are on different shapes, size and texture
11. Coconut spathes, palm caps etc
12. Forest twigs infested with white ants and driftwood
13. Dried vegetables like okra
14. Minor forest products like stems, twigs, bark, thorns/spines, roots, lichens, mosses, selaginellas, ferns etc.
15. Onion peel
16. Twines and twigs of forest weeds
17. Other washes like broken china ware and terracotta pots
18. Coloured seeds of ornamental trees such as *Delonix regia*
19. Pine cones
20. Dropped seeds coats of wild almond
21. Inflorescence of wild Celosia and Amaranthus.

All the items can be used in dry flower arrangement including pot pourri. Broken China ware and terracotta pots are quite suitable as bases in flower arrangement. Dry flower activity, whether collection of waste materials of its utilization in dry flower arrangement is labour intensive, leading to generation of job opportunities for many people. Trade of finished products also generates direct and indirect employment.

7.3 Architectural Landscaping

Landscaping is a branch of ornamental horticulture having Aesthetic and beautifying value which freshens up the atmosphere, enhances the look of the environment and improves beauty of land. In the area of landscaping, it is beneficial to know about ground covers (grasses etc), hedging plants, and focus plants that will complement one another.

A garden by definition is a piece of land devoted to growing flowers, fruits, vegetables, shrubbery and turf. Gardens brighten their surroundings and they add to the beauty of the landscape. The types of flowers that can be grown in a garden depend on the size of the garden, its location and the amount of sunshine and shade it gets.

Essential Components of Landscaping

The essential components of landscaping are hedges, lawn, flowerbeds, shrubbery and trees etc.

Hedges: A garden becomes much more attractive when its boundary is delineated by a hedge rather than a wall. The two most common shrubs used for making up hedges in Indian gardens are henna and hibiscus. Periodic trimming of the hedges is essential for these species. A hibiscus hedge takes up more space than the slip and straight henna. The yellowish green foliage of *Duranta* is also making popular as a hedge row plant. Bougainvillea plants also make good hedges, and also bears magnificent bunch of flowers in various hues.

Flowerbeds, shrubbery and trees: It is always advisable to keep one type of flowering plant confined to one bed or one set of pots, arranged in an attractive pattern and kept well-trimmed. The maintenance of these plants like height management and uniformity is important. Planting annual flowering varieties in beds and seasonal in pots can be displayed only when in full bloom (returned to the greenhouse when dormant) is a practical option. It saves manpower and the flower beds remains in full bloom throughout the year.

Arrangement of flower beds: The spacing of different flowering plants is of vital importance. A garden can be made more attractive if instead of treating all flowering plants equally; prominence is given to one variety for instance to add emphasis of these main plants. The intermingling of flowering plants at random without following any pattern of arrangement will affect adversely the beauty of the landscape garden. In selecting larger trees for the garden, instead of the usual ashoka and gulmohur, one can plant *Nycanthes* (parijat), *Compaita guencensis, Michelia champaca*, and the plants which have fragrant blossoms. 'Pride of India' *Lagerstroemia speciosa* is another good option, whose purple flowers are a treat for the eyes. If creepers are preferred, jasmine and *Passiflora* are a sensible option.

Lawns: A lawn is an expanse of closely mowed, grass covered land. Apart from its visual appeal, lawns absorb and hold water, which helps reducing water run-off and improves water quality in the garden soil. Lawns also have a significant cooling effect, provide oxygen, trap dust and dirt, promote healthful micro-organisms, prevent soil erosion and filter out rainwater contaminants.

Pathways: Where the garden is fairly large, as in most hotel properties, care should be taken to provide pathways among the flowerbeds. These afford more visibility to the flowers as well as making the approach to the plants easier for visitors. Small shrubs with attractive flowers or leaves should be grown on either sides of the pathways so as to act as a border for both the flowerbeds and the pathways.

Selection and sowing of seeds: Seeds that are older than one season can become inferior in quality and should not be used. Seeds sold by a reputed supplier or nursery should be preferred. Never wash roughly or 'treat' the seeds unless instructed by the supplier. Sow seeds in a shallow trough or tray, lightly mixed with soil in such a way that some seeds are exposed and some buried. Do not water until the next day, when a slight sprinkling of water is required. Water the soil fully only when the surface soil begins to lose its dampness; but do not let the soil dry up either.

When the seedlings have grown to nearly 1 inch, replant them in another trough, separating the seedlings into regular, spaced rows, with a gap of at least 2 inches between seedlings. Before attempting to uproot the seedlings, make sure that the soil is damp. While handling the seedlings, pull them by the leaf and not by the stem, since the tender stem can break beyond repair. In areas where there is a menace of locusts or birds, it is advisable to cover the seedlings with wire netting or other appropriate coverings that do not hinder light and air. When the seedlings grow to about 4 inches in height, they can be replanted in garden beds or pots, singly or in twos.

Pots and containers: Three following layers should be laid down inside the pot:

Gravel: The lowest layer should be filled with gravel, consisting of large stones. This is to avoid water logging. The gravel, in conjunction with the drainage hole, helps to remove excess water from the pot.

Fibrous layer: Just above the gravel layer, there should be a layer of plant fibre, ideally coconut husk. The fibre layer store a fair amount of water, but does not allow waterlogging. Its function is to act as a filter for the excess water in the soil above it.

Soil: The soil is the top layer, in which the sapling is planted. The soil should always be moist and loose. A sufficient amount of sand should be mixed into the soil layer. To this, an ample amount of manure should be added to get an ideal pot.

Sapling selection: While buying potted saplings, one should aim to buy those that are neither too small nor too big for their pots. Never buy a sapling that has roots growing out of the drainage hole in the pot. This means it has already outgrown its pot and the root ball is too dense. Also avoid any plant whose foliage is spilling over the rim of the pot. When buying a sapling in a polythene bag, check the quality of the soil in it, soil should not be too wet or too dry. Make sure that there is no fungus on the sapling or on the surface of the soil. There should not be any green 'film' on the soil surface either. Buy saplings and plants from a reputed nursery.

Soil: Tillage of the soil is equally important. This provides adequate aeration, which is necessary for the roots of the plants to breathe. While tilling soil on which plants are already standing, utmost care should be taken that it should not harm the roots of the standing plants. Watering the soil before tillage is essential and try not to rake close to the stand plant.

Manuring/Composting: Compost and dung make ideal manure for gardens. The urine of the cow is also ideal for plants. The use of chemical fertilizers should be discouraged. It has been proved that these fertilizers in the long run 'harden' the soil. Compost is formed by the decomposition of organic matter by the action of a mixed population of micro-organisms in a warm, moist, and aerobic environment over a period of time. The use of compost should be encouraged in preference to chemical fertilizers. The benefits of using compost are:

1. Compost improves the soil texture and structure of both clayey and sandy soils.
2. It increases the organic matter (humus) in the soil.
3. It rectifies the micronutrient deficiency in the soil.
4. It acts as a soil conditioner and maintains soil health.
5. It reduces the susceptibility of top soil to wind and water erosion.
6. It increases crop flower and fruit yields.
7. It increases the uptake of macro and micro nutrients by the plants.
8. It saves the cost of fertilizer by more than 10 per cent.
9. It balances the pH value of the soil and is eco-friendly.

Vermicompost : Another eco-friendly option is the use of vermicompost. Vermicompost is natural organic manure composed of the excreta of earthworms fed on scientifically decomposed organic wastes such as the dung of cattle and other animals, coir pith, farm wastes, urban garbage such as paper and rags and a variety of agro-industrial waste. It enriches the soil as well as promoting plant growth, and confers on the plants all the benefits of the more common garden compost.

Bio-fertilizers: The use of bio-fertilizers is also beneficial to plants. These are distinct strains of micro-organisms that enhance the productivity of the soil, whether by fixing atmospheric nitrogen, or by dissolving soil phosphorus so as to make it available to plants, or stimulating plant growth through the synthesis of growth promoting substances. Bio-fertilizers have the ability to mobilize nutritionally important elements from non-usable forms into usable ones. Indian soils normally have a low population of nitrogen fixing bacteria.

Watering: The water requirements of a plant are not the same throughout its life. Here are some thumb rules regarding the watering of plants: 1) **Check the soil humidity:** slight pressure on the soil surface leaves a finger imprint on the soil and the soil looks damp and dark, watering can be avoided for that day. On the other hand, if the soil surface crumbles at the touch and the surface looks cracked, it shows that watering is needed. 2) **Be consistent in watering:** Too much water will only result in flooding and the washing away of manure and nutrients. Adequate and consistent watering for nearly a week is the only way to reliably restore plant health. 3) **Water just enough, and not more:** When a plant is over-watered, its roots begin to rot and results in yellowing of the leaves. When a plant is under-watered, its leaves begin to crumble and dry up. In case of potted plants, care should be taken to sprinkle only as much water on the soil surface as will penetrate the soil in the pot to a halfway depth and not reach the bottom. 4) **Water leaves in the evening:** Spraying of leaves must be done only in the evening. Some leafy plants however can grow even in shade or indirect sunlight. Where direct and strong sunlight poses a threat to plants, adequate arrangements should be made to give them enough shade. Exposure to strong sunlight for a prolonged period may prove harmful to delicate plants.

Planning a good landscape

The landscape should be (1) functional (2) maintainable, (3) environmentally sound, (4) cost effective and (5) visually pleasing.

Landscaping starts with a base plan, which is developed from the information collected about the site. Information is obtained from many sources and involves communicating with many people. The base planning process includes site surveys, site analysis, and study of site plans, structural and utility blueprints.

Landscape Design: Once the base plan is ready, the landscape designing sequence begins. There are four steps in the landscape designing sequence: (1) bubble diagrams, (2) concept plans, (3) draft designs, (4) final landscape design.

(1) **Bubble diagrams:** A bubble diagram defines the spaces that are identified on the base plan. Initially, the bubbles on it roughly correspond to what

will eventually be a specific physical space in the landscape, but they are not specific and are without detail. A designer may sketch many bubble diagrams before the most suitable one is identified. Space that need to be located on the bubble diagram include patios and decks, entryways and gardens, ponds and water features, lawns or turf, shrubbery and flower beds, container grouping, and so on.

(2) **Concept plans:** Concept plans are more detailed than bubble diagrams; the shapes of the spaces now begin to look like what the actual spaces in the completed landscape will look like. While developing effective spaces in a concept plan, large spaces should be planned first. The larger spaces that should be considered first in a concept plan are ponds, woods, lawns, large areas of ground cover, and parking lots. Smaller spaces that are impacted by these larger spaces include decks and patios, walkways and paths, pools, plant beds and borders.

(3) **Draft designs:** This stage continues to define in greater specificity what has been envisages in the concept plan. The rough draft is reviewed and revised until the designer is satisfied with the results. The spaces created in the concept plan now have specific forms and functions. It is important to assign specific spaces to the plants to be used in the draft design. The plant spaces are usually identified by a specific classification (tree, shrub, annual flowers, etc) or by their function (screen planting, foundation plants). The location of these plant spaces on the draft design helps determine the types of plants or plant grouping. Plants with important functions and larger trees are usually located first on the draft design.

(4) **Final landscape design:** In finalizing the completed landscape design, the designers use graphics and symbols rather than words. Different symbols are used to indicate different types of plants- evergreens, deciduous trees, groundcover etc.

7.4 Indoor Plants

Indoor plants are appreciated for their ability to add charm and liveliness to the public areas such as lobbies and corridors. They should be chosen with care, so that their colours, shapes and size fit in the space. One should not hesitate to take advice from an expert horticulturist, gardener, or nursery manager on matters such as the suitable types of plants for a space or any special treatment they may require.

Care of Indoor Plants: Most of indoor plants require regular attention like watering, re-potting, and cleaning. In addition, indoor plants should generally be placed away from draughts as far as possible and never kept near a window or doorway on cold nights without placing a layer of newspaper between the plant and the glass panes.

Watering: The amount and frequency of watering depends on the kind of plant, the weather, and the type of heating in the room. Always use water that is neither too chill nor too warm, preferably rainwater and pour it into the soil, not onto the foliage. Too much water can be dangerous to many plants and it is a good idea to help drain the soil by putting a few stones at the bottom of the pot. On the other hand, the soil should never be allowed to become dry and powdery either.

Potting and re-potting: It is best to consult experts and to refer to a reliable book on these important points. In general, use a light soil mix for potting plants a good mixture is made of equal quantities of leaf mould and a peaty soil containing plenty of fibre with half the quantity of sharp sand. If the roots form a close network within the soil and begin to come out of the pot, the plant probably needs re-potting compost.

Placement of Indoor Plants: Small plants look nice grouped together, in case of more exotic plants, a shelf in a warm place is ideal. Attractive and inexpensive jardinieres are available in metal and cane. Climbing plants can often be trained across a wall or up a frame made of cane and bamboo. An ordinary garden trellis can be used as a room-dividing screen, with plants trained up it or hung from it in holders.

Popular indoor plants: Some popular flowering and non flowering indoor plants are discussed below:

1. Climbing plants: *Cisus antarctica 'grandidentala' and Cissus straita; Philodendron, Plumbago capensis, Rhoicissus rhomboidea (grape ivy).*
2. *Trailing or spreading plants: Chlorophytum elatum 'variegatum' (spider plant), Hedera (ivy), Peperomia glabberima, Tradescantia (silver queen).*
3. Low-growing plants: *Begonia rex*, Japanese fatsia and Irish ivy, *Maranta, rubber plant (Ficus elastic), Cacti and other succulents.*
4. *Greenhouse and florists's plants: Azalea, Begonia, Cineraria, Cyclamen, Hydrangea, Primula etc.*

Some popular flowering and non flowering indoor plants are discussed below :

Climbing plants Some common climbing plants are as follows :

Cisus antarctica 'grandidentala' and Cissus straita These are fast-growing plants with notched, oval leaves. They need a cool room, rich soil, and good light.

Philodendron Most species in this genus are well adapted to growing indoors. They have glossy, leathery leaves and aerial roots that can be trained up a wall or trellis. These plants prefer warmth, but will stand cool conditions; they like plenty of water.

Plumbago capensis This quick-growing plant has small, oval leaves and blue flowers. It does not tolerate temperatures below 7^0C.

Rhoicissus rhomboidea (grape ivy) This tendril-climber with glossy leaves arranged in threes requires a fair amount of water and rich soil.

Trailing or spreading plants Let us now look at some trailing and spreading plants used in hotels.

Chlorophytum elatum 'variegatum' (spider plant) The rosettes of long, narrow, pale-green leaves striped with white or silver are very adaptable, and particularly good for a north facing aspect.

Hedera (ivy) These trail very gracefully and can also be made to climb. The species *H. helix* is hardier than many others of this genus and is best for an unheated room - but all the ivies are very easy to manage.

Peperomia glabberima This plant has red stems and long, fleshy flowers with spikes; other varieties have trailing stems with small leaves. In a warm, moist atmosphere, they produce flowers, but also thrive in cooler conditions. Low-growing and bushy varieties of Peperomia are also available.

Tradescantia (silver queen and wandering Jew species) Excellent trailer and easily grown in baskets, this plant has pale green leaves with silver- white veins.

Low-growing plants Low growing plants are discussed below :

Begonia rex Its attractive foliage needs constant warmth, humidity, and frequent spraying, grows best in country districts.

X Fatschedera lizei A hybrid of Japanese fatsia and Irish ivy, this plant with pointed leaves is hardy and easy to grow.

Maranta The attractively marked leaves of these plants need heat and moisture; but if kept in a constant temperature, can survive fairly cool conditions.

Tolmiea menziesii (piggyback plant) This plant has pale green, heart-shaped leaves. Given some shade and plenty of water, it is very easy to grow.

India-rubber plants These popular indoor plants have become a part of the contemporary interiors owing to their statuesque apearance and undemanding habit of growth.

Ficus elastica This typically has shiny oval leaves; the F. elastica 'decora' has larger leaves with red undersides. Other plants in the genus are F. elastica 'variegata', with yellow markings, and F. chauvieri, which has wavy- edged leaves with yellow veins. They prefer warmth, but will bear cool conditions. They need plenty of water in spring and summer but very little in winter.

Cacti and other succulents These can be grown successfully without constant warmth, but they do need as much sun as possible, so keep them in a south-facing window. They like dry air and a minimum of watering.

Greenhouse and florists's plants Lovely as these are, these hothouse types are not easy to manage. Their period of flowering is usually fairly short and, failing a greenhouse, they cannot be easily made to flower again. Their short lives can, be prolonged by proper care.

Azalea Keep the root ball moist by standing the pot in a bowl of water. Stand it is an evenly warm temperature, out of draughts. On no account give it water containing lime.

Begonia Water frequently and spray.

Cineraria Water frequently. It will stand fairly cool temperatures.

Cyclamen Best bought in early autumn. Avoid wetting the tuber when watering. To revive a flagging plant, stand the pot on a block of wood in a large bowl and pour boiling water round the block; the stem will revive the plant, which can then be watered throughly. Pull out any decayed leaves and flower stalks by their sockets.

Hydrangea This set of plants need plenty of water and overhead spraying, but they like dry air, yet hate draughts.

Primula These comparatively long-flowering plants may survive from year to year if kept at a cool temperature; watered frequently but drained well; and, if necessary, transferred to a large pot.

Pest and diseases

Some insects are so small that their presence is not noticed until the plant shows signs of ill health. Suspicious symptoms are : mottling or yellowing of leaves; a fine white network like a cobweb; or mildew which produces a whitish powder on the leaves.

Professional Maintenance of Indoor Plants

The executive housekeeper must ensure that the following factors are kept in mind for the professional maintenance of indoor plants :

Arrangement Plants and flowers should be arranged according to the original plan, which should include a detailed description of which plants go where. The light and heat requirements of the plants should be considered at the initial stage. Foliage textures should be specified and each plant should have the structure, shape, appearance, size, and edging that had been specified.

Correct Height Selection of plants of the correct height is important. In case of groupings, the shorter plants should be in front. If the grouping can be seen from all sides, it must be well balanced throughout and built up at the centre. Keep the scale of the surroundings in mind when choosing the plant heights -- a three foot plant is good for a position next to a desk, but a plant of at least six feet height must be chosen if it is meant to be viewed from the point of entry into a room or restaurant across the room.

Containers Plant containers must be appropriately selected to blend with the overall design of the area. While choosing containers for different areas, the light, temperature, humidity, and desired soil condition must be considered. Large containers, with big plants inside, must be top dressed with moss or grass covering so as to avoid soil exposure.

Watering schedules Separate schedules for watering in winter and summer are required to keep plants in good condition. Contrary to popular belief, even the watering of plants requires specific skills and knowledge. Choose a can with a long, thin spout so that the water can be directed onto the soil without splashing the plant itself.

Misting and spraying Misting is beneficial for a lot of plants. A small hand-held spray bottle with nozzle should be good enough to do the job of keeping them healthy.

Reconditioning schedules Feeding is important to all plants. For this, they need to be taken back to the greenhouse and exxchanged with another set of plants. After each set of plants has been indoors for around two weeks, it needs to be taken to the greenhouse and reconditioned to keep it healthy and growing.

Trimming and dead-heading The regular grooming of plants is very important in a hospitality property. All dead flowers and leaves need to be removed regularly.

Treating An occasional light spray of eco-friendly pesticides will keep plants safe from pests.

7.5 Bonsai

Bonsai is a horticultural art that is believed by some authorities to have originated in China, from where Buddhist monks spread this art to Korea and then to Japan. The use of bonsais to beautify interiors is an innovative trend and now a day's bonsai development is gaining special attention. The idea was originated in Japan, though potted plants were grown in China as early as 1000 BC, the art of true bonsai making started only around 600 BC. The ancient proponents of this art believed that the miniaturization and training into auspicious shapes of trees and plants conferred certain divine powers on them. *Bonsai* literally means 'a plant in a tray'. It is a creative art where the raw material is a living thing, a tree or a plant. The art of bonsai differs from the simple growing of potted plants in many aspects. In bonsai development, the shape and properties of a full-grown tree or a plant as found in nature are sought to be copied exactly in miniature.

The practice of bonsai development incorporates a number of techniques either unique to bonsai or, if used in other forms of cultivation, applied in unusual ways that are particularly suitable to the bonsai domain. These techniques include:

- *Leaf trimming*, the selective removal of leaves (for most varieties of deciduous tree) or needles (for coniferous trees and some others) from a bonsai's trunk and branches.
- *Pruning* the trunk, branches, and roots of the candidate tree.
- *Wiring* branches and trunks allows the bonsai designer to create the desired general form and make detailed branch and leaf placements.
- *Clamping* using mechanical devices for shaping trunks and branches.
- *Grafting* new growing material (typically a bud, branch, or root) into a prepared area on the trunk or under the bark of the tree.

- *Defoliation*, which can provide short-term dwarfing of foliage for certain deciduous species.
- *Deadwood bonsai techniques* called *jin* and *shari* simulate age and maturity in a bonsai.

Elements of Bonsai: Three elements that make a good bonsai form are *pot, soil, and the plant.* These should be in the proper proportion and should complement each other.

Pots: Pots for holding bonsai should be chosen carefully. Both ceramic and terracotta pots are available. In Japan and China, ceramic pots are used for bonsai making. These pots come in various shapes like round, oval, square, triangular and hexagonal. The pot selected should suit the tree that is to be made into a bonsai. If the tree is tall and slender, the length of the pot should be two-third or three-fourth the height of the tree. If the tree is short with low spreading branches, then the pot should be three quarters of the width of the tree. Upright and gently slanting trees are often placed in a rectangular or oval pot whereas, thick trunked trees and those with dark foliage look best in heavy pots.

Soil: The ideal potting mixture for bonsai is river sand, red soil, and compost in the proportion 2:1:4.

The tree/plant: Most important element in bonsai making. Any tree or shrub can be made into a bonsai, but those with small leaves look better as bonsai. Even succulents can be made into bonsai. Plants of the *Ficus* genus also give early results. *Ficus benjamina, Ficus bengalensis* and *Ficus religiosa* from this family are some of the popular species for bonsai. Junipers make excellent bonsai, with their beautiful foliage. Fruit bearing and flowering plants are also good for bonsai making.

Converting a tree into a Bonsai: With some aesthetic sense, patience and a pinch of common sense, anybody can make a bonsai of any tree that is common in that geographical region. The trees or plants having aesthetic value are generally used for bonsai making. In addition, trees with small flowers and fruits are favoured. Open spaces between the branches and foliage masses are also aesthetically necessary. Transplanting of plants in bonsai containers after cutting roots, trees growing in the wild may be stunted by nature followed by pruning and cutting into attractive shapes.

Care of Bonsai: Once the tree has been planted in the container, it needs constant attention. Watering is very important even for succulents, which generally need less water. The pot being shallow, ideally watering should be done three times a day during summer; chemical fertilizers should be avoided and only dried and powdered cow dung, bone meal, and neem cake are ideal food for bonsai.

Repotting the plant should be done after pruning the excess roots. The pot should be filled with a new potting mixture, surrounded by a layer of sand so that the new roots can grow easily. It is a sign that the bonsai has become pot bound when the leaves turn yellow, the plant looks unhealthy, and new roots are not coming up. Re-potting can be done once or twice a year. The first re-potting can be in June-July and the next in January-February.

The bonsai can be shaped according to one's own imagination by using aluminium wires or copper wires. Wiring helps the tree to look naturally 'weathered', though it needs much time and patience.

Styles of Bonsai: Bonsai can be arranged in different styles. Some of the popular styles are listed here.

1. **Informal upright style:** In this style, a single tree grows straight up.
2. **Windswept style:** In this style, the bonsai appears like a tree that grows near the coastline and has been constantly battered by the wind.
3. **Root-over-rock style:** Trees growing over rocks, exposing some of their root structure, are always fascinating. *Ficus* spp are more suited to this style of arrangement.
4. **Exposed root style:** Here, the roots can be seen above the pot rim. *Adenium*, though a succulent, is best suited to this style.
5. **Cascade style:** In this style, tall pots are used so that the branches are hanging down below the rim.
6. **Multiple-trunk style:** This can be created in a number of ways. For instance, it may be achieved by cutting a deciduous tree almost down to the ground and letting it spring up again and again.
7. **Broom style:** This style looks like a broom when the plant shed off all its leaves in winter.

7.6 Lawn Management

A quality lawn is one of the strongest elements in any landscape design. It can be both beautiful and functional. A turf will prevent soil erosion by wind and by water and also beautify the land. The grass, by giving off water in a process called transpiration, will keep the air cooler around your home. Turf grasses are often divided into two groups: warm season and cool-season grasses.

The common warm-season grasses are bermuda, carpet grass, centipede, and zoysia. Examples of cool-season grasses are bent, bluegrass, fescue and rye.

A lawn is a closely mown, grass covered land. Apart from its visual appeal, lawn absorbs and holds water, which helps reducing water runoff and improves water quality in the garden soil. Lawns also have a significant cooling effect, provide oxygen, trap dust and dirt, promote healthful micro-organisms, prevent soil erosion and filter out rainwater contaminants. The basics of maintaining a healthy lawn are:

Soil: Lawns grow best in loamy soils that have a mix of clay, silt, and sand. Addition of organic matter, such as compost and grass clippings, benefits any type of soil. The soil's pH checked with a pH tester, should be between 6.5 and 7.0 which is just slightly acidic. If the soil is too acidic, it will need a sprinkling of lime. Sulphur can be added to soil which is not acidic enough.

Selection of grass: Choose a locally adapted grass. Grasses vary in the type of climate they prefer, the amount of water and nutrients required, shade tolerance etc. An experienced gardener can recommend the grass best adapted for use in given area. Some turf species (hybrid Bermuda grass, Zoysia grasses) are limited to vegetative propagation by sod, sprigs or plugs because seed is not available or does not germinate true-to-type. Other turf species establishment by seed are bahia grass, centipede grass, carpet grass, common Bermuda grass, tall fescue, bluegrass and ryegrass). A quality lawn can be established by either method if the site is properly prepared and maintained.

Comparison of the major grasses grown for lawns:

	Bermuda	Carpet	Centipede	Tall Fescue*	Zoysia
Establishment methods	sod, sprigs, plugs, seed	seed, sprigs	seed, sod, sprigs, plugs	seed	sod, sprigs, plugs, seed
Maintenance level	High	low	low	Moderate	High
Mowing ht. (in)	¾ to 1½	1 to 2	1 to 2	2½ to 3½	¾ to 2
Mowing frequency	very high	low	low	high	low-medium
Soil condition	wide range	acid	acid	wide range	wide range
Color	Medium dark	light	light	Medium dark	Medium dark
Texture	fine	medium	medium	medium to coarse	medium-fine
Disease tendency	low	low	low	moderate	moderate
Drought tolerance	excellent	very poor	fair	fair	excellent
Salt tolerance	excellent	poor	poor	good	Good to excellent
Cold tolerance	fair	poor	poor	good	fair-good

Mowing: Mowing the lawn properly will do more for quality than will anything else. Mowing keeps down unsightly growth and builds up a vigorous, fine-quality grass turf. This should be done often, but the grass should not be mourn too short. In mowing very short, the surface roots become exposed, the soil dries out faster and surface aeration is reduced. The grass should not be cut off by more than one third of its length at any time. Most turf species are healthiest when kept between 2.5 and 3.5 inches tall. If the lawn is mowed before the grass gets too tall, the clippings left on the lawn will quickly disappear.

Watering: Water your lawn to a depth of 3 to 6 inches to encourage a deep root system. Thorough watering encourages the lawn to develop deep root systems, which make the lawn hardier and more draught-resistant. Avoid over-watering, which can in fact be more damaging than under-watering. You can water any time of the day if diseases are not a problem. If diseases are a problem, water in the early morning. Sprinkling every day or two is a bad practice. It leads to the spread of certain weeds and causes the grass to have a shallow root system. The colour of the grass should be dull and footprints should stay compressed for more than a few seconds before a lawn needs to be watered. The best time for watering is in the early morning, so that less water will be lost through evaporation.

Different grass types and their watering needs

Type of grass	Watering interval
Bermuda grass, Bahia grass, St Augustine grass and centipede grass	12-21 days
Carpet grass, fine fescue, kikuyu grass, tall fescue, and Zoysia	8-12 days
Ryegrass, Kentucky bluegrass and bentgrass	5-7 days

Controlling thatch: Thatch is the accumulation of above-soil runners put out by the grasses. This layer should be about 1.25cm on a healthy lawn. The proportion of thatch-to-lawn should be kept in balance by natural decomposition, earthworms and mico-organisms. Too much thatch prevents water and nutrients from reaching the grass roots. Excess thatching can be reduced by harrowing with a steel rake.

Fertilizing: The lawn should be fertilized once or twice a year. This is sufficient for an attractive lawn. Avoid using fast-acting fertilizers, as some nutrients may get washed away with watering or rain and the wasted fertilizer then pollutes groundwater supplies. Compost is the best option. Grasses use nitrogen more than any other nutrient. Nitrogen stimulates leaf growth. Apply nitrogen in the spring and in the summer but not in the late fall. Grass should be dry and the soil moist when you add fertilizer. Never add fertilizer to a lawn when it is raining.

Controlling weeds: A non-toxic by-product of corn processing, corn gluten kills weed seedlings within days of application. It also adds nitrogen to the soil, thus acting as a fertilizer.

Warm-season grasses are best established in late spring or summer. Establish cool-season grasses only in the fall. Before planting, prepare your site, clean up the area, but save top soil of the lawn area. Spread fertilizer and lime onto the site as indicated by a soil test. Hand racking is important after adding fertilizers. You can start a lawn in three ways: sodding, seeding or planting small pieces called sprigs or plugs. Use top-quality seed that is fresh and certified for purity and percentage germination. The seed of many turf grasses are extremely small and difficult to plant. Mix five parts moist sand with one part seed in a dry container for better results. After planting, cover grass seed with 1/8 inch of soil. Seed germination will be more rapid if you water the planted area immediately after planting and keep it moist during germination. Covering the lawn with clean straw will help keeping the young grass seedlings from drying out. Grasses may be propagated asexually by sodding, plugging, or sprigging. Sod should be 3/4 to 1 inch thick. Lay the pieces of sod as a solid mass or in strips 2 to 4 inches wide spaced 1 foot apart. Keep it moist until it is well established. In plugging, cut the sod into 2 to 4 inch round plugs, and place these plugs about 1 foot apart. Sprigging is the planting of individual plants. The spacing is governed by how fast the grass spreads, by how fast you want coverage, and by the amount of planting material you have available.

Maintenance: Once you establish a lawn, you must maintain it by mowing, watering, feeding, and weeding. Turf grasses need sunlight. A thick covering of leaves left on the lawn for several weeks may result in dead grass.

Irrigation: When normal rainfall does not provide enough moisture during the growing season, grass goes dormant and turns brown. To ensure a high-quality lawn, the lawn must be watered. Signs that a lawn needs water include **footprints remain while walking across the lawn, a slight change in colour to dark blue-green and grass blades folding inward.**

Weeding: Control weeds first by promoting a healthy, vigorous turf that won't allow weeds to grow and second by the proper use of control chemicals called herbicides. Along with killing harmful pests, chemical pesticides also kill the soil organisms that contribute to a healthy lawn. Use neem-based natural pesticides instead of chemical fertilizers for best results in Indian conditions.

Thatch: Thatch is a layer of organic matter made up of decaying grass leaves, stems and roots that build up in between the lawn and soil surface. It is a common problem on Kentucky bluegrass lawns that have been established for several years and over-watered and over-fertilized. Thatch harbours insects and diseases. Thatch can restrict grass roots from growing into the soil root zone, resulting in a shallow rooted lawn. Thatch interferes with water infiltration.

Weed Management: A thick, vigorous lawn is the best prevention against weed invasion. Low mowing encourages broadleaf weed invasion and invasion from grassy weeds such as creeping bentgrass and annual bluegrass. Lawn should be mowed at the proper mowing height, fertilized regularly and irrigated properly. Control weeds by hand-pulling, hand-raking, mowing to prevent seed formation, applying corn gluten meal product for pre-emergence control of crabgrass.

Insect and disease management

A healthy, well-maintained lawn is the best defense against insect invasion. Insect damage is usually less severe on well-watered lawns. Insects that infest home lawns are generally difficult to notice and their presence goes undetected until significant damage has been done. Insect damage can often be mistaken for drought damage. If the lawn remains brown or shows signs of thinning out despite watering, try closer examination for insects. Regular inspection of the lawn including leaves, stems, roots, thatch and soil will help to determine if the problem is insect-related. The most common lawn insect pests are: hairy chinch bugs, grubs, sod webworms, European crane fly, bluegrass billbug and turfgrass scale.

Detail of lawn-damaging insects.

Insect	Description	Damage	Detection/Control
Hairy Chinch Bug	Start as brick red nymphs in June/ early July. As they mature they turn grey, adults are 4 mm long and have an X on their backs.	The turf appears sunken. The bugs suck plant juices from the grass, leaves and stems. In case of heavy infestation, large areas of turf may die and dead turf does not pull out easily, it can destroy the entire lawn.	Cut the ends off a metal can to make a cylinder and force it into the lawn. Fill the can with water and chinch bugs will float or a 6-10cm^2 piece of turf and place it in a bucket of water. Turf species containing endophytic fungi show resistance to chinch bug feeding.
Grubs	C-shaped larvae with brown heads 1-3 cm in size. They feed on turf grass roots and the lawn lifts up like a carpet.	Cut 3 sides of a square and lift to uncover grubs.	Apply beneficial nematodes for marginal control
Bluegrass Billbug	Adults are weevils about 5 mm long, larvae are small, white and legless with brown heads.	The damage starts as small areas of yellow grass that pull away above the thatch.	Sawdust excrement is found where the bill bugs are feeding, turf species contains endophytic fungi show resistance to billbug feeding.
Sod Webworm	Adult is a fawn-coloured moth, the caterpillar is tan in colour.	Feed in September in thatch. Turf pulls away like a carpet.	Soft green pellets found in dead grass area where grass can be easily pulled away. Turf species containing endophytic fungi show resistance to worm feeding.
European Crane Fly	The adults resembles large mosquito, larvae are called leather jackets, greenish grey with no distinguishing feature.	Leather jackets feed in May and early June, causing damage by chewing grass blades back to ground level.	Examine the top of the thatch in thinned areas, and leather jackets will be visible in spring.
Turfgrass Scale	Typical scale insect resembles an egg cut in half. Brown with yellow striped center immature crawler stage of pin head size.	Small patches of dead grass that do no green up in spring, mainly on sodded lawns damage occurs in the spring.	During early July, crawlers can be found on shoes when you walk through the lawn do not cause much damage.

Disease problems in home lawns are minimal. Excessive fertility can cause succulent growth that is more susceptible to diseases. When establishing or renovating a lawn area, select varieties that are resistant to various diseases. Improper irrigation also contributes to lawn diseases. Make sure to water in the early morning to minimize the length of time that the lawn stays wet.

Common lawn diseases

Name	Description	Conditions favouring disease	Control
Fairy Ring	Circles or arcs of dark green grass or dead grass, may be mushrooms growing in the ring.	Decaying organic matter in soil	Repeated deep cultivation and drenching with water.
Leaf Spot	Begins as small oval reddish-brown spots on leaves in early spring. Under hot and humid condition spots can spread to kill stems and crown, even causing death of lawn.	Hot, humid conditions and heavily fertilized lawns are prone. Kentucky Bluegrass is most susceptible.	Raise mowing height, fertilize lightly to encourage recovery and irrigate in the mornings only.
Necrotic Ring Sot	Appears as roughly circular patch often with green tufts of grass.	Wet, cool condition in spring promotes disease. Symptoms appear during a drought condition, often a problem of sodded lawns.	Encourage deep rooting, water lightly and frequently during dry periods.
Powdery Mildew	Greyish-white colour powder appears on leaves and stems.	Shaded areas that are kept moist and have poor air circulation	Decrease shade and improve air circulation, It usually thins turf but does not completely kill it.
Rust	Yellow flecks on leaves with reddish- brown pustules on underside of leaves that produce reddish-yellow spores during a heavy infection, found on shoes and mower blades.	Stress caused by low nitrogen and drought, perennial ryegrass is the most susceptible.	Fertilize and water infrequently, mow high and frequently.

7.7 Post-Harvest Problems of Cut Flowers and Foliage

Bent Neck

It is a common post-harvest problem observed in roses and is due to the following reasons:

* Water deficiency in the neck tissue which is controlled by the transpiration rate, the rate of water uptake and the ability of different organs on the cut flower shoot to compete for water (Van Doorn, 1997).
* An increase in the stem flow resistance of cut blooms due to vascular occlusions of metabolic origin (Zieslin, 1989).
* Appearance of plugging materials like pectin,cellulose, and microbes van Doorn, 1997).
* Lack of development of secondary thickening and lignification of the vascular elements in the peduncle area subtending the flower head (Zamski *et al,* 1991).
* It has also been found that the growth and rigidity of rose peduncles are gibberellins and auxins and the activity of phenyl alanine ammonia lyase in the peduncle tissue (Zicslin, 1989).
* Extreme temperature during shipping or storage.

Control: Use of de-aerated and micro-organism-free water and wetting agents reduce the extent of bent neck (Van Doorn, 1999).

Limp Neck

A type of disorder in roses caused by water stress in the area just below the flower head. The affected flower buds bend down due to the weight of the top. Insufficient stored energy of flower heads may be one of the reasons.

Bull Head

Thrips infestation; insufficient carbohydrate supply to developing buds and hard pruning cause bull head in roses. Affected roses have shorter shelf life.

Blind Shoot

Blind shoot in roses is due to failure of the shoot to initiate flower buds, or due to flower bud atrophy or bud abortion. Inadequate carbohydrate supply, unfavourable temperatures and light conditions during bud initiation at the early stages of development are associated with blind shoot production.

Calyx Splitting

Calyx splitting in carnation is a factor of quality. The sepals beneath the flowers are unable to form a cylindrical calyx tube, which supports the base of the petals. During bud opening, the calyx may split either half or completely.

Reasons are (I) genetic, (2) high doses of nitrogenous fertilisers, (3) high day temperature and lower night temperature, and (4) high density planting.

Sleepiness

A disorder in carnation, caused by exposure of the flowers to ethylene gas or water stress. The extent of this disorder is much higher when flowers are stored for long periods or when they are kept at high temperatures.

Topple

Topple in gladiolus is characterised by breaking of spikes after opening of the florets in the vase. The spikes harvested from calcium-deficient soil have higher incidence of topple.

Negative Geotropism

A post-harvest disorder of gladiolus and antirrhinum, it occurs during storage and shipping. The spikes curve upward if they are placed horizontally. Differential distribution of auxins are responsible for this phenomenon. Transport of cut flowers in upright position is the remedy.

Flower Bud Blasting

A disorder found in tulip that is caused by dry storage or forcing of bulbs. It has been reported that a change in the plant's hormonal status, which regulates the distribution in carbohydrates and other organic materials within the plant, is the main reason for blasting.

Petal Discoloration

Low night and day temperatures are correlated with accumulation of pigments and is accompanied by blackening of petals and often stimulated by penetration of ultraviolet radiation through the materials covering the greenhouse (Mor and Zieslin, 1988; Schayer *et al.* 1987: Tjosvold, 1987). Bluing during storage is attributed to breakdown of proteins, release of free ammonia and a concomitant increase in pH. Bluing of red rose petals is increased by the use AOA but reduced by the use of STS (Mor *et al,* 1989).

Flower Bud and Petal Abscission

It is caused by ethylene evolution, formation of an abscission layer, activity of cell wall hydrolytic enzymes, shaking, wounding and high temperatures, pollination and fertilisation causing ethylene production. Remedial measures are: Use of ethylene inhibitors, spray with NAA (30 to 50 ppm), application of MH (200 to 400 ppm) and citric acid (500 ppm) through cut stem. Treatment with AOA reduces abscission.

Foliage Discoloration

Placing cut flowers in the dark at high temperatures causes yellowing, whereas oxidation of native phenols, mainly leuco-anthocyanins, results in darkening of foliage. Insufficient carbohydrate supply and water stress cause leaf blackening in *Pro tea nerifolia* (Newman *et al,* 1990; Paull and Dai, 1990). Ethylene has been implicated in the yellowing of some species, since endogenous ethylene enhances it and AVG reduces it (Mattoo and Aharoni, 1988). Exogenous ethylene has been found to increase leaf yellowing in potted plants like *Dieffenbachia. Dracaena, Euphorbia, Hibiscus, Pelargonium, Rhaplidophora* and *Yucca* (Weltering, 1987). Spray with cytokinin and STS-pulsing and treatment with GA_3, AOA or AIB had been found to reduce leaf yellowing and darkening (Van Doorn and Weltering, 1991).

Petal Wilting

The wilting of petals following ethylene exposure is a characteristic of only a limited number of plant families (Woltering and Van Doorn, 1998) and the Caryophyllaceae is the family which displays petal wilting in response to ethylene. This family includes the commercial important flowers like carnations (Nichols, 1966) and Gypsophila (Van Doorn *et al,* 1991 b). STS pulsing, inclusion of AOA, cytokinin and AIB (a-amino isobutyric acid) in the vase solution reduces petal wilting.

Bud Drying

In Asiatic hybrid lilies, the apparent desiccation and shrivelling of flower buds followed by abscission is a common problem. This problem is solved by STS pulsing.

Premature Leaf In-Rolling and Bract Discoloration

This occurs in *Heliconia psittacorum.* Vascular blockage is the reason behind it (Kalpo *et al,* 1989). Application ofGA_3 (0.1 mM) and ABA (0.000 I to 0.001 mm) delays leaf rolling by 2-3 days (Van Doorn, 1999).

Water Stress

Water stress causes wilting of *Cymbidium* and *Phalaenopsis.* Low rate of transpiration associated with low uptake of water are major factors involved in such problems (Van Doorn, 1999).

Leaf Wilting

A lower rate of water uptake caused by bacterial plugging is prevalent in chrysanthemum. Placement of the stems in cold water overcomes the problem (Van Meeteren, 1989).

Scape Bending

This phenomenon of cut gerbera is caused by excessive bacterial growth in vase solution which reduces longevity (Van Doorn and De Witte, 1994). Different varieties respond to different extents (Van Doorn *et al,* 1994).

Lack of Flower Opening

An interaction between ethylene and gibberellins is involved in controlling flower opening of *Pharbitis nil* (Raab and Koning, 1988). In *Petunia hybrida,* gibberellins from the anthers were found to regulate flower development (Weis and Halevy, 1989). Flower opening in Iris is controlled by elongated growth of the pedicel, which is inhibited by low concentrations of ethylene and stimulated by STS or gibberellins (Swart, *1981).* Reid *et al* (1989) showed that extremely low concentrations of ethylene accelerated or inhibited flowering in cut rose buds. The effect of ethylene is counteracted by STS. In lily flowers, the opening of flowers in the vase is often inhibited by endogenous ethylene, which is counteracted by STS treatment. In *Euphorbia fulgens,* ethylene treatment reduces flower opening, while STS treatment promotes growth and opening of flower buds. In freesia, STS treatment promotes growth and opening of flower buds. Lack of flower opening in gladiolus hybrids, Gypsophila and roses are overcome by the addition of sucrose in the vase solution. Goszczynska *et al* (1990) reported that gibberellins are involved in opening of cut roses.

Low Water Uptake

The rate of water uptake will depend on the transpiration pull and on the temperature and composition of the solution. Some reports state that ionic composition of the vase solution is a determinant of the rate of water uptake. The rate of water uptake of freshly cut flowers may initially be high when the plant has a low water potential at cutting. The rate of uptake will reach a steady state corresponding to the rate of transpiration but, depending on the species, during vase life the rate of transpiration also declines but tends to be higher than the water uptake rate. This results in a negative water balance (= rate of uptake-rate of transpiration), a decrease in water potential and in stomatal closure. When the rate of water uptake remains lower the rate of transpiration of the flowers or leaves, or both, may show turgor loss.

The rate of change of turgor (P) with a change in water potential depends upon the elasticity of the cell wall and the osmotic potential. The reduction of water uptake in cut roses is a result of occlusion in a large variety of xylem conduits

Treatments for Increasing Water Uptake Into Cut Stems

Re-cutting Under Water: Re-cutting of stems under water removes blockage and wilting of several cut flowers.

Increase of Pressure: Increasing pressure above the water results ii- recovery of cut flowers.

Decrease of Pressure: Wilted stems that are placed in water rapidly recover when the water is placed under sub-atmospheric pressure which facilitates removal of air from the stems.

Degassing of Water: Degassing of vase water through boiling and then cooling to ambient temperature can show rapid rehydration of cut flowers.

High Water Temperature: Wilted flowers placed in warm water regain turgidity more quickly, normally at 35-40° C. The use of warm or tepid water after re-cutting of the stems is often recommended to consumers. Sacalis (1993) advised the use of warm water for rehydration of many flowers including *Dahlia, Delphinium, Eustoma, Forsythia, Freesia, Gladiolus, Gypsophila, Hippeastrum, Lathyrus, Liatris, l.ilium Limonium, Matthi ol a,Narcissus, Nerine, Paeonia, Protea, Strelitzia, Syringa* and *Tulip.* In Holland, the use of warm water (about 50° C) is advised for the rehydration of *Phalaenopsis* flowers.

Low Water Temperature: Cut roses placed in water at 2° C rehydrate much more rapidly than roses placed in water at 23° C (Durkin, 1979b). Placing fronds of *l'teris* ferns in water at 4° C shortly after harvest has been found beneficial (Carow, 1981). The water uptake of fronds from the leather leaf fern *(Rumohra adiantiformis)* is similarly improved by placing is found in dry stored chrysanthemum flowers (Van Meeteren, 1989).

Decrease of Solution: Low pH has been shown to be favourable for rehydration of dry stored roses and chrysanthemums (Durkin, 1979a, 1979b, 1980). Rehydration of flowers in retail shops with a citric acid solution is recommended by Sacalis (1993) for flowers such as *Acacia. Aistroemeria, Antirrhinum, Argyranthemum frutescens, Bouvardia, Callistephus chinensis, Delphinium, Dendranthema, Freesia, Gladiolus, Gyps oph ila, Heliconia, Iris, Lilium, Paeonia, Protea* and *Syringa,* while for roses a pH of3.0 is recommended. The acid treatment is usually advised to be combined with warm water treatment. Low pH is known to increase the rate of flow in isolated 5 em stem segments of rose flowers (Durkin, 1979a). This may relate to the dissociation constant of carboxyl groups. Cellulose contains numerous carboxyl groups which is the main reason why the xylem wall is negatively charged. In aqueous solutions above pH 3.0, the carboxyl groups are dissociated and, therefore, negatively charged. Water is a partial dipole and forms a mantle around each of the carboxyl groups and, especially in the narrow pit membranes, these mantles may impede water flow. At pH 3.0, the carboxyl groups become protonated and uncharged and the water mantles are thus lost.

Decrease of Surface Tension: The addition of surfactants to the vase solution is very effective in counteracting the occlusion that develops during dry storage (Durkin, 1980). Pulsing with Tween-20 or Tween-80 alleviates the blockage in dry stored rose stems (Van Doorn *et al,* I 993a). A pulse treatment of roses with a solution of Agral-LN prior to dry storage is effective in promoting water uptake after dry storage (Perik and Van Doorn, 1988). Linear alkylethoxy surfactants have been identified as non-toxic to flowers and are biodegradable (Pak and Van Doorn, 1992). A pulse treatment with Triton X-I 00 prior to dry storage increases the length of vase life of roses, *Bouvardia* and Astilbe (Van Doorn *et al,* 1993a). The mechanism of action of surfactants is based on a decrease in surface tension (Myers, 1991). In dry stored stems, the decrease in surface tension facilitates the entry of water into the air filled lumen of xylerr: conduits (Van Doorn *et at.* 1993b).

Vascular Occlusion in Cut Flowers

The vase life of cut flowers is often very short because of water stress symptoms such as wilting and bending of segments just below the flower head and, in turn, low water potential is called vascular occlusion. A number of factors are attributed to the plugging of stems of cut flowers and the consequent reduction of water uptake.

* Physiological blockage is inherent in the stem, factors such as outflow upon cutting of latex, gum, mucilage and resin (Fujino and Reid, 1983; Vander Molen *el at.* 1983; Mauseth, 1988).

* The deposition of mucilage into xylem vessels by adjacent cells or the formation of tyloses (Van Doorn and Reid, 1955; Systema-Kalkman, 1991; Henny, 1982; Vaughan, 1988).

* Air embolism of the vascular systems due to cavitation in the stems (Dixon *el at.* 1988; Dixon and Peterson, 1989; De Stigter and Broekhuysen, 1989; Van Doorn, 1989; Van Doorn and Cruz, 2000).

* Bacterial plugging, both bacterial and fungal (Van Doom *et al,* 1989; Van Doom and Perik, 1990; Van Doorn *et at.* 1991c; Put and Clerkx, 1988; Put, 1990; De Witte and Van Doorn, 1988; Nooh *et al,* 1986; Van Doom *et al,* 1994; Put and Klop, 1990).

* Uptake of toxic compounds leaking from the stems and leaves (Woltering, 1987).

a) Physiological Blockage

The stems of many families such as Apocyaceae, Asclepiadaceae, Asteraceae, Euphorbiaceae, Liliaceae, Convolvulaceae and Papilionaceae contain latex which consists of high molecular polyterpenes that are' deposited in the vacuole. Gums are found in several families, including Araceae, Convolvulaceae, Magnoliaceae and Musaceae. Mucilage, an aqueous mixture of olysaccharides, is extruded from the cut surface of plants of many families including Cactaceae, Lauraceae, Malvaceae, Sterculiaceae and Tiliaceae, and in genera such as *Aloe, Althaea* and *Ulmus.* Resins mainly, consisting of terpenes mixed with volatile oils, are found in Araucariaceae, Cupressaceae, Pinaceae, Taxaceae, Taxodiaceae, Rosaceae and Anacardiaceae. After cutting of the stem, these substances cover the cut surfaces and enter into the xylem vessels and tracheids. Another mechanism of blockage is the deposition of mucilage into xylem vessels by cells adjacent to the xylem and tracheids.

b) Formation of Tyloses

Tyloses are outgrowths of cells that form a balloon-like structure in the lumina of the xylem conduits and may completely fill the conduit lumen (Zimmerman, 1983). They may function as a means for blocking the entry of microorganisms. Tyloses generally originate from ray cells, occasionally from paratracheal parenchyma cells. Gums, resins, mucilage seem to be accompanied by the production of large molecular weight substances that may account for lack of water flow in the stem with tyloses. The presence of tyloses has been investigated in a few cut flowers such as *Prunus* sp., roses and lilacs.

c) Air Embolism (Cavitation)

Upon cutting of the stem, air will flow into the xylem and tracheids. When placed in water after cutting, the water will compress the air in the opened conduits, thus forming a bubble. Usually, these air bubbles do not cause occlusion. The unopened xylems and tracheids can also become filled by gas bubbles in a process called 'cavitation'. Two types of cavitation can be distinguished (I) those in which air is pulled into a conduit, and (2) a spontaneous cavitation in which no such transfer takes place. There is a difference between species and cultivars in the time until the number of cavitations is high enough to hinder water flow. Microbial plugging of stem bases cause development of secondary air embolisms of stem vessels.

d) Microbial Plugging

Water always contains bacteria, and the cut surface of stems supplies food for them. Sugary substances will flow for some time out of the opened phloem cells. Bacteria are found to multiply first on the phloem of the cut surfaces. All other cells at the cut surface are also opened, thereby similarly providing food for bacteria. Bacteria grow on the cut surface, but they also grow in the vase solution, and these will be taken up with the water that flows into the stem. Bacterial plugging is composed of several components like living bacteria, extrapolysaccharides produced by living bacteria, dead bacteria and the macromolecular products that are formed upon the degrading of dead bacteria. The bacterial concentration found in vase water at consumer sites is 10^7 – 10^8 c.f.u/ ml a few days after placing the stems in the water. Toxic microbial compounds are excreted in the vase water and accelerate senescence. These toxic metabolites cause disruption of cell membranes. At a concentration of 3×10^9 bacteria per ml of water, the roses wilt within an hour. Bent neck is observed at this high bacterial number. The bacteria that are predominant in the vase water and cut surface of cut flowers have been isolated and identified by various research workers. They belong to the genera *Pseudomonas, Alcaligenes faecalis, Enterobacter, Aeromonas, Bacillus, Flavobacterium, Acetinobacter* sp., *Achromobacter* sp., *Erwinia* sp. and *Corynaeb acteria.* Fungal plugging of xylem vessels of cut flowers has been reported by various researchers. The predominant fungal species isolated and identified from vase water are *Botryt is cinerea, Fusarium oxysporum, Aspergillus niger, Mucor* sp., *Penicillium* sp., *Acremonium strictum* and *Rhizopus stolonifera.*

e) Uptake of Toxic Compounds Leaking from Stems and Leaves

Compounds leached from the stems and leaves into the vase water are shown to cause breakdown of the stem cells and induce stem plugging by the products of cell degradation. Beside sugars and proteins, leached substances also include polyphenols which reduce the longevity of cut flowers. Other factors associated with vascular occlusion are (1) the effects of water temperature, (2) cavitation as a result of bacterial blockage, and (3) the importance of cavitation repair. At low temperature, water can aid in restoring the rates of water uptake following a period of dry storage, apparently by absorbing some of the air in the stems 'Following the extended period of dry storage, the keeping of the cut flowers in water at 40° C also helps in restoring the rate of water uptake. Cavitations in stems are detected whet placed in water with a high bacterial count. The presence of a higher number of cavitate: conduits reduces water uptake. Cavitations are formed due to blockage of the basal end of the cut stems, either by bacteria or by particulate matter. The repair of cavitation is slowed down when the number of cavitations is higher and cavitation repair is the factor that is limiting the rate of water uptake following a period of dry storage. Cavitation repair is faster when the period of dry storage is shorter and very fast when a surfactant is added to the vase water.

Control of Microbial Populations

Antimicrobial compounds that delay wilting without being toxic to cut flowers include

* Salts of copper, zinc, cobalt and nickel (Reddy, 1988; Reddy *el al,* 1988; Van Doorn *et aI,* 1991 g).

* Quinoline compounds such as HQC or HQS (Jones and Hill, 1993; Van Doorn *et al.* 1990a; Ketsa and Boonrote, 1990; Joyce *et al,* 1993; Sytserna-Kalkman, 1991; Stamps and Neill, 1983; Van Doorn *et al,* 1991 d).

*Chlorine compounds such as sodium hypochlorite, slow release chlorine chemicals and chloramine- T (Joyce *et al,* 1993; Jones and Hill, 1993; Van Door *et al,* 1991 g; Van Doorn *et al,* 1990a; Accati Garibadi and Deambrogio, 1988; Jones *et al,* 1993; Faragher, 1986).

* Quaternary ammonium compounds such as benzalkone, Physan-20.

* Chlorinated hydrocarbons such as dichlorophan and chlorhexidine.

*Antibiotics like streptomycin, kanamycin, tetracyclin (Zagory and Reid, 1986 De and Bhattacharjee, 2002).

Other antimicrobial compounds which are commonly used in combination with sugar for prolonging vase life of different cut flowers and foliage greens are AI_2(S04)' (Mugge. 1983); $COCI_2$ (Pardha Sarathi, 1989); $AgN0_1$ (Awad *et ai,* 1986; Abdul Kader and Roger: 1986; Stenitz, 1982); HQC or HQS (Woodson, 1987; Faragher, 1989; Ketsa, 1989; Kader and Rogers, 1986; Downs *et ai,* 1988); sodium hydrochlorite (Joyce *et ai,* 1993), DICA (Faragher 1989); DDMH (Van Doorn, 1997), Physan-20 (Kofranek, 1986; Lacey, 1983); Benzalkone. Dichlorophen (Van Doorn, 1997).

7.8 Damask rose (*Rosa damascena* Mill) - An Alternate Value-added Commercial Crop

Introduction

Rose basically a temperate plant belongs to family Rosaceae and genus Rosa. The number of species under this genus varied from 120-200. Out of several species of rose only *Rosa centifolia* Linn., *Rosa moschata* Hook, *Rosa borboniana* Desp, *R.* Replets, *Rosa alba* and *Rosa damascena* Mill have been exploited commercially for rose oil and allied products in various countries. The last is the major Bulgarian commercial species of rose used for the isolation of rose oil. In India, *Rosa damascene* (Shaptri in Sanskrit) is mainly grown for production of rose oil and rose water and commonly known as Fasil or Chaiti gulab.

Rosa damascene is an vigorous shrub with exquisite fragrance, attains a height of about 2.5 to 3 m. Foliage soft grey-green, the leaflets oval and simply toothed, usually 5 to a leaf. Branches very prickly with hooked spines as well as prickly bristles. Flowers borne in large clusters, semi-double, sweet scented, variable in colour, bluish-white to deep pink, the pedicels being long and covered with glandular bristles and small prickles. Some of the better known varieties of this species are Triginipetala, Celsiana, Pazanlik. Other varieties, which perform well in Himachal are Jwala and Himrosa. Two species namely *Rosa moschata* and *R. macrophylla* grow wild in H.P.

From 10th to 17th century, the damascene rose industry was centred in Persia. From here, the industry gradually spread to India, Arabia and North Africa. In India, the rose industry got an empetus during Mugal rule as the King had a fancy for the delicate perfume. Noorjahan, the queen of Mugal emperor Sahangir, is said to have discovered the rose oil accidentally in 1612 AD.

Distribution

Rosa damascena is cultivated in Bulgaria, Italy, Turkey, Morocco, France and USSR on commercial scale. Major supplies of oil in world market comes from Bulgaria. The plant is native to Persia and appears to have been introduced from there in the state of Uttar Pradesh at Kannauj and subsequently, at Aligarh, Ghezipur and Ballia. During Mugal rule and possibly in the later years, it found its way to places of Maharaza of Chittor, from where, it spread to the villages in Haldighatti of Rajasthan. Babar introduced this plant Via port of Bussosrah in year 1526. At present, in India, major areas taken under the cultivation of scented rose are UP, J&K, parts of Bihar and Rajasthan. In H.P., *Rosa damascena* is suitable for mid hills from an altitude of 3000-7000' amsl.

Climate

Rose needs a plenty of sunshine for the proper growth. High air humidity (above 60%) and moderate temperature (15-20 °C) yields a large rose harvest. Although, a mild temperature climate is the ideal, but the plant does well under sub-tropical climate also. It needs protection from frost during January-February months. The plant survive better on the Mediterranean climate with moderate rainfall.

Soil

Rosa demascena can be grown on a variety of soils, but it prefers well drained soil with good human content. It can tolerate wide range of soil pH conditions ranging from 6.5 to 9.0 and silty clay-loam to sandy loam soils. Soils which loses water more quickly requires frequent irrigation. Clay or clay lime stone soil, freshly exposed, more or less pebbley, slightly sandy and fairly rich in humus are best.

Value added products and their uses

Besides rose oil, other products made from fresh flowers are rose water, attar – a sandal wood oil based product; gulroghan – a hair oil, gulkand – a conserve of rose petals with sugar; pankhuri – a shade dried petals; dried rose buds; concrete and absolute. The various rose products are used in cosmetics, beverages, cold drinks, food stuffs, tobacco flavouring, fruit flavours, soft drinks, alcoholic liquors and pharmaceutical preparations.

Nursery technology

Propagation:Damask rose is propagated through one year old stem cuttings. Stem cuttings are collected at the time of pruning. About 20 cm long, 0.75 to 1.50 cm thick cuttings (3 to 4 eyes) are planted in nursery. 2/3 of length is inserted into soil to get maximum number of sprouts. Seradix No.3 or IBA @ 200-250 ppm is used for promoting rooting. The cuttings are planted from November-January in rows with a distance of 10 cm from plant to plant and 20 cm row to row. The sprouting takes place within three months and cuttings are ready after one year for transplanting. Besides cutting, this rose can be propagated through division of old plant, lateral sprouts with roots and seeds. The divisions are obtained by uprooting the plants and separating the roots with shoots from the clumps.

Plantation techniques

Planting time: Early monsoon (June-July), Winter season (December-January)

Transplanting: Rooted stem cutting, Pit size: 45 cm^3 or In poorer soils pit size = 60 cm^3. Spacing: Plant to plant = 1.5 m, Row to row = 1.5 m.

No. of plants/ha = 5000

In spacing of 1x1 m^2, 10,000 plants/ha will be accommodated. The transplanting is also done in trenches about 1 m deep and ½ m wide. The trenches are filled with FYM. The plant has a life span of 15 years. It is useful to put about 3 to 4 kg FYM, 20 to 25 g NPK mixture and 20 g aldrin powder per plant in the pits before planting. The pit is watered so that the entire soil is drenched and is kept moist. The plant is then allowed to grow.

Precautions

(i) Plant only one sapling per pit

(ii) The main root should be straight

(iii) Plant in upright position upto collar level

(iv) Plant to the right depth, slightly deeper than its depth in the nursery

Manuring and fertilization

Damask rose is a soil exhausting crop which remain in the field for more than 15 years, so it requires liberal manuring. The quantity of fertilizer and manures should be applied on soil test basis considering various factors like basic fertility of soil, organic control, soil texture, moisture supply, soil pH etc.

First and 2nd year

FYM 18 to 20 tonnes/ha

100 to 125: 60:40 kg NPK mixed fertilizers in split doses

After 2nd year

100 to 125 kg N: 60 kg P: 40 kg K mixed fertilizers/ha in split doses.

Annual application of fertilizers is applied after pruning. In general nitrogenous fertilizer is given in 2 split doses at an interval of 3 to 5 week to ensure better utilization. In alkaline soils containing high sodium and pH upto 9.0 calcium ammonium nitrate results in better flower yield than ammonium sulphate and urea and fertilizer requirements are generally higher (about 10 to 20%) than normal soil (pH 7). The nitrogen should be given through cowdung manure plus any nitrogenous fertilizer while phosphorus and potassium through any phosphatic and potash fertilizers as top dressing on the standing crop. In all foliar spray 0.1% teepol should be used as wetting agent for proper distribution and absorption of the nutrition through leaves.

Special care

(i) Ferric sulphate @ 0.1 to 0.2% may be sprayed in iron deficient soils

Or A spray of 0.1 to 0.2% ferric chloride solution may be used for its control.

(ii) Zinc sulphate @ 0.5% or 20 to 25 kg/ha (soil application).

(iii) IAA 50 ppm and 1% agromin spray at 10 to 15 days interval for increased flower yield from January onward till the start of flowering.

Irrigation and drainage

Young plantation of rose require frequent irrigation particularly in summer month. January-March is critical when proper soil moisture is required for vegetative growth. However, when plants are established properly after two years, frequency of irrigation may be reduced. In all 10-12 irrigations are sufficient. Roses can tolerate moist soil conditions but water logging is harmful.

Intra-cultural operations

Though weeding and hoeing are required after pruning every year in January-February. Atleast two weedings, two hoeing and one sickling are required every year. Frequent hoeing are done after and before irrigation and essential during month of January and February to obtain a good harvest of flowering. To control the seasonal weeds and grasses in rose plantation, the 2,4-D @ 2 kg/ha a.i., Senazin @ 3 kg/ha a.i., Diuron @ 2.5 kg/ha are used.

Plant protection measures

Pest control

Aphids, thrips, chafter beetle, red sealem mites, termites, caterpillars, rose leaf hopper and rose leaf rolling, saw fly are the commonly known insect pest of *Rosa demascena*. For the control of these insects, sprays of metasystox 25 EC @ 750 ml/ha, dimecron 100 EC @ 250 ml/ha, malathion 50 EC @ @ 1500 ml/ha, endosulfan 100 EC @ 1500 ml/ha may be applied alternatively after pruning to the end of flowering. Nuvan @ 1.5 litre/600 litre water/ha is quite effective against aphids and thrips. These spray also destroy the insect vectors which are responsible for transmission of viral disease of *Rosa damascena*. Aldrin dust (5%) @ 20 g/plant is useful against termite or aldrin 35 EC @ 8 ml/plant dissolved in one litre of water may also be used.

Diseases

The common diseases of roses are black spot, powdery mildew, downy or black mildew, rust, crown gall, rose mosaic, full heads and blind shoots. The following schedule of chemical control is recommended. One spray with rogor (0.10%) soon after pruning followed after a week by another spraying wilt captan (0.2%) should be done. Prophylactic sprays of Bavistin @ 0.10% during August to October help in controlling black spot disease.

Pruning

It is important operation in *Rosa damascena*. It requires a dormant or resting period before flowering. In temperate climatic conditions, the dormancy requirement is met out naturally due to low winter temperature when plant goes under dormancy and shed its leaves. In succeeding years, new shoots appears on which flower buds take place. In the region of sub-tropical climate, the rose plants are essentially pruned to induce artificial dormancy. The other purposes of pruning are to train plants into desired form, to keep the desired size, to remove the injured and diseased parts, to remove the terminal buds and change the growth habit to encourage bushy roses, to provide more horizontal expansion and finally, production of more flower buds.

Time, number and height of pruning are main factors for consideration. During first year of plantation, light pruning is sufficient in the month of December-January. During second year, plant should be pruned twice in a year. Once in the month of August at 50 cm plant height and again in November-December at 75 cm plant height. Further, pruning should be done once in a year in November-December at one meter plant height. Excessive water shoots should be checked to grow, otherwise, size of bushes becomes unmanageable.

Flowering

Summer Damask rose (*Rosa damascena* var. Trigintipetala) flowers from early March to mid of April in North Indian plains, from 10th April to 20th May in mid hill of Himachal Pradesh and early May to early June in Srinagar valley. Exact flowering time depends upon prevailing temperature in the locality. Autum Damask rose (var. bifera) also flowers during September to November and yield small quantities of flowers. The total flowering period of *Rosa demascena* is about 25 to 35 days but major part of yield (about 75%) is received within 15 days of peek flowering period.

Plucking

The flowers are harvested in the early hours of day when they begin to open pluckings starts from 4 O'clock in early morning continue until all flowers are plucked. Flowers are plucked by hands being nipped of just below the calyx. The work is done by contract by local villagers. On an average 2 to 3 kg flowers are plucked by a plucker per hour manually. The flowers are collected in cotton or polythene bags and transferred to well airy wooden baskets before processing within 3-4 hours. Flowers stored for more than 12 hrs loose their half oil yield. The flowers (with calyx) possess maximum essential oil at the cup form stage and should be picked up for distillation. There should be minimum time lag between picking and distillation.

Yield: In an average, a well maintained rose plantation yields about 30-40 quintal flowers/ha/year. Agro-climatic conditions like foot hills and valley of north-west Himalayan sloppy hills, having traces of ferrous salt, slightly moist, free from acids, well drained and easily permeable soils can yield 5 to 6 tonnes/ha of fresh rose flowers.

Economics of cultivation of ***Rosa damascena***/extraction on pilot plant

A. Economics of cultivation/ha

S.No.	Particulars	Expenditure (Rs.)		
		1st yr	2nd yr	3rd yr
1.	Preparation of land	1000	-	-
2.	Preparation of beds (15 labourers,	900	-	-
	Rs.60/- labourer/day)			
3.	Digging of pits 100 labourers/day @ Rs.60/-	6000	-	-
4.	Cost of fertilizers/manure/put filling			
	Charges before planting			
	i) Farm yard manure (2.5 to 3 kg/pit) or	6000	-	-
	125 to 150 q/ha @ Rs.40/- per q			
	ii) BHC power 2 q @ Rs.400/q	400	-	-
	iii) Mixing of manure and filling in pits			
	(20-25 g of NPK/pit) (125 kg/ha)			
	Cost of CAN: Rs.4.22/kg	527.50	-	-
	Cost of SSP Rs.2.50/kg	312.50	-	-
	Cost of MOP Rs.7.40/kg	925	-	-
	Filling of pits (20 labourers/day @ Rs.60/-)	1200	-	-
5.	Carriage charges of manure/fertilizer	400	-	-
6.	Cost of rooted cutting (5000 @ Rs.5/plant)	25000	-	-
7.	Planting of rooted cuttings 30 labourers	1800	-	-
	@ Rs.60/day			

8.	Fertilizers/manures			
	FYM: i) 1st yr (20 t/ha) FYM @ Rs.40/-	8000	2400	2400
	ii) 2nd yr and 3rd yr (6 t/ha)			
	Fertilizers			
	1st and 2nd yr 100:60:40 NPK/ha			
	In 3rd yr NPK – 200:90:60 kg/ha	422	422	844
		150	150	225
		296	296	444
9.	Carriage charges	400	400	500
10.	Application of fertilizer/manure	1800	1800	1800
	30 labourers/day @ Rs.60/-			
11.	Irrigation (12, Rs.100/irrigation) 1st yr	1200	1100	800
	2nd year (11, Rs.100/irrigation)			
	3rd yr (8, Rs.100/irrigation)			
12.	Hoeing/weeding, 20 labourer @ Rs.60/-	1200	1200	1200
13.	Pruning 30 labourers @ Rs.60/-	-	1800	1800
14.	Cost of herbicides	1500	1500	1500
15.	Cost of insecticides/fungicides	1000	1500	1500
16.	Harvesting of flowers, 6 labourers/day	500	2000	4000
17.	Extraction cost of oil (Rs.3/kg)	1500	7500	15000
18.	Miscellaneous	1000	1000	1000
	Total expenditure (1 to 18)	65445.50	14568.00	17013.00

Expenditure in three years 65445.50+14568.00+17013.00 = Rs.97026.50

Average/ha/annum: Rs.32342.10

B) Economic of extraction

Rosa damascena extraction cost on pilot plant

1.	Price of pilot plant	4.5 lakh
2.	Life	15 years
3.	Salvage value	45000
4.	Working hrs per 10 months in a year	4864 hrs
5.	Capacity	350 kg
6.	Recovery/batch	100 @ 0.028%
7.	Distillation time	8 hrs

Sr.No.	Particulars	Amount (Rs.)
1.	Capital expenditure (capacity 350 kg)	450000
2.	Recurring expenditure (fixed charges	

Sr.No.	Particulars	Amount (Rs.)
	i) Depreciation	Rs.27000
		$\frac{\text{Total value of} - \text{Salvage Unit value}}{\text{Life (in years)}}$
	ii) Interest @ 10%	$\frac{45000+45000}{2} \times \frac{10}{100} = 24750$
	iii) Repair and maintenance @ 3.5%	$\frac{\text{Total cost x } 3.5}{100} = 15750$
	iv) Lubrication @ 0.25%	$\frac{450000\text{x}0.25}{100} = \text{Rs.}1125$
5.	Shelter 1%	$\frac{450000}{100} = \text{Rs.}4500$
6.	Insurance @ 0.25%	$\frac{450000 \text{ x } 0.25}{100} = 1125$
	Total fixed charges	Rs.74250
	Cost per	$\frac{74259}{4814} = \text{Rs.}15.27$
	Cost per batch	15.27x8 = Rs.122.12
	iii) Operating charges	
	i) Electric motor charges/batch	Rs.800
	Labour charges for extraction of oil/batch	Rs.120
	Total operating charges	Rs.920
	Total charges = fixed charges + operating charges	920+122.12 = Rs.1042.12
	Cost of 100 l of oil	Rs.1042.12
	Cost of extract of 1 l of oil	Rs.10421.2
	1.5 L of oil	Rs.15631.80
	350 kg = 1042.12	
	1 kg = 1042.12 ------------------ = 2.98 350	
	Inputs (Rs./ha/year)	32342.10
	Expected output of	500 kg (1st yr)
	Flower yield (kg/ha/yr)	2500 kg (2nd yr)
		5000 kg (3rd yr)
	Total yield	8000 kg
Income		
i) From rose flowers (when flowers are sold without processing)		
	a) Total yield of flowers in three years	8000 kg/ha

Sr.No.	Particulars	Amount (Rs.)
	b) Sale of 8000 kg flower @ Rs.50/kg in three yrs	400000-97026.5
	Minus cost of cultivation in three years	302973.50
	c) Income/annum/ha	100991.16 or 1.0 lac
(ii) From rose oil		
	a) Flower production in three years	8000 kg/ha
	b) Oil recovery after distillation @ 0.028%	2.2 L
	c) Price of 1 L of oil (estimated)	Rs.3.00 lac
	d) Price of 2.2 L oil	6.6 lacs
	e) Net profitn (price of 2.2 L oil in	(66000-97026.5-24000)=
	Three years cost of cultivation in	
	Three years-cost of extraction)	538973.50 or
		5.3 lac
	Average profit/annum/ha	1.79 lac

Processing of ***Rosa damascena*** Mill for rose oil and its allied products

Rosa damascena is a fragrant species cultivated commercially for extraction or distillation of rose oil, rose water, rose attar, rose hair oil, concrete and absolute besides making other allied products i.e. gulkand, pankhuri, etc.

Rose oil: Rose oil is an important commercial product obtained from rose petals, sepals and whole flower. Apart from sweet fragrance, it has medicinal property and is often used in Ayurveda. Rose oil has antibacterial property against *Shigella dysenteqiae* and *Mycobacterium tuberculosis*. The rose oil is obtained by hydrodistillation, steam distillation and hydro steam distillation. Its quantity depends upon the quality of rose flweors picked, species and cultivar, stage and time of picking and method of oil extraction, hydro steam method of distillation is used for better yield of oil.

Generally, 1 kg oil is obtained from 3000-4000 kg flowers. To obtain good quantity of rose oil, the flowers are to be harvested early in the morning, as the percentage of oil decreases with advancing day. In dry weather, the oil content of open flowers decreases whereas the oil yield increased in wet cool weather. Rose oil at the rate of 3 drops three times daily may be used for treatment of gall stones. In present day rose oil forms one of the most valuable natural material used in perfumery, flavour and cosmetics industry all over the world. The presence of higher contents of rose oxide and phenyl ethyl alcohol are responsible for value addition. The rose oil finds its importance in human psychology. It stimulate the nervous system, dreams become more frequent, brighter and longer concentration of healthy subjects. It accelerates the working rate and improve the capacity of work. Rose oil preparation are used in the treatment of fatty dystrophy of the liver and as a support for hypoenergy diet reducing resum levels of total lipids, chlorestrol. And triglycerides. Rose oil/vit A preparation called Girosetal is successfully applied in the treatment of cholelithiasis and liver steatosis.

Oil yield at laboratory scale (using clevenger's apparatus)

Petals = 0.053%

Sepals = 0.043%

Whole flower = 0.045%

Total alcoholic constituent = 80%

Oil yield at semi commercial scale (by hydro steam distillation) = 0.028%

Physico-chemical properties

Colour: Light greenish/colourless

State: Liquid

Sp. Gravity: 0.8670

Congeiling pt.: +19 to +22°C

Refractive index: 1.468

Optical rotation: -2° to -3°C

Ester number after acetylaction: 194.98

% of alcohol as geraniol : 58.68

(i) Maceration: This process consists of the extraction of flowers in a hot fat.

Procedure: A cloth is tied on the color of a wide mouthed vessel. The flower are kept on the clsoth "Sesame seed oil" heated to about 80°C is poured slowly on the flowers. The oil takes the perfume from flower and filters down in the vessel. The exhausted flowers are replaced with fresh flowers. The filtered oil is taken out from the vessel, poured on fresh flowers. This process is repeated till oil gets saturated with rose perfume i.e. Rose hari oil (petals are treated with wet sesamum oil or gulroghan.

Gulroghan: Gulroghan is a type of hari oil produced by maceration of rose flowers with warm sesamum seed oil or type of hair oil prepared from rose petals by cufleorge with wet sesamum seed oil.

Solvent extraction

Concrete: Waxy essence obtained by extracting odorus material with volatile solvent like petroleum ether and then evaporation of the solvent.

Or

Concretes which are usually waxy solids, are odorous concentrates obtained from fresh plant material of resinous content by extraction with a volatile non-aqueous solvent, followed by the removal of the solvent by evaporation at moderate temperature and under partial vacuum. The rose flowers are processed by solvent extraction.

Petroleum ether (40-60°) is an ideal solvent for extraction. Normal Hexame 65° food grade is also used.

Procedure: The flowers are immersed in the solvent for the extraction. The perfume passes on the solvent. The solution of perfume called extract is drained out. Three extractions of a charge like this are made.

In 1st extraction, flowers are dipped for 30-36 minutes. In 2nd extraction the flowers are dipped for 20 to 25 minutes and in the 3rd 15 to 20 minutes.

1st and 2nd extractions are combined and 3rd used for the 1st extraction of fresh charge. The solvent for 1st and 2nd combined extraction is distilled off at about 70°C. then contents are transferred to a condenser which is solvent distillation unit with shallow retard last traces are removed under vaccum.

The residue left is a crude extract of perfume is called concrete: in addition to perfume, the concrete contain wares and colouring matter etc.

Absolutes: It is alcohol soluble part of concrete which is obtained by solvent extraction of odorous material. It is highly concentrated from the perfume.

Or

Absolutes are highly concentrated perfumery material obtained from concrete by repeated extraction with ethyl alcohol followed by chilling of the extract, filtration of the remaining alcoholic solution and finally removal of the most of the alcohol by evaporation at moderate temperature and under partial vacuum. Absolute are as a rule liquids and are usually soluble in alcohol.

Absolutes: Concrete is processed for the preparation of absolutes.

Procedures

The concrete is dissolved in high proof alcohol and the contents are chilled at -25°C. The waxes and other substances get solidified and are separated by filtration. From the filterate, the solvent is distilled off under vacuum and residue left behind is called absolute and possesses true fragrance of flowers.

Rose water: This is the main stem of production from flowers in India. 80 per cent production of flowers is used for rose water. It is an important commercial product obtained from rose petals. Distilled during flowering, stored to 2 to 3 months for maturation of odour, than diluted and bottled. Price of rose water varies according to concentration of oil in it. Two quantities are sold in the market (1) Ekmana, (2) Do-mana.

Uses: Rose water used for flavouring confectionery, syrups, soft drinks and tobacco. It has properly of cooling the body and is often used in eye lotion and eye drops for its sorting quantities. In India, widely used in temples for sprinkling on gathering on ceremonial occasions. Rose water is obtained by water distillation of rose flowers.

Rose attar: is obtained by water distillation but the distillate is passed through sandal wood oil.

Uses: It is used as a perfume on Agarbattis and also for flavouring of tobacco, particularly shuffs and chewing tobacco.

Otto of rose: This is also known as Ruh-Gulab, obtained by the water distillation of rose flower by Re-distillation. The distillate two or three times, till it gets saturated with oil dissolved in it, then chilled, oil drops floating on surface water are removed. Yield comes 0.045% on fresh weight basis in improved stills. The yield is 0.01 to 0.016%. At Lucknow 0.03 to 0.04% oil.

Uses: Uses in confectionary, flavouring of tobacco, soft drinks and alcohol liquors.

Gulkand: It is a preserve of rose petals in sugar. Preserved by mixing the rose petals with white sugars (equal portion of petals with white sugar.

Uses: It is good time and has lucerative properties.

Pankhuri: Dried rose petals are known as pankhuri and dried rose petals used in making cool summer drinks.

By products (Wastes utilization)

Water: by water distillation, the flower cannot be completely exhausted of their perfume. So, the flowers petals left after the distillation contain a light odour.

Uses: Used in Agarbattis and incense after drying and grinding.

Pruned material: is used as full by natives in the growing year. One ha plantation yields about 140 g of green wood in a year. Also used to supplement the fuel for firing the distillation units.

Other uses: Jam, Jellies, syrups. Rose vinegar, rose petal wine, rose squashes, rose jam can be made. Fruits can be used for hot drinks like Tea and popular wine.

7.9 Propagation Techniques for Horticulture Crops

Propagation of plants may be defined as the controlled reproduction of plants by man to perpetuate selected individual or groups of individual plants which have specific value to him. Or

Propagation is the perpetuation of plants as independent units by means of seeds, bulbs, layers, cuttings, or grafts.

Propagation methods

A) Seed or Sexual propagation: The reproduction may be done by using seeds and known as sexual reproduction.

B) Vegetative/Asexual propagation: Propagation by using a plant part itself

A) Seed or Sexual propagation: Sexual propagation is the method of raising plants by means of seeds which are formed due to the fusion of male and female gametes within ovule of a flower. Plants raised from seeds are called seedling.

Advantages of Sexual propagation

1) Seedling trees are hardy, long lived, easier to propagate, and bear more heavily.
2) Plants which are difficult to propagate by vegetative method can only be propagated by seeds e.g; papaya, phalsa, mangosteen etc
3) In breeding for evolution of new varieties, the hybrids are first raised from the seed and it is therefore essential to employ this method in such cases.
4) The root stocks on which the fruit varieties are budded or grated are usually obtained by means of sexual propagation. The rootstocks required should be hardy and develops better root system.
5) Seedlings are mostly free from virus diseases.
6) Seeds if stored properly can be kept for longer duration for future use.

Disadvantages of Sexual propagation

1) The seedling trees (progenies) are not always uniform in their growth, yielding capacity and fruit quality as compared to plants propagated vegetatively.
2) Seedlings take more time to bear the first crop.
3) It is not possible to perpetuate the exact character of any superior selection through seed.
4) To multiply superior hybrids or chance seedlings, vegetative methods thus have to be employed.
   - **Seed**: A seed has been defined as a young plant packed ready to start growing when required.
   - **Apomixis**: Development of seeds without the complete sexual process is known as apomixes and seed produced in this manner is called apomictic seeds.
   - **Seed dormancy**: The embryo of the seed remains in inactive stage from the time of its development to the time it germinates. This failure of the embryo is termed as dormancy of the seed.
   - **After-ripening**: Some seeds germinated fully when freshly harvested, but they germinate after a period of dry storage. The change taking place in such seeds are known as after-ripening.

Basic parts of seeds

1. **Embryo:** The embryo is a new plant resulting from the union of male and female gametes during fertilization.
2. **Storage tissues**: The food material of seed may either be stored in cotyledons or endosperm.
3. **Seed coat or covering**: The seed coat known as testa is usually in two layers, the outer being dry and hard and the inner being membranous. The seed coat provides mechanical protection for the embryo. The seed covering sometimes plays an important role in dormancy of some seeds.

Apomixis: The embryo is generally produced by sexual reproduction but there are certain cases in which the embryo is produced by an asexual process. The phenomenon in which in the place of the normal sexual reproductive process, the asexual reproductive process occurs is called apomixes. Common types of apomixes are:

1. **Recurrent apomixes**: In recurrent apomixes, the female gametophytes develop apparently as in normal way excepting the meioses does not take place. The embryo develops directly from the egg nucleus without fertilization.

2. **Adventitious embryony:** (Nucellar embryony or polyembryony): In this case, the embryos do not arise from the gametophytes but arise from a group of cells in either the nucellus or the integuments. A number of embryos may develop along with a sexual embryo developed by normal reproductive process. At maturity the seed may contain one, two or more embryos enclosed within a single seed coat.

3. **Vegetative apomixes:** In this case, instead of flowers the vegetative buds or bulbils develop in the inflorescence.

The process of apomixes is of more use in horticulture it makes it possible to raise uniform root stock, seedlings. In most citrus plants and in some varieties of mangoes the phenomenon of polyombryony is observed.

Propagation media for seeds: For propagation of plants, several media are used. The media should have following qualities:

1. Sufficiently firm to facilitate the holding of seeds or cuttings in place.

2. It should not shrink excessively when dry. The volume should remain constant when dry or wet.

3. In order to avoid watering at frequent intervals, the medium should be fairly retentive of moisture.

4. For proper drainage of excess water, it should be sufficiently porous. This would provide adequate aeration.

5. The medium should be free from weed seeds and disease organisms.

6. The medium should have a pH level suitable for the plants to be propagated.

7. Commonly used media are soil, sand, leaf mould, sphagnum moss, vermiculite and sawdust.

Commonly used media

Soil	Soil alone is seldom used as a medium for growing plants. It is usually mixed with farmyard manure in varying proportion depending upon the type of soil and the plant to be grown.
Sand	Pure sand is used for rooting of soft wood cutting; it is also used for mixing soil for proper drainage of the excess water.
Leaf Mould	Prepared by placing layers of leaves one above the other, mixed with soil. A small quantity of ammonium sulphate is added. The mixture is watered to maintain the decomposition action. The compost gets ready in 12-16 months.
Sphagnum Moss	It is used most commonly for propagation of plants by air layering, on account of its high water holding capacity. It is also light in weight and can absorb 10-20 times its own weight of water.
Vermiculite	A micaceous mineral, light in weight (6-10 Ibs. Per cu. ft.), neutral in reaction, and is able to absorb large quantities of water, that is 3-4 gallons per cu. ft.
Sawdust	This is a by-product of saw mills, having good water holding capacity.

Containers for propagation: Different types of containers are used for the propagation of plants as well as for growing plants. The common types of containers used are:

Earthern Pots	Wooden Trays	Baskets
The pots may be of different types, designs and sizes. The common types are (a) Parli (b) Madki (c) Khobda (d) Nand (e) Pela (f) Kundi (g) Gamla	Used for propagation of plants by cutting or for raising seedlings.	These may be either made of bamboo or of wire. These are most commonly used for ornamental plants.

Seed dormancy: The embryo of the seed remains in an inactive stage from the time of its development to the time it germinates. This failure of the embryo is viable and is termed as dormancy of the seed. This dormancy sometimes may be due to unfavourable external factors like lack of moisture, favourable temperature or oxygen. Dormancy caused by these factors is referred to as **external dormancy**. Sometimes even if the external factors are favourable, the seeds fail to germinate due to certain internal conditions of the seeds called **internal dormancy.**

1. **Embryo dormancy:** Conditions existing within the embryo.
2. **Seed coat dormancy:** Influence of some of the enclosing seed parts on the embryo e.g; the seed coat may mechanically inhibit water uptake and restrict movement of gases or embryo expansion.
3. **Inhibitory dormancy:** Some substances in parts of seed or fruit may chemically inhibit the germination. Abscissic acid is responsible for

dormancy in seeds of most of temperate fruits like apple, peach, pear and walnut.

4. **After-ripening dormancy**: Seeds fail to germinate when freshly harvested, but they germinate after a period of dry storage. Such seeds are known as after-ripening dormant seeds. This is due to the physiological changes taking place in embryo.

Seed Coat Dormancy: A common cause of dormancy is the impermeability of seed covering to water. Seed with hard seed coat is commonly met with in legumes. The seed coat is easily decomposed if the soil contains sufficient moisture and has warm temperature. Seed coat softening can be affected by addition of nitrates to the medium. The seed coats usually get ruptured by the expanding embryo put in some cases the seed coats are so hard that they offer mechanical resistance to embryo expansive.

Inhibitory dormancy: In this, the inhibiting action of endosperm has been observed. Even a small portion of endosperm in contact with embryo prevents germination.

Treatments to overcome dormancy

In order to overcome the various types of seed dormancies explained above and in order to facilitate germination the seeds require certain pre-germination treatments. The various pre- germination treatments given to the seeds are as follows:

Chemical treatment	The seed covering can be rendered more pervious to water by treating the seeds with certain chemicals like Sulphuric acid (used in strengths varying from 50% to 25%) has been found effective.
Soaking and Scalding	The soaking of seeds in water hastens germination by making the seed coats soft and also helps in removing the inhibitory factors. Soaking period depends upon the hardness of the seed coat. Scalding is the treatment in which seeds are immersed in hot boiling water and are allowed to soak in the gradually cooling water for 12-24 hours.
Mechanical Scarification	This treatment consists of rubbing the seeds in folds of sand paper or filing the seed coat, the object used to make the seed coat permeable to water. Examples of such seeds are chiku, canna and ber.
Stratification	Exposing the seeds to low temperature for a considerable period helps in accelerating the process after ripening and breaking of dormancy resulting into stimulation of the germination. This cold treatment is known as stratification or moist chilling. The seeds are arranged in alternate layers of moist sand or soil and are stored at 32°F to 45°F for 1-4 months. The seeds of apple, pear and cherry need to be given this treatment before they can germinates.

Seed sowing: Seeds of citrus species used as rootstocks are sown on raised beds. Mango stones are sown in madkis or small pots. The seeds of papaya and mango do not require pre-germination treatment. The seeds of other fruits should be sown on beds in nursery. The beds are prepared by pulverizing the soil and mixing it with farmyard manure. The seed should be covered with sand or fine soil and water well. In-situ sowing: in ber, mango, pecannut and walnut, the tap root system is very vigorous. So during the process of transplanting, rot system is disturbed which ultimately affects their establishment in the field.

B) Asexual or Vegetative method of propagation: Asexual propagation is the reproduction by means of vegetative parts of the plant, such as roots, shoots or leaves.

Advantages of asexual method of propagation

1. As there is no change in the genetic makeup of the plant propagated by this method the fruit plants propagated vegetatively are true to type and results in uniformity in growth, yield and quality of fruit, which make harvesting and marketing easy.
2. Some fruits such as banana, pineapple and some guavas being seedless the only way of further propagation is vegetative method.
3. Vegetatively propagated fruit trees come into bearing earlier.
4. Certain varieties of some fruit plants are susceptible to certain diseases. By budding or grafting them onto a resistant rootstock, these varieties can be grown without pest or disease incidence.
5. Hardiness to cold and other unfavourable condition as draught etc. can be obtained.
6. Trees can be considerably dwarfed by using proper rootstocks. Methods like bridge grafting can be used for healing of the wounds caused by rodents.
7. By top working, the inferior quality fruit trees can be converted into superior quality fruit trees.
8. It is possible to grow two or three varieties on the same plant by using asexual propagation e.g. one can get 3 to 4 varieties of roses on the various branches of the stock plant.

Disadvantages of asexual propagation method

1. The vegetatively propagated plants are generally not so vigorous and long lived as seedlings.
2. No new varieties can be evolved by vegetative propagation.

Methods of Asexual Propagation: There are two main methods of asexual propagation like:

a) methods based on plants own roots, and

b) methods based on roots of other plants.

These methods can be further sub-divided into various specific methods based on particular technique or specific plant part to be utilized for propagation.

a) Methods based on plants own roots

i) Parts not detached before rooting like Suckers, Runners, Layering

ii) Parts generally detached before rooting like;

By separation- Bulbs, Corms

By division- Rhizomes, Crown, Offsets, Tubers

iii) Parts always detached after rooting- Root cuttings, Leaf cuttings, Stem cuttings

b) Methods based on roots of other plants

i) **Grafting**: Inarch grafting, Tongue grafting, Saddle grafting, Whip grafting, Veneer grafting, Crown grafting, Side grafting, Bridge grafting.

ii) **Budding**: Shield budding, Patch budding, Forkert budding, Ring budding.

a) Methods based on plants own roots

i) Parts not detached before rooting like Suckers, Runners, Layering

Suckers: These are plant parts which arise from the base of the mother plant e.g. in pineapples, the suckers emerge from the leaf axis near roots. These are cut neatly with attached roots and planted directly in the field. Date-palm and Chrysanthemum are examples.

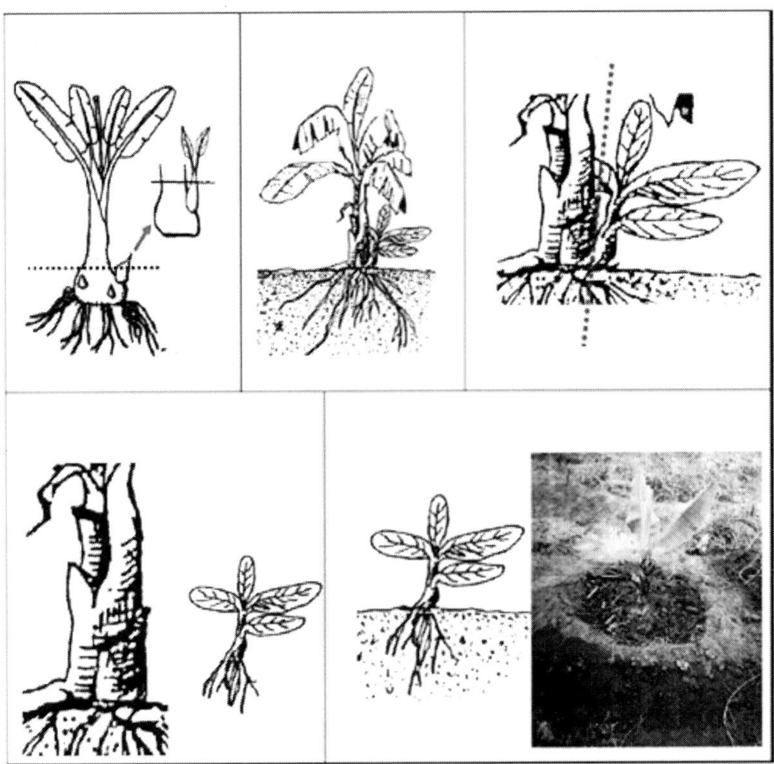

Runners: Strawberry is an example of such runners. Runners are parts of mother plants each of which is capable of producing roots in contact with the soil while connected with the mother plant. These also can be cut from the mother plant and planted directly in the field.

Runner production in Strawberrry plants

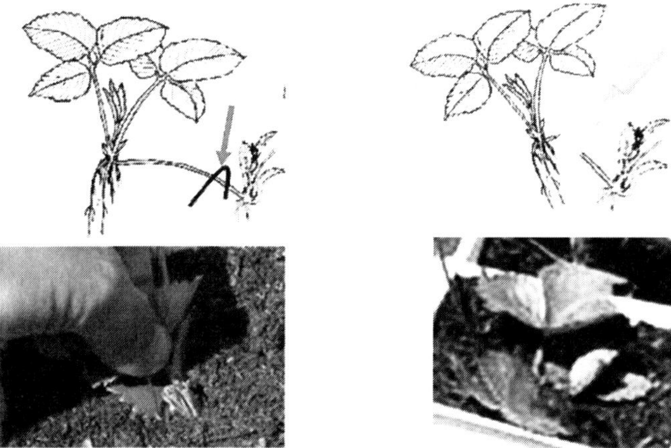

Layering: Layering is the development of roots on a stem while it is still attached to the parent plant. The rooted stem is then detached to become a new plant growing on its own roots. A layering stem is known as a layer. Different methods of layering are:

1. **Tip Layering**: In this case, the tips of shoots are buried 1" to 2" in the soil. The shoot tip begins to grow downwards into the ground but recurves to produce a sharp bend in the stem from which roots develop. This method is commonly followed for raspberry.

2. **Simple Layering**: Branches that have formed roots in one area only are called simple layers. The procedure followed in propagating plants by this method is as follow: A mature branch of one season's growth is selected close to the ground. A sharp slit of 1" to 1" is made slanting towards the tip about 2 to 2½' from the cut portion away from each other. Then this branch is buried in the soil. After about 3 to 4 months when the roots have formed the layered plant is severed from mother plant and is ready for planting in the field. The guava, lime lemon jasmine are propagated by this method.

3. **Continuous or Trench Layering**: This method consists of completely covering a branch under soil. This method is adopted in the propagation of own rooted apple and pear. This method is also known as the etiolation method of layering. In this method about 1 year old plants intended to be multiplied are planted in a slanting position forming an angle of 40° to the ground. When the plants are established in this position, they are bent over and pogged down in a shallow trench and covered with a thin layer of soil. As the buds begin to swell along the burled parts of the stem, more soil is thrown over the stem gradually. From these blanched or

etiolated parts roots emerged and the rooted growths are finally detached and planted out leaving sufficient number of the buds on parent plant for the formation of future layers. Thus, the layering beds when once established become more or less permanent, producing a succession of new plants.

4. **Compound or serpentine layering**: Long shoots that are alternately covered and exposed over their entire length are known as compound layers. They normally from roots at each node where they are covered and develop new shoots from buds at nodes that are not covered.
5. **Mound or stool layering**: This is a modification of etiolation method. In this the plants to be multiplied are cut back to almost ground level. The fresh growths which result are etiolated by gradually heaping earth around them as they grow up. The new shoots are thus burried gradually up to not more than about half their length. After rooting they detached.

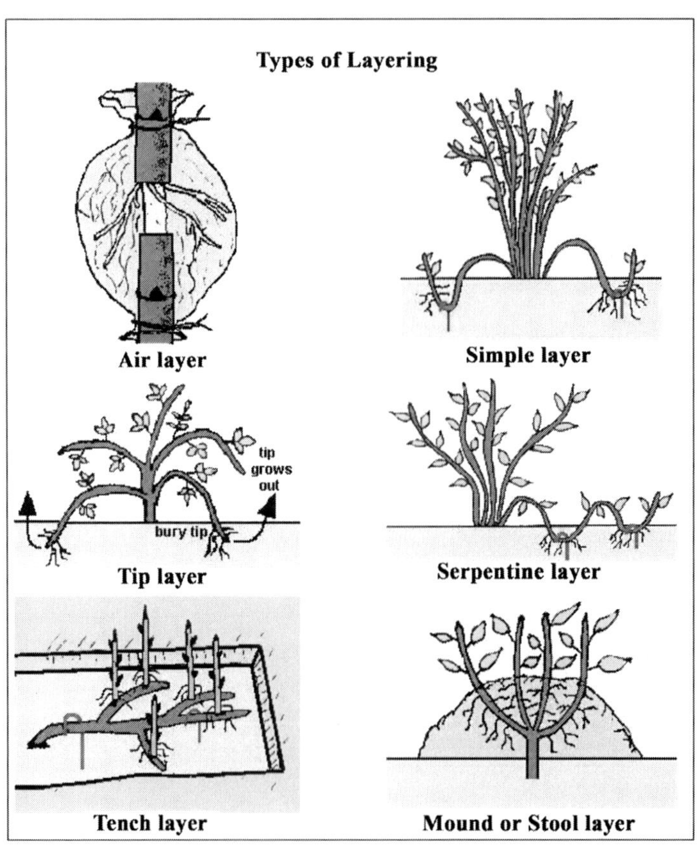

6) **Air Layering**: If the branches or shoots are far above the ground level and do not lend themselves to bending, they are layered by using a suitable medium in evidence rooting in their aerial parts. At the desired position the branch a circular strip of bark up to an inch in width is complete removed, leaving the wood as such. Sphagnum moist is packed round this portion and tied with a polythene sheet. The polythene sheet keeps the medium moist and prevents the loss of water by evaporation. Rooting occurs in six to eight weeks. Guavas, chiku, figs, and pomegranate are propagated by this method. Rooting in layered branches is induced by surrounding them with a moist porous medium. When the roots are visible through the polythene wrap the plants are detached from the parent plant.

Advantages of layering

1. This is a rather certain method of inducing rooting.
2. Some plants that cannot be satisfactorily started from cutting, e.g; guava, can be propagated with relative ease from layers.
3. The cuttings which have been detached from the mother plant often do not remain alive until roots are formed. But a layer on other hand in supported by the parent Plant.
4. By using a large branch, a much larger plant can be obtained in the first instance.

Disadvantages of layering

1) Slow and cumbersome process.
2) Interference with cultivation.
3) Limited number of plants can be propagated.
4) Requires more individual attention.

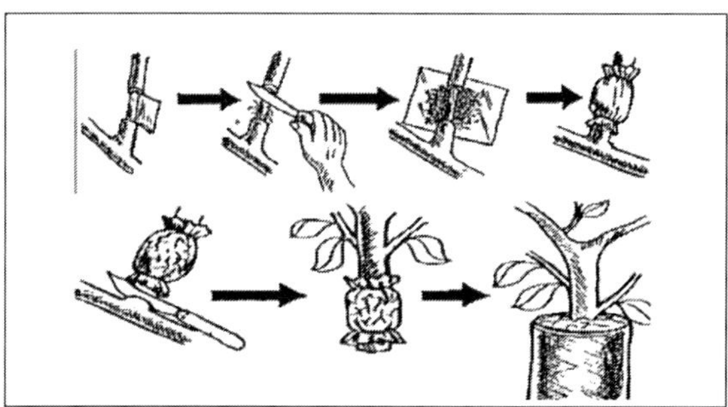

Fig. 1: Steps involved during Air layering of plants

Root formation in layers: Root formation during layering is stimulated by various stem treatments which cause an interruption in the downwards translocation of carbohydrates, auxin and other growth factors from leaves and growing shoot tips. These materials accumulate near the point of the treatment and rooting occurs in this area even though the stem is attached to the parent plant. Water and nutrients are supplied to the layered shoots, because the stem is not cut and the xylem remains intact. The root formation takes place in simple, serpentine and air layering in this way. Etiolation is another means by which the internal condition of the developing shoot can be modified during layering to stimulate rooting. The absence of light is favourable for initiation of root primordia in the stem tissue. The root formation takes place in mound and trench layering.

ii). Parts generally detached before rooting

This type of vegetative propagation is further divided into two groups. These are (a) Separation, in which plant parts like bulb of onion or garlic are separation, into independent units and (b) Division, in which plant parts like rhizomes, tubers etc are divided into small sections before they are planted.

(a) Separation

Bulbs: The bulbs may be tunicated or scaly: in tunicated bulbs the fleshy leaves are completely unsheathed in the inner axis e.g; onion. In the scaly bulbs the fleshy, leaves which form the storage organs are protected by thin scaly leaves e.g., garlic. These bulbs are separated from mother plant and used for propagating new plants. This type of propagation is commonly not found in fruit trees.

Corms: A corm is a modified stem in which the central axis is short and compact. The entire structure, when dormant, consists of fleshy axis. The corm differs from the bulbs in that the dormant corm is solid, without leaves or scales. Examples of corms are Gladiolus and Calendula. This type is also not commonly found in fruit crop.

(b) Division

Rhizomes: Rhizomes is a stem growing in horizontal direction below the surface of the soil. It has the same general structure as typical stem, nodes and internodes, axillary buds, and a terminal growing point e.g., Rhizomes of Canna and Ginger.

Crowns: In pineapple there are tuft of leaves on the top of the fruit. These are called as crowns. For propagating pineapple these crowns can be used.

Tubers: Stem tuber is shortened and thickened underground stem. The 'eyes' of the tuber are the modified auxillary buds e.g., potato.

Root Tubers: Fleshy roots differ from stem tubers in that they do not have organized buds present on any part of them. The root tuber can be used for propagation only if the tuber is accompanied by a portion of the stem.

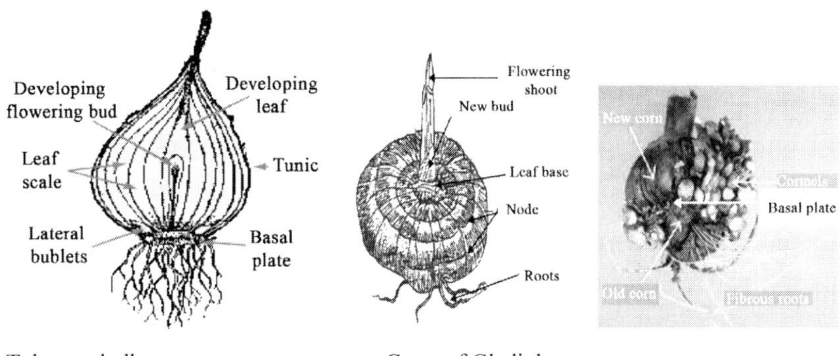

Tuberose bulb

Corm of Gladiolus

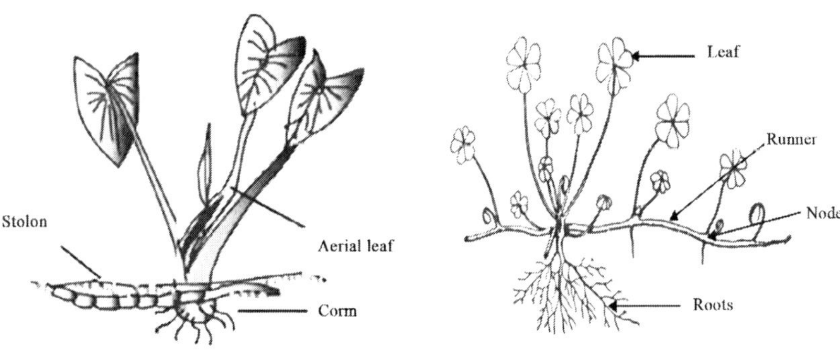

Stolon

Runners

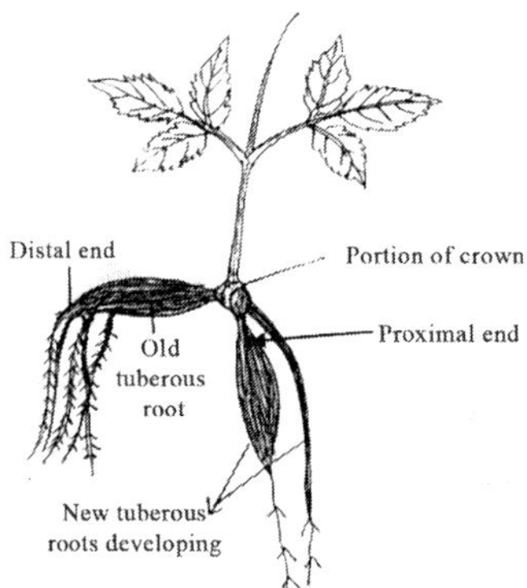

Tuberous roots of Dahlia

iii) Parts always detached after rooting

This class includes root, leaf and stem cutting. Cutting is the process of propagating plants by the use of vegetative parts that, when detached from mother plant and placed under suitable conditions will develop into complete plants. The main advantages of propagation by cutting are (i) Larger number of plants can prepared from a few plants, (ii) it is inexpensive, quick, simple and does not require any special technique, (ii) There is no problem of compatibility with rootstocks.

Root Cutting: These are cut pieces of roots about 4"-10" long which are usually planted in horizontal position in sand or soil. Guava can be propagated by root cuttings but this method is seldom followed.

Leaf Cuttings: Many plants with fleshy leaves can be propagated leaf cuttings. The leaf is detached from the mother plant and planted with petiole and half of the leaf covered with soil. This method is not followed in fruit tree propagation.

Stem Cuttings: These are further classified as Hard wood, Soft wood and Semi-hard wood cutting.

b). Methods based on roots of other plants

The methods of propagation described above were those in which only the mother plant or a part thereof was involved. The methods described below involve the union of two plants, the stock of rootstock and the scion. Scion is that part of the mother plant which is used in grafting and budding to develop the future tree. The plant or part thereof on which the scion is worked upon to produce the final tree is the rootstock or stock. There are two groups of grafting:

1) Scion grafting or commonly referred to as grafting, and
2) Bud grafting or commonly referred to as budding.

When the stock and scion plants are brought together by anyone of the methods described later the union between the two takes place in the following steps:

1) Freshly cut scion is brought into secure, intimate contact with freshly cut stock tissue in such a manner that the cambium regions of each are in close proximity.
2) Temperature and humidity conditions must be such as to promote activity in exposes and surrounding cells.

3) The outer exposed layers of cells in the cambium region of both scion and stock produce parenchyma cells which soon intermingle and interlock. This is commonly called callus tissue.

4) Certain cells of this newly formed callus tissue which are in line with the cambium layer of the scion and stock differentiate into new cambium cells.

5) These new cambium cells produce new vascular tissue, xylem towards inside and phloem towards the outside, thus establishing vascular connection between the scion and stock, a requisite for successful graft union.

Graft Incompatibility

The inability of the stock and scion to produce a successful graft union and the resulting single plant to develop satisfactorily is termed incompatibility or sometimes uncongeniality. The opposite of this is compatibility or congeniality. Incompatibility means stock and scion fail to unite and the graft dies rather quickly. Uncongeniality would include cases when the combination lives, but some modification of stock or scion occurs. There are commonly two theories put forth to explain the causes of incompatibility.

a) Growth reaction at the bud union: The different growth characteristics of the stock and the scion are associated with incompatibility i.e. if marked differences occur in vigous or in the time of starting or completing vegetative growth for the season, incompatibility may be expected.

b) Incompatibility may be due to physiological and biochemical differences between the stock and the scion. In some cases it is believed that one of the partners of the graft form toxin which either inhibits the growth of or actually kills the other.

Stock-scion Relationship: The rootstock influences scion or the resulting tree and the fruit in many aspects. The important ways in which the rootstock influences the combination are:

1) The most noteworthy reactions between stock and scion are intimately related to growth rate and usually can be plainly seen by an examination of the trunks at the point of the union. In some cases, the scion overgrows the stock or sometimes the stock may overgrow the scion. The reaction at bud union represents the congeniality or affinity between the stock and scion. A smooth bud union indicates a uniform balance of physiological function and growth rate between the stock and the scion.

2) Growth of the scion top: On certain stocks the trees become dwarf e.g. the sweet orange tree grown on trifoliate stock becomes dwarf. The shape and form of the trees is also sometimes affected by the stock e.g. the Milton Pump on Wayland stock has upright, narrow base form whereas on the Marianna roots the trees are low, round headed, bushy with thick spreading dwarf tops. However the same stock may react differently with different scion variety e.g. sweet oranges, Valencia of sour oranges are bigger in size as compared to sweet orange on sour orange.

3) The rootstock influences the yield of the scion varieties grafted on them. The trees of sweet orange on Mokari yielded significantly less crop than on rough lemon in Punjab. The yield of kangpur lime stock is more than Jamberi and other stocks.

4) Precocity or early fruiting: Generally the stocks which have dwarfing effect tend to stimulate precocity or early fruiting e.g. santra trees on Rangpur lime bear at an earlier age as compared to other stocks.

5) Fruit maturity: Slow growing stocks tend to hasten fruit ripening e.g. Trifoliate stock is generally considered to secure early ripening in oranges.

6) Quality of the fruit: The quality of fruit as expressed by juice content and acid or sugar content is greatly affected by the stock. In Punjab it has been found that plants produced on vigorous rootstocks like rough lemon and Gajanimma produce thickly skinned fruits. In Punjab, the fruits of Sweet Orange on Nasnaran had a higher sugar content than on other citrus stocks.

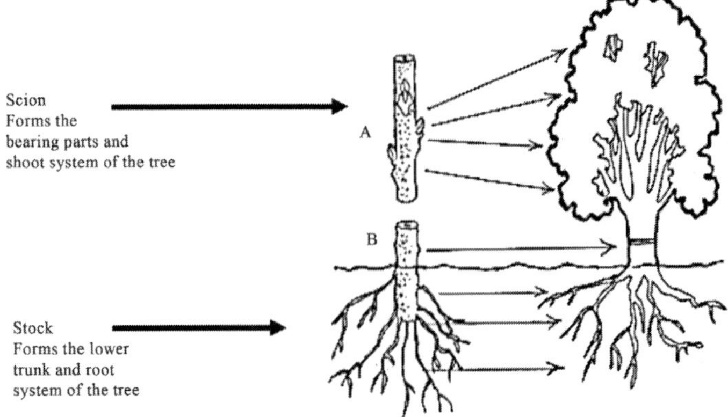

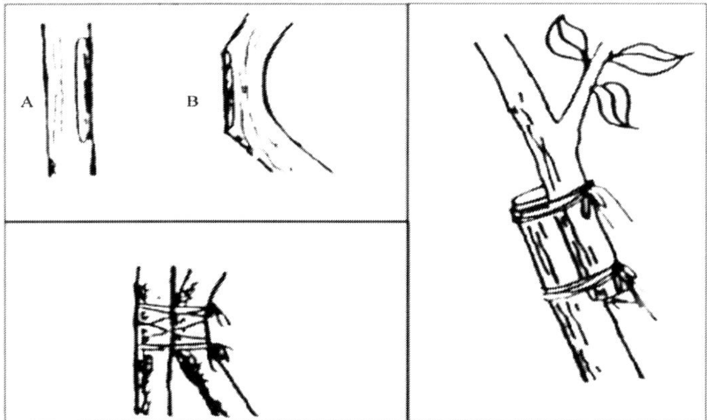

Process of Grafting: Scion-stock relationship

Methods of grafting

1. **Inarch grafting** (grafting by simple approach): Inarching consists of uniting the stems of two separate plants which are propagated with considerable difficulty by other methods. One year old terminal twig of the scion tree of the desired variety of about 1 to 2 feet in length having the same thickness as that of the stock is selected. A healthy and well established potted seedling of the same size (lead pencil size) is selected. The selected potted seedling is carried near the scion tree and the scion branch is first bent like an arch and is operated and united at the place where it can be tightly join. A thin slice of bark and wood, about two inches long, nearly a third of an inch in breadth and a twelfth of an inch deep, is removed with a sharp grafting knife both from the stock and the scion branch. The cuts thus made should be absolutely flat, clean, over an smooth. Both the cut surfaces are brought together under pressure and face to free without leaving any hollow interspaces between them. They are tied firm first with a flat tape of banana leaf sheath and then with a jute string (sutali). The bandage is made waterproof and air-proof by covering it with grafting wax or cow dung-clay plaster. The graft is removed to shady place where it is nursed, hardened and cured for a period of about three to six months prior to its final planting at a permanent place. The operation can be done when the sap in the plants is in good flowing condition which helps in quick healing. A hot dry period as well as heavy rains during the inarching period is not favourable.

2. **Tongue or approach grafting**: The selection of stock seedlings and scion branch is almost the same as in the case of simple grafting. For

this method, a long deep slice is removed from both the components to be joined. The slice varies according to the diameter of the plant part used and is deep enough to remove a portion of the central wood or xylem region. Diagonal tongue shaped cuts half to three-fourth of an inch in length are made on both the scion and the stock in such a way as to permit perfect interlocking. The two parts are then tied with a string. After the union is complete, the scion is served below the graft union and the rootstock is cut just above the joint as is done in case of the inarch grafting. This is usually practiced with mango sometime in the monsoon season i.e. August to October.

3. **Saddle Grafting**: This method is sometimes followed in the case of mango though it is not as popular as inarching. Care should be taken to select the stock and scion of equal thickness. The rootstock is de-headed at a height of about 8% taking two diagonal cuts opposite one another to meet at the centre to form a wedge shape. A cleft equal in length to that of the wedge of the stock is cut on the outer side the selected scion branch to expose the cambium and fix in the wedge of the stock. The depth of the cut in the scion goes more than half way through the scion. The joined parts then tied over firmly. The proper season to do this operation is from August to October.

4. **Whip Grafting**: This method of grafting is used to join together plant parts which are under one inch in size. This method is not commonly used. It is useful when it is not convenient to take the stock seedling to a scion tree which may be far away. The stock and scion should be of equal thickness and in vigorous growth having the sap in a free flowing condition. The scion branch of about 9” length from matured wood previously defoliated leaving a portion of the petiole, is selected. It is also given a slantwise cut of the same size as that of stock piece and is then brought in contact with the stock and tied firmly at the operated part with the help of banana fibre (sopat) and jute string.

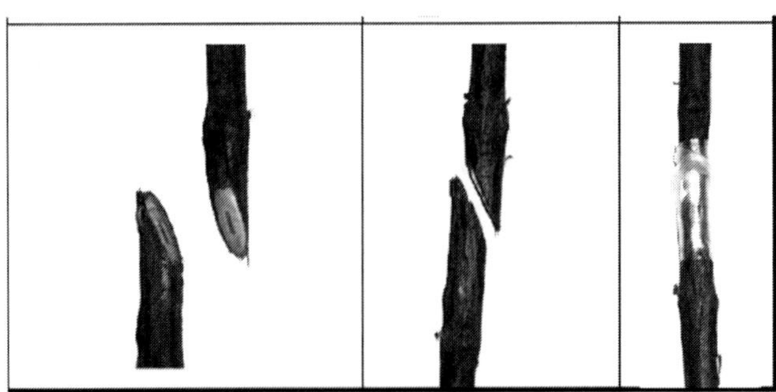

Whip Grafting

5. **Veneer Grafting**: Veneer grafting is now practiced in West Bengal on Mango in preference to inarching. In this method, the scion terminal shoots of 10 to 15 cm length and of pencil size thickness are cut to use as scion. Terminal shoots with plump and swollen buds that are about to sprout in a fortnight are considered ideal. Immediately after cutting, the scion shoot is given a slanting cut of 5 cm long on one side of the cut end removing bark and wood to half its thickness. Skill is necessary in making a clean cut. A notch is made in a selected mango seedling up to 5 cm deep in an oblique manner on any convenient side. The cut end of the scion shoot is placed in position and wrapped very tightly with 1 cm wide polythene film tape keeping the terminal shoot and free. The seedlings are kept moist so as to ensure good sap flow for promoting speedy union. September to October is considered favourable for veneer grafting. It takes about three months for veneer grafting plants to become ready for planting in orchard.

6. **Side Grafting**: This is another method of grafting in which the terminal shoots of scion plants are used. The scion shoot is first defoliated upto 4" to 4 1/2" length, a week before its separation. Then these shoots are cut away from the parent tree and grafted to the side of stock seedling of the same thickness. Two planting cuts are made at the base of the scion shoot forming a wedge and this is fitted into a notch like cut made on the side of the stock seedling. A firm bandage is then made on the side of the stock seedling. The scion material separated from the desired variety of mango should be kept moist by wrapping it with wet gunny cloth.

7. **Bridge Grafting**: It is not mean of propagation in the true sense as the other methods. It is principally employed to join living tissues of trees which are girdled partially or completely by rodents, animals, implements due to mechanical injury, cold or cracking. Eventually all roots die since no food returns to them

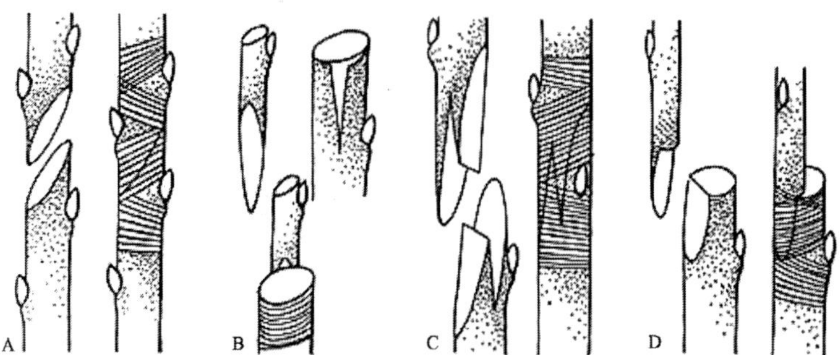

Grafting: a) Whip grafting b) Rind grafting c) Tongue grafting d) Saddle grafting

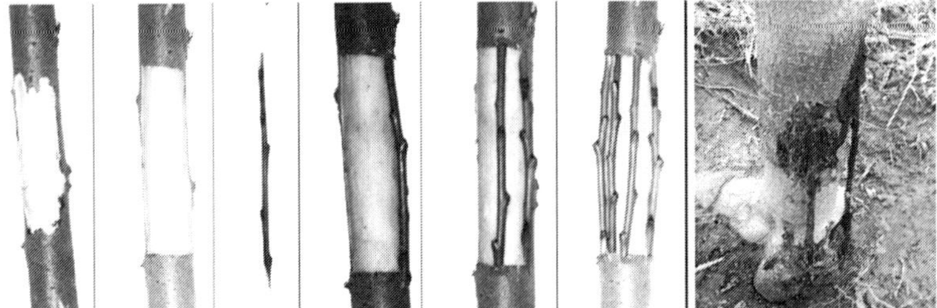

Bridge Grafting

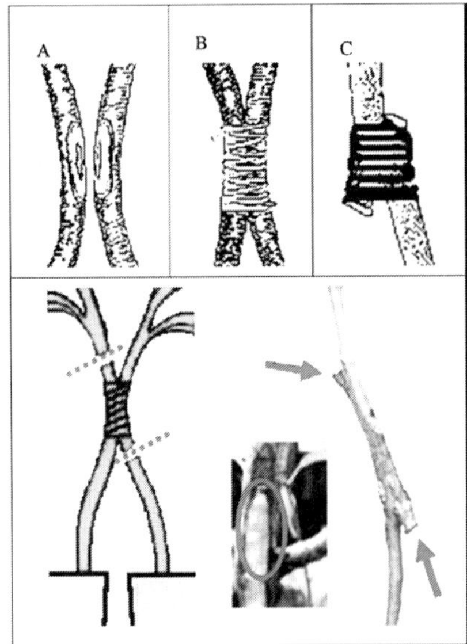

Approach grafting

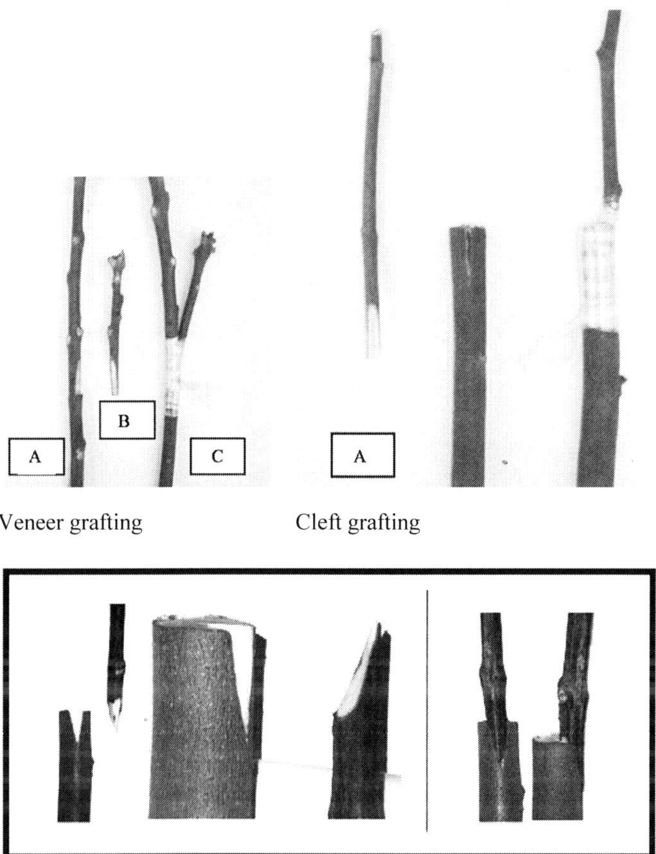

Veneer grafting

Cleft grafting

Wedge Grafting

through the bark. The bridging of the damaged or injured portion of the limbs, stem or trunks of the tree is done to save it. The sap flow on both sides of the injury is thus established by causing congenial circumstances to unite the scions with the tree both above the below ends. The girdle in such a way is bridged to fill the gap. This is commonly done when the tree is in sap flowing condition. The selection of the scion wood is practically done the same way as in other types of grafting. Congeniality is the pre-requisite. Scions are cut in such a way that, when they are in position, both ends extend well in the healthy tissue. Both the ends of the scion are joined to a length of 2 to 3 inches of the wounded tree. Initially the rugged edges of the injured region are trimmed over by making a clean cut into the living tissue, above and below the wound. The portion so cut is slightly shorter than the scion is marked out at two inches interval around the trunk so that the entire wounded area is bridged and to facilitate a perfect fit the components are finally nailed in place.

The scion is inserted with larger diameter end towards the ground and thus both ends are nailed in position. Since the scions are little longer than the channels cut for them, they bow slightly. The scions and the injured surfaces are painted with the grafting wax to prevent drying. After the union is complete, a few buds on the scion may sprout. Cut these off early. Inter-change of elaborate food material manufactured in the leaves and nutrients absorbed by the root system, takes place immediately.

Equipments for Grafting

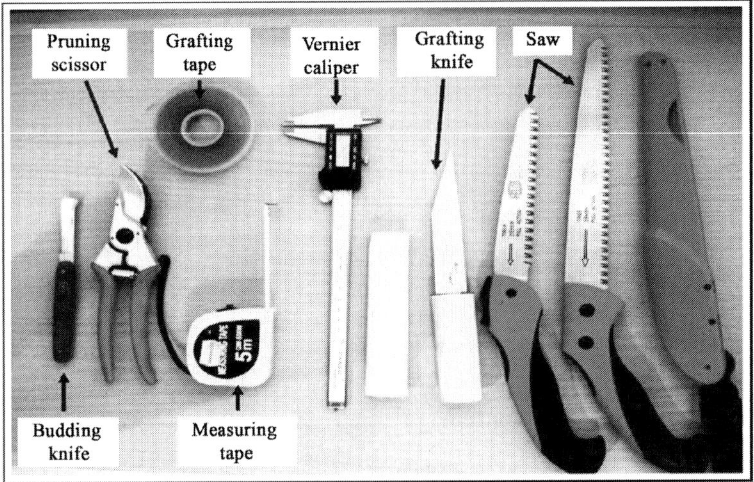

ii). **Budding**: It is yet another propagation technique where a vegetative bud is excised from a mother plant and used as the scion material. The technique involves,

1. The removal of selected vegetative bud along with a patch of bark from the scion plant and inserting it on to the stock plant.
2. The graft is further tied to keep the bud in place and maintained till the union takes place.
3. After the union is ensured, the portion of the stock above the bud union is removed and the sprout from the scion bud is encouraged to grow further.

Different budding techniques such as Shield budding, Patch budding, Ring budding, Forkert budding are seen in use, in which the scion material (shield, or a small rectangular patch, or a ring) is inserted on to the stock plant. The method of budding is the most common technique for plant propagation in commercial nurseries. First, one must graft a single bud attached to the stem of the rootstock. The stem or branch may not be thicker than 2 cm diameter. Therefore, this method is only applicable for young rootstock plants or smaller branches of large plants.

Use bud wood or bud sticks which are of a vigorous current season growth for best results. Remove the top and bottom part of the branch, because the tip buds are too immature and the bottom buds may be a cluster of buds or they are too weak to use for budding. The length of the stick is approximately 30 cm. Remove the leaves leaving a 1-1.5 cm long of leaf petiole on the stem. The time for budding comes when the bark peels easily on the stock. Irrigation a few days before budding helps to slip the bark. One should bud graft into the root neck, or into a higher part of the plant. Normally, budding should be done about 15-20 cm above the root neck avoiding the possibility that the scion will root into the soil.

T-budding: The "T" cut on the stock is done about 20-25 cm above the surface with a 2 cm long vertical cut and a 7-8 mm long horizontal cut on the stock. A slight twist with the budding knife may open the two flaps of bark. The bud is then inserted under the two flaps of bark by pushing downward. If part of the bud remains above the horizontal cut, it must be cut off. This will allow the flaps to be closed tightly. Finally, the incision should be closed with budding tape, which should be wrapped tightly around the stem. Tying must start at the bottom or the top end of the incision. After 3-4 weeks, the tape should be removed. If the shield is shrivelled and the petiole does not fall off at the touch, the bud is possibly dead and the budding process should be repeated.

Inverted "T"-budding: The inverted T-budding technique is exactly same as the normal T-budding method with the exception that the horizontal cut is made on the bottom end of the incision. In this case, the bud is cut from the bud stick by starting above the bud and exiting below it. Currently most fruit trees are propagated with the T-budding method. However, the use of inverted T-budding technique is much more effective due to the downward flow of hormones that are intercepted below the bud. Therefore, the union will be stronger and the healing process will be faster.

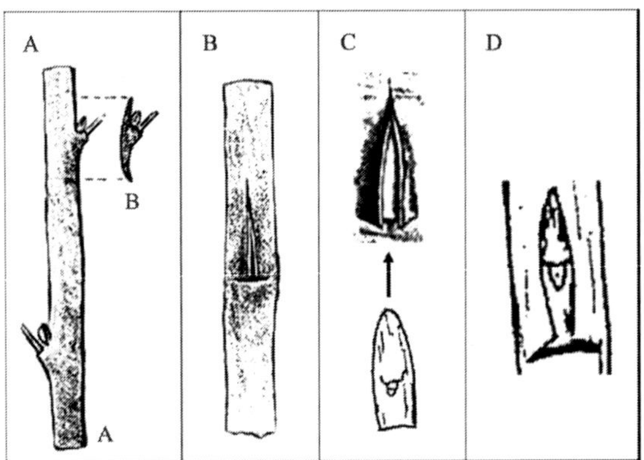

Inverted T-Budding

Chip-budding: Chip-budding does not use the protective bark flaps as T-budding does, but it also does not use slipping bark. A thin slice of wood with a scion bud is removed by making a smooth downward cut for a distance of 2-3 cm (1 in.) and just into the wood. A second cut is made at the base of the first one, forming a notch. A chip is removed from the stock in the same manner. Only 2 thin lines of cambial tissue on both the stock and scion are present for healing, so it is important that matching occurs on both sides. However, matching along one side of a small scion is often adequate. The scion is then wrapped so that all cut edges are completely covered. The stock and scion must be placed together in such a way that allows the cambium of the bud and stock to match together as much as possible.

Patch budding: It is used on plants in which the bark is either too thick or too brittle to allow easy insertion of a bud shield. A 2-bladed patch-budding knife can be used to make 2 parallel, horizontal cuts 2-3 cm (1 in.) long on the stock. These cuts are connected at the ends by 2 vertical cuts and the bark patch is peeled off and discarded. The patch of bark containing the scion bud is cut from the bud stick in the same manner. The cut scion should not be lifted but slid off sideways to avoid damage. The scion patch is then inserted on the prepared stock and securely wrapped, being careful that all cut edges are covered.

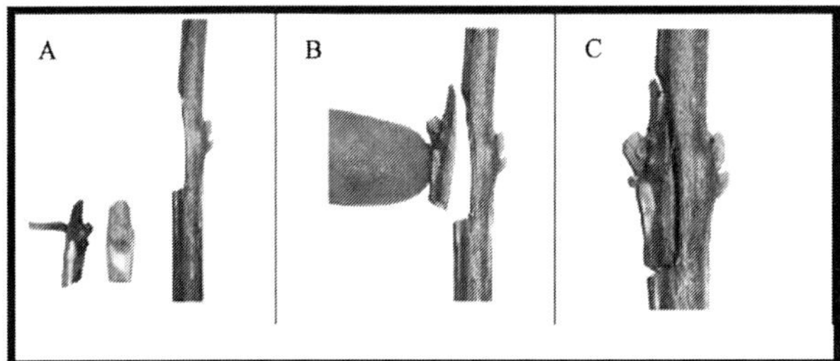

Chip Budding

Propagation Techniques for Mango

Mango is a cross pollinated and highly haterozygous fruit crop. Therefore, propagation by seeds (called stones in mango) lead to variability in the progeny and is a limitation for commercial orcharding. Hence, vegetative methods of propagation are adopted for getting true-to-type plants. Seed propagation is still the chief method of multiplication of rootstocks.

Propagation of rootstocks: Rootstock plants are raised from stones. Most of the commercial varieties in India are mono-embyronic but some varieties from South India are poly-embryonic which give true-to-type seedlings from nucellar embryos. Stones collected indiscriminately give poor germination but provide a lot of variation. The viability of mango stones is lost very quickly. Freshly collected stones from canning units give high germination but when these seeds are stocked or kept in sun for a large period, they lose germinability. The germination of mango stones is 80% when sown within a month of extraction but none thereafter. The selected stones are spread on raised nursery beds and covered with leaf mould or FYM for better germination. Germination starts within 12 - 15 days and continues up to 3 weeks. Seedlings are transplanted to pots or polybags as soon as they turn green and these are nursed and prepared for grafting. When polyembryonic seeds are sown, nucellar seedlings are separated within a month and planted separately.

Vegetative propagation: Propagation of rootstocks by vegetative methods is advocated to eliminate variation. These methods are not commonly used probably due to absence of standard rootstock type.

1. *Cutting:* The hardwood leafy cuttings are used for rooting. Cutting from younger trees rooted better than those from old trees. Rooting as well as subsequent survival has been improved by using juvenile shoots, etiolation and ringing of shoots and application of IBA in lanolin paste on the ringed portion. A medium containing peat moss and sand (1:1)

proved better and such cuttings have to be kept under mist for rooting. For Deshehari cuttings dipped in 5000 ppm IBA and planted in sphagnum moss and sand mixture resulted in 97 per cent rooting compared to only 15 per cent without bottom heat. Pre-planting treatment with phenolic compounds such as hydroxybenzoic acid, coumaric acid and ferulic acid generally promoted auxin-induced rooting in cuttings.

2. *Air layering:* Etiolation of shoots before layering resulted in more fibrous roots than without etiolation and application of IBA + NAA improved rooting. The success of air layers was markedly improved by use of growth regulators like 5000 to 20000 ppm NAA and IBA in lanolin paste.
3. *Stooling:* In stool layering, after about two years of growth, the mother plant is headed back at 10-12 cm above ground to induce emergence of several shoots below the cut end. Vigorous shoots are ringed and IBA (5000 ppm) in lanolin is applied on the ringed portion about a week before earthing up. Rooting takes place in 4 to 6 weeks and these are separated from the mother plant. The same mother plant can be utilized for about ten years to obtain genetically uniform rooted plants of a given clone. This is the easiest and fastest method for vegetative propagation to multiply mango rootstocks.
4. ***Budding:*** Various budding methods, namely, patch forkert, shield, chip and T-budding are successful in mango. However, the success varies depending on geographical location and season.
5. ***Grafting:*** Inarching or approach grafting, veneer grafting, wedge or whip grafting, epicotyl grafting or stone grafting and softwood grafting are the most extensively used methods.

Advantages of Budding/Grafting

1) Change varieties or cultivars. An older established orchard of fruiting trees may become obsolete as newer varieties or cultivars are developed.
2) The newer varieties may offer improved insect or disease resistance, better drought tolerance, or higher yields.
3) As long as the scion is compatible with the rootstock, the older orchard may be top worked using the improved variety or cultivar.
4) Optimize cross-pollination and pollination. Certain fruit trees are not self-pollinating; they require pollination by a second fruit tree, usually of another variety. This process is known as cross-pollination.

5) Portions of a tree or entire trees may be pollinated with the second variety to ensure fruit set.

6) Take advantage of particular rootstocks, certain rootstocks have superior growth habits, disease and insect resistance, and drought tolerance.

7) Benefit from interstocks: An interstock can be particularly valuable when the scion and rootstock are incompatible. The interstock that is compatible with both rootstock and scion is used.

8) Produce certain plant forms. Numerous horticultural plants owe their beauty to the fact that they are grafted or budded onto a standard, especially those that have a weeping or cascading form.

9) Increase the growth rate of seedlings. The seedling progeny of many fruit and nut breeding programs, if left to develop naturally, may require 8 to 12 years to become fruitful. However, if these progeny are grafted onto established plants, the time required for them to flower and fruit is reduced dramatically.

10) Another way toincrease the growth rate of seedlings is to graft more than one seedling onto a mature plant. Using this procedure as a breeding tool saves time, space, and money.

Plants That Can be Propagated by Root Cuttings: *Breadfruit (Artocarrpus altilis), blackberry (Rubus sp.), fig (Ficus carica), garden phlox (Phlox paniculata), Japanese pagoda tree (Sophora japonica), lilac (Syringa vulgaris), Malus sp., oriental pear (Pyrus calleryana), Rosa spp.*

Plants That Can be Propagated by Leaf Cuttings

African violet (Saintpaulia ionantha), Begonia spp., Bryophyllum spp.), Crassula spp., *Kalanchoe* spp., *lily (Lilium longiflorum and L. candidum), Oxalis* spp., *Peperomia* spp, *Sedum spp., snake plant (Sansevieria trifasciata), sweet potato, wax plant (Hoya carnosa). Generally, these plants have thick leaves. Jasmine (Jasminum sambac) and dracaena (Dracaena godseffiana) have also been propagated experimentally by leaf cuttings.*

Plants That Can be Propagated by Stem Cuttings

Acerola (Malpighia glabra), bamboo, black pepper (Piper nigrum), cacao (Theobroma cacao), cassava (Manihot esculenta), citrus (Citrus spp.), coffee (Coffea spp.), eggplant (Solanum melongena), grape (Vitis vinifera), guava (Psidium guajava), passion fruit (Passiflora edulis), pineapple (Ananas comosus), rubber (Hevea brasiliensis), sugarcane (Saccharum officinale), tomato (Lycopersicon esculentum).

Plants That Can be Propagated by Air Layering

Bell fruit, water apple (Syzygium aqueum), black pepper (Piper nigrum), cacao (Theobroma cacao), cashew (Anacardium occidentale), citrus (Citrus spp.), coffee (Coffea spp.), grape (Vitis vinifera), guava (Psidium guajava), jackfruit (Artocarpus heterophyllus), litchi (Litchi sp.), mango (Mangifera indica), mangosteen (Garcinia mangostana), sapota (Manilkara zapota), star apple (Chrysophyllum cainito) and tamarind (Tamarindus indica).

Propagation Techniques for Citrus

The sexual as well as asexual (vegetative) methods of propagation are used to raise plants of different species in citrus. The seedlings of acid lime and mandarins are still planted in southern and north-eastern region of India.

Seed propagation: The number of seeds per fruit varies between different citrus species and cultivars. Seeds obtained from healthy, virus-free old trees which have a pedigree performance of producing vigorous, uniform seedlings should be used.

Polyembryony: Seeds of most citrus are polyembryonic and thus nucellar seedlings are used both for raising uniform rootstocks as well as for direct planting, especially in acid lime and mandarins. This also helps to raise healthy plants as citrus viruses are not transmitted through seed. Kama Khatta, *Citrus jambhiri, C. aurantium* and *Poncirus trifoliata* associated with polyembryonic nature, except in *P. trifoliata* with polyembryony varying from 35.5 to 54.2 per cent.

Viability: Since *Citrus* seeds generally have no dormancy and if they are allowed to dry and the cotyledons separate, the seeds fail to germinate. Therefore, it is essential to sow the seeds immediately after extraction.

Raising seedlings: *Citrus* seeds are to be sown on raised and well manured beds at 2.5 cm apart in rows spaced at 15 cm. In commercial nurseries, sowing is done during mid August to February.

Vegetative propagation

Cutting: Many species of *Citrus* can be successfully raised from cuttings and it is a very useful method of propagation especially when a species is desired to be colonally propagated on its own root system. However, there is wide variation in the rooting ability of different *Citrus* species. While limon and citron are easy to root, mandarin oranges, sour orange and grapefruit root with considerable difficulty. Synthetic auxins (IBA, NAA and IAA) and phenolic compounds help in rooting of cuttings. However, age and physiological status of mother plant, type of wood, time of planting and media composition for planting of cuttings determine the extent of success.

Air-layering: Air-layering is fairly common and is used to propagate pummelo, lime and sweet lime. Certain rootstocks like C. *karna, C. jambhiri, C. pennivesiculata, C. assamensis* and *C. megalocarpa* can easily be raised from the air-layers even without treatment of growth regulators.

Budding: Budding is the most common and widely used method of vegetative propagation of *Citrus*. T-budding is probably the best method and is successful with many species of *Citrus*. In Punjab, the bud take of Kinnow on *C. jambhiri* was 98% with better subsequent growth when round buds without wood were used than by using angular buds with or without wood. The time of budding affects bud take and subsequent growth of-plants. Now polythene strips are commonly used as wrapping material instead of jute twine.

Propagation Techniques for Jackfruit

Seed propagation is an old method of multiplication which is planted *in situ* or raised in pots. Now, vegetative propagation is the commercial method of jackfruit multiplication.

Seed propagation: This method is mainly used for the production of rootstocks. Soaking of seeds in NAA 25 ppm for 24 hours resulted in highest germination percentage as well as good seedling growth.

Vegetative propagation

Cutting: The highest percentage of rooting (84%) and survival (75%) was obtained in cuttings from invigorated and etiolated shoots treated with 5000 ppm IBA and kept under intermittent mist. (Etiolation and ringing for 15 days prior to planting also caused rooting in large number of cuttings which otherwise failed to strike roots.

Air-layering: Application of IAA, IBA and NAA significantly increased the percentage of rooting and IBA was most effective and produced large mass of roots in all the treated air – layers.

Stooling: Success in stooling of one year old jackfruit plants was reported. Soil is heaped upto 10 cm round the basal shoots for 15-20 days, after which it is removed. A ring of bark is taken from each etiolated shoot and IBA (5000 ppm) in lanolin is applied. At callus formation the shoots are again earthed up. About one month later, the rooted shoots are separated.

Grafting: Though jackfruit was successfully propagated (84% success) by inarching on seedling rootstock. This method of propagation is cumbersome. Soft wood grafting is the commercial method of propagation and is 100% successful under high humid conditions of coastal areas. Wherever the conditions are not favaourable, the soft wood grafting was highly successful under intermittent mist.

Budding: Patch budding is very successful (100%) when done in middle of June while the success was less (90%) when performed in May or July. Similar success with patch budding in June.

Propagation Techniques for Litchi

Seed propagation: This method is not desirable since the trees raised from seeds have long juvenile period, fail to produce true-to-type plants and often produce fruits of inferior quality. Propagation by seed is used mainly for rootstock propagation and breeding. The seeds of litchi have a very short viability, usually less than 5 days.

Vegetative propagation

Cuttings: Propagation by cuttings is possible, but the plants produced are less vigorous and this method is not generally recommended.

Air-layering: The main commercial method of propagation and rates of success may be as high as 95% under ideal conditions. Air-layered trees normally produce commercial crops after 3-6 years.

Grafting: Due to the limited and unpredictable activity of the cambium, which is related to the onset of leaf flushing, grafting is not always very successful. There is also possibility that some scion/stock combinations may be incompatible. However, approach grafting is generally successful.

Propagation Techniques for Mangosteen

Seed Propagation: The best known practice for the propagation of mangosteen is by seeds and when fresh seeds are sown, they germinate in 10 to 15 days. Since the seeds are of asexual origin, they produce trees identical to the mother. If the seed is dried or kept outside the fruit for several days before planting, germination is drastically reduced. However, the seeds can be maintained for 3 to 4 weeks within the fruit. The best way to carry seeds is by transporting the entire fruit. The size of the seeds is highly variable.

Vegetative propagation: Many attempts have been made to develop stronger, more rapidly growing mangoseen trees with a short juvenile phase through cutting, air-layering, Forkert budding, approach grafting and cleft grafting but the results were not promising. All the propagation methods tried did not show any real advantage over the seed propagation method.

Plant cloning: Cloning can produce high yielding crops. A cloned plant can yield a thousand new plants from one parent plant. This means that farmers can produce more crops without a lot of seeds. However, it promotes homozygocity in the absence of linkage, as in sexual reproduction. Cloning can produce drought and pest resistance crops. Cloning can also be very much welcome, producing crops with higher nutrition in them, for instance, *Golden Rice*, material which has high vitamin A content. Cloning can lead to selected crops with perfect size and high nutritious value; maximum output in every harvest. DNA material can be manipulated in order to select specific features of different plants (colour, shape, vitamins, and minerals). Cloning a plant means you can choose the best plants to clone. An entire crop of healthy plants can be cloned from one strong parent plant. Cloned plants grow at the same rate, so harvesting can become streamlined.

Kiwifruit (***Actinidia deliciosa):*** Kiwi vines are propagated commercially mostly by grafting cultivars to seedling rootstocks because grafted plants are believed to be more vigorous and to come into bearing sooner than those started as rooted cuttings. However, kiwis may also be propagated by leafy, semi-hardwood cuttings under mist, hardwood cuttings, and root cuttings.

Seed: Seedling plants have a long juvenile period and their sex cannot be determined until

fruiting at 7 years or more. Seed should be taken from soft, well-ripened fruit, dried and stored at 5°C (41°F). After at least 2 weeks at this temperature, subject seed to fluctuating temperatures 10°C (50°F) night and 20°C (68°F) day for 2 or 3 weeks before planting.

Cuttings: Leafy, semi-hardwood cuttings taken from apical and central parts of current season's growth in late spring and midsummer may be rooted under mist in coarse vermiculite with 6,000 ppm IBA. Hardwood cuttings, taken in midwinter and planted in a greenhouse, require higher IBA concentrations.

Grafting: Seedlings are grafted successfully by the whip graft in late winter using dormant scion-wood; T-budding in late summer is also successful. Seedlings are grown 1 year in the nursery. Collect dormant wood in previous winter and store. Use 1-bud scion with a whip graft. Wrap completely with budding rubber to make an air-tight seal.

Micropropagation. Kiwifruit can be propagated by using short meristem tips or longer apical shoots as the initial explants.

Jackfruit ***(Artocarpus heterophyllus):*** A medium-sized tropical tree with fruit of unique flavour has many related genera and species including breadfruit *(Artocarpus altilis).* Although grown mostly by seed, cultivars are available. The seed has limited viability and must be germinated within 1 month. Propagated by cuttings when stock plants are etiolated, and cuttings treated with IBA and rooted under mist. Grafting, including inarching, epicotyl grafting, and various budding methods, including chip budding, are successful. Can be propagated by air layering.

Pecan (***Carya illinoinensis):*** Pecans are native to the southwest United States and northern

Mexico where many natural seedling groves exist. Commercial growers use selected cultivars grafted to pecan seedling rootstocks.

Seed: Pecan seeds of certain cultivars may show vivipary, which ruins the pecan crop. Seeds start to germinate in the hulls before harvesting and lose their viability in warm, dry storage. To maintain viability, seeds should be stored at 0°C (32°F) at 5 percent moisture immediately after harvest and until planted. Pecan seeds should be stratified for 12 to 16 weeks at about 1to 5°C (34 to 41°F) to ensure good, rapid germination. Young seedlings are tender and should be shaded against sunburn. In the summer, toward the end of the second growing season, the seedlings are large enough to bud.

Grafting: Cultivars are propagated by budding or grafting to two-year-old pecan seedling rootstocks. Patch budding in the nursery is the usual method. After the budded top grows for 1 or 2 seasons, the nursery tree is transplanted to a permanent location. Young pecan trees have a long taproot and must be handled carefully when digging and replanting. Seedlings may be crown grafted with the whip graft in late winter or early spring.

Citrus (***Citrus* spp.**): Includes cultivars of *C. aurantifolia* (lime), *C. limon* (lemon), *C. maxima* (pomelo), *C. medica* (citron), *C. reticulate* C. sinensis* (tangor), C. *paradisi* (grapefruit), *C. reticulata* (mandarin orange), *C. sinensis* (sweet orange), *C. paradise x C. regiculata* (tangelo), and related citrus species used for rootstock.

Seeds: Polyembryony occurs in seeds of most citrus species used as rootstocks due to nucellar embryony. The sexual seedlings present within the embryo tend to be weak, variable, and are usually rogued out. The apomictic seedlings, which arise from the nucellus, are usually uniform and have the same genotype as the seed tree. As commercial plants, nucellar seedlings not only have a long juvenile period but are also vigorous, thorny, upright-growing, slow to come into bearing, and undesirable as an orchard tree. Citrus seeds generally have no dormancy but are

injured if allowed to dry. Consequently, seeds should be planted immediately after being extracted from the ripe fruit. Seeds may be stored moist, in polyethylene bags at a low temperature [4°C (40°F)]; before storage they should be soaked for 10 minutes in water at 49°C (120°F) to aid in eliminating seed-borne diseases.

Grafting: The most important method used in commercial production of citrus is to bud or graft onto nucellar seedling rootstocks. T-buds, inverted T-buds, or modified cleft grafts can be used. In micro budding, a very small sliver of stem bearing the bud is inserted under the bark of the rootstock.

Propagation of Flower Plants

Carnation: carnations which are recommended for pot culture are:

Spider type: Purple Rain (purple)

Pot carnations: Maldeves (pink), White Sunny (white), Charm top (red), Pinky (red).

Methods for propagation: Perpetual carnations are multiplied vegetatively by stem cuttings while seed propagation is normally practiced in raising plants of marguerite carnations and border carnations as well as for the purpose of hybridization. Specialist propagators use micro-propagation for producing disease free plants commercially.

Terminal cuttings (10-15cm) from healthy, disease-free mother plants are taken and lower 1-2 pairs of leaves are removed. There should be at least 3 nodes on a cutting. Treat with Bavistan (0.1%) + Dithane M-45 (0.25%) for 5-6 minutes and shake them properly to remove the solution and treat the cut ends with NAA (500ppm) for 10-12 seconds. Plant cuttings at 3cm x 3cm distance in trays or propagation beds containing sterilized sand.

Rooting is obtained in 25-30 days with manual misting in a polythene chamber.

After rooting, the cuttings should be transferred in a hardening chamber containing a mixture of sand, farmyard manure, rice hulls and ash (1:1:1:1 v/v). Keep the cuttings under mini portable tunnels of 3m x 1.5m size covered with a layer of hessian cloth or 50% shading net and transparent polythene as required. Supply of nutrients during the rooting period is not necessary if the stock plants are maintained at an adequate level of nutrition. Overhead fogging unit is best for obtaining intermittent mist and is applied on bright days at an interval of 10 seconds out of every 10-15 minutes. Carnations can be propagated round the year provided temperature inside the polyhouse is maintained at 20°C with 75-80% relative humidity. The rooting and hardening media should be treated with 5% commercial formalin before planting (one litre of formalin in 7 litres of water). After treating the media with formalin, it should be covered with polythene for 7 days. Later on, it must be raked daily for 10 days to release the formalin gas.

Gladiolus: Gladiolus is propagated through corms and cormels, seed and tissue culture.

Propagation methods

Corms: Propagation of gladiolus through corms and cormels is most common and commercially used method. A single corm of gladiolus produces an average of 1-3 flower grade daughter corms in a season depending upon its size and cultivar. Normally large-sized corms may produce more daughter corm; than small-sized ones. Large and medium-sized corms are used for production of cut spike, whereas small-sized corms are used as planting stock for the production of flower grade corms for the subsequent planting season. Most varieties produce 1-2 flower grade daughter corms from the single parent corm. Gladiolus varieties Suchitra, Jackson Ville Gold, American Beauty produce up to 3-4 daughter-corms/corm. The number of daughter corms/corm can also be increased by pre-planting (pre-storage or post-storage) treatment of corms with ethrel (500-5,000ppmfor 30 min.). Ethrel breaks apical dominance and promotes the sprouting of lateral buds which eventually increases the number of daughter corms. Multiplication of gladiolus through corms is, however, a slow process and sometimes leading to high incidence of diseases in the daughter corms.

Cormels: Multiplication of gladiolus through cormels is an inexpensive and rapid method. The cormels also escape diseases or viruses even if the parent corm is infested.

Therefore, corms produced through cormels are usually healthier than those raised from the corms. The number of corms is produced by a corm varies with the cultivar and planting time. The cultivars producing 10 or less cormels are poor multipliers, whereas those producing >10-25, >25-50 and >50 cormels/ corm can be categorised as moderate, fast and very fast multipliers. Production of cormels can be improved by shallow, planting of corms, removing of flowering spike at an early stage, proper nutrition and improved cultural practices. Cormels are planted closely (3-5cm apart) in rows or ridges

about 15-20cm apart and 2.5-3.5cm deep. Cormels should be planted early in the season which results in bigger-sized corms. Best time of planting cormels in north Indian plains is early to mid-September. In hilly areas (temperate region), the cormels should be planted in early spring. Before planting, the cormels should be soaked in water (150-20°C temperature) for at least 24hr to facilitate their uniform germination. The large cormels show higher germination than the smaller ones. Cormels can also grow faster by pre-soaking in an aqueous solution of gibberellic acid (100ppm for 24hr). Waterlogged conditions are however harmful for production.

Corm dormancy: Corm/cormels of gladiolus undergo a period of dormancy or rest during which they do not sprout. Dormancy is more pronounced in cormels and corms produced under warmer climates than those produced under cooler climates. On the other hand they possess very little or even no dormant period. The dormancy of corms/ cormel can be broken by storing them under low temperature (40-5°C) for 3-4 months. The period of dormancy differs in different cultivars. Physiological basis of corm or cormel dormancy has been ascribed to the accumulation of growth inhibitory substances, especially abscissic acid (ABA) in tissue as well as the scales encapsulating them. Dormant cormels contain as much as 5-10 times ABA than the non-dormant ones. The dormant corms can also be made to sprout by treating them with growth-regulatory substances like ethylene chlorohydrin, ethrel (1000ppm) and gibberellic acid (100-500ppm). Descaling also stimulates germination of dormant cormels.

Chrysanthemum: Chrysanthemum is propagated by seed, cuttings and suckers. It is mostly propagated by cuttings and suckers. All varieties do not set seed. Only a few varieties set seed in large-flowered chrysanthemums, whereas more varieties set seed in small flowered ones.

Seeds: Small-flowered varieties are grown from seeds; suckers and cuttings due to its polyploidy and heterozygous nature, a wide range of variations are observed from seedlings. Garden chrysanthemums do not reproduce true-to-type from 'seeds. Seeds are collected during last week of December or first week of January when blooms are dried. The seeds are sown after 15 February either in earthen pots or nursery beds. The seeds are covered with a thin layer of leaf-could and soil and watered. They germinate within 7-10 days. Seedlings are read~, for transplanting, within 40 days.

Suckers: Rooted suckers are planted in field during January for stock plants. Regular pinching is performed in these plants for vigorous and profuse branching. Some of these stock plants are used for potted plants for flower show and other display. The first pinching is performed in April, second in May and third in June. After third pinching, cuttings are taken from these mother plants otherwise, pinching continued in other lot of stock plants. Fourth pinching is performed during August and the final pinching of stock plants is completed by mid-September.

Cuttings: Terminal cuttings of stock plants are taken in June. They are transplanted after rooting in 15cm (6") pots during June-end. These plants are ready for pinching during July-end or beginning of September. When a plant attains 8-10 leaf stage first pinching is done by removing the terminal portion (with 2-3 leaves). Lateral shoots develop from below the cut.

Rose: Hybrid Tea and Floribunda roses are generally propagated by budding, whereas climbers, ramblers, polyanthas and miniatures can be multiplied by stem cuttings.

The commonly used rootstock for budding is *R. bourboniana* in northern plains and *R. multiflora* in coastal areas, West Bengal, Bihar, Karnataka, Maharashtra, Andhra Pradesh, Tamil Nadu and sub mountainers regions of Dehra Dun and Nainital (Uttarakhand); Another rootstock *Rosa indica* var. *odorata* has now become quite popular in northern plains. It is tolerant to powdery mildew and high soil pH. The rootstocks used in India are propagated by stem cuttings. December-February is ideal time for budding (T-budding) in northern plains; October-November and January-March in the eastern region; and February-March/April in the hills.